THE NEW CAMBRIDGE SHAKESPEARE

GENERAL EDITOR
Brian Gibbons

ASSOCIATE GENERAL EDITOR
A. R. Braunmuller, *University of California, Los Angeles*

From the publication of the first volumes in 1984 the General Editor of the New Cambridge Shakespeare was Philip Brockbank and the Associate General Editors were Brian Gibbons and Robin Hood. From 1990 to 1994 the General Editor was Brian Gibbons and the Associate General Editors were A. R. Braunmuller and Robin Hood.

KING JOHN

King John had a distinguished life on the eighteenth- and nineteenth-century stage but for most of this century the play has been undervalued.

The introduction to Professor Beaurline's edition presents the fullest account to date of the stage history, with accompanying illustrations to suggest the dramatic potential of the script. The play's political importance, its rich and varied language, and its skilful design suggest that *King John* deserves a high place among Shakespeare's historical tragedies. Professor Beaurline points out that late in the play the Bastard Falconbridge's character assumes some of the attitudes of Montaigne, especially his mixed feelings about the affairs of this world.

The textual analysis examines several disputed emendations to the text. In the appendix Professor Beaurline surveys the arguments about the dating of Shakespeare's *King John* and the anonymous *Troublesome Reign of King John*, and presents new evidence for the possibility that Shakespeare's play was written first. In that case, *King John* would be an early composition and *Troublesome Reign* an adaptation of it.

THE NEW CAMBRIDGE SHAKESPEARE

All's Well That Ends Well, edited by Russell Fraser
Antony and Cleopatra, edited by David Bevington
As You Like It, edited by Michael Hattaway
The Comedy of Errors, edited by T. S. Dorsch
Coriolanus, edited by Lee Bliss
Cymbeline, edited by Martin Butler
Hamlet, edited by Philip Edwards
Julius Caesar, edited by Marvin Spevack
King Edward III, edited by Giorgio Melchiori
The First Part of King Henry IV, edited by Herbert Weil and Judith Weil
The Second Part of King Henry IV, edited by Giorgio Melchiori
King Henry V, edited by Andrew Gurr
The First Part of King Henry VI, edited by Michael Hattaway
The Second Part of King Henry VI, edited by Michael Hattaway
The Third Part of King Henry VI, edited by Michael Hattaway
King Henry VIII, edited by John Margeson
King John, edited by L. A. Beaurline
The Tragedy of King Lear, edited by Jay L. Halio
King Richard II, edited by Andrew Gurr
King Richard III, edited by Janis Lull
Love's Labour's Lost, edited by William C. Carroll
Macbeth, edited by A. R. Braunmuller
Measure for Measure, edited by Brian Gibbons
The Merchant of Venice, edited by M. M. Mahood
The Merry Wives of Windsor, edited by David Crane
A Midsummer Night's Dream, edited by R. A. Foakes
Much Ado About Nothing, edited by F. H. Mares
Othello, edited by Norman Sanders
Pericles, edited by Doreen DelVecchio and Antony Hammond
The Poems, edited by John Roe
Romeo and Juliet, edited by G. Blakemore Evans
The Sonnets, edited by G. Blakemore Evans
The Taming of the Shrew, edited by Ann Thompson
The Tempest, edited by David Lindley
Timon of Athens, edited by Karl Klein
Titus Andronicus, edited by Alan Hughes
Troilus and Cressida, edited by Anthony B. Dawson
Twelfth Night, edited by Elizabeth Story Donno
The Two Gentlemen of Verona, edited by Kurt Schlueter
The Two Noble Kinsmen, edited by Robert Kean Turner and Patricia Tatspaugh
The Winter's Tale, edited by Susan Snyder and Deborah T. Curren-Aquino

THE EARLY QUARTOS

The First Quarto of Hamlet, edited by Kathleen O. Irace
The First Quarto of King Henry V, edited by Andrew Gurr
The First Quarto of King Lear, edited by Jay L. Halio
The First Quarto of King Richard III, edited by Peter Davison
The First Quarto of Othello, edited by Scott McMillin
The First Quarto of Romeo and Juliet, edited by Lukas Erne
The Taming of a Shrew: The 1594 Quarto, edited by Stephen Roy Miller

KING JOHN

Edited by
L. A. BEAURLINE

CAMBRIDGE
UNIVERSITY PRESS

CAMBRIDGE UNIVERSITY PRESS
Cambridge, New York, Melbourne, Madrid, Cape Town,
Singapore, São Paulo, Delhi, Mexico City

Cambridge University Press
The Edinburgh Building, Cambridge CB2 8RU, UK

Published in the United States of America by Cambridge University Press, New York

www.cambridge.org
Information on this title: www.cambridge.org/9780521293877

First published 1990
5th printing 2012

A catalogue record for this book is available from the British Library

Library of Congress Cataloguing in Publication data
Shakespeare, William, 1564–1616.
King John / edited by L. A. Beaurline.
    p.   cm. – (The New Cambridge Shakespeare)
Bibliography.
ISBN 978-0-521-22196-2 (hbk). – ISBN 978-0-521-29387-7 (pbk.)
1. John, King of England, 1167–1216 -- Drama.   I. Beaurline, L. A. (Lester A.)
II. Title.   III. Series: Shakespeare, William, 1564–1616.   Works.   1984.
Cambridge University Press.
PR2818.A2B4   1989
822.3'3 – dc19   88-26739 CIP

ISBN 978-0-521-22196-2 Hardback
ISBN 978-0-521-29387-7 Paperback

THE NEW CAMBRIDGE SHAKESPEARE

The *New Cambridge Shakespeare* succeeds *The New Shakespeare* which began publication in 1921 under the general editorship of Sir Arthur Quiller-Couch and John Dover Wilson, and was completed in the 1960s, with the assistance of G. I. Duthie, Alice Walker, Peter Ure and J. C. Maxwell. *The New Shakespeare* itself followed upon *The Cambridge Shakespeare*, 1863–6, edited by W. G. Clark, J. Glover and W. A. Wright.

The New Shakespeare won high esteem both for its scholarship and for its design, but shifts of critical taste and insight, recent Shakespearean research, and a changing sense of what is important in our understanding of the plays, have made it necessary to re-edit and redesign, not merely to revise, the series.

The *New Cambridge Shakespeare* aims to be of value to a new generation of playgoers and readers who wish to enjoy fuller access to Shakespeare's poetic and dramatic art. While offering ample academic guidance, it reflects current critical interests and is more attentive than some earlier editions have been to the realisation of the plays on the stage, and to their social and cultural settings. The text of each play has been freshly edited, with textual data made available to those users who wish to know why and how one published text differs from another. Although modernised, the edition conserves forms that appear to be expressive and characteristically Shakespearean, and it does not attempt to disguise the fact that the plays were written in a language other than that of our own time.

Illustrations are usually integrated into the critical and historical discussion of the play and include some reconstructions of early performances by C. Walter Hodges. Some editors have also made use of the advice and experience of Maurice Daniels, for many years a member of the Royal Shakespeare Company.

Each volume is addressed to the needs and problems of a particular text, and each therefore differs in style and emphasis from others in the series.

PHILIP BROCKBANK
General Editor

CONTENTS

ILLUSTRATIONS

PREFACE

My debt to former editors is far greater than the notes can record, especially to
E. A. J. Honigmann and to R. L. Smallwood. Both kindly read a draft of the
introduction, and Professor Honigmann read the appendix. When I began thinking
about the vexing problems in *King John*, I was influenced by the critical studies of
Emrys Jones and Wilbur Sanders, and that respect has deepened steadily. Stanley
Wells's judicious books *Modernizing Shakespeare's Spelling* (1979) and *Re-Editing
Shakespeare for the Modern Reader* (1984) have shaped many decisions in the text.

My friends and colleagues, Verdel Kolve, David Vander Muelen, Daniel Kinney,
Gordon Braden, Fredson Bowers and Arthur Kirsch have answered questions about
the text and interpretation. Special thanks go to Mike Stanford, Scott Boltwood, and
Brent Harris, who helped check the commentary, and to Deborah Shea for putting
the text and commentary on a word processor.

Professor Philip Brockbank helped me generously with the unruly introduction,
and at Cambridge University Press Paul Chipchase's copy-editing has improved
almost every page of this edition.

Staff at the Folger Library, the Harvard Theatre Collection, the Huntington
Library, the Royal Shakespeare Gallery, the Victoria and Albert Museum, the
Weimar National Theatre, Yale University Art Gallery, and the British Museum
Department of Prints and Drawings have found fugitive material and have generously
allowed me to reproduce pictures from their collections. The most delightful part of
making this edition has been the spirited correspondence with Walter Hodges. His
splendid drawings and his fund of theatrical knowledge have enriched the edition
incomparably.

My deepest debt is to my wife, who has put up with my groans and questions for
more than seven years. If there are any good sentences in the introduction, she has
shaped them.

University of Virginia   L. A. B.

ix

ABBREVIATIONS AND CONVENTIONS

Shakespeare's plays, when cited in this edition, are abbreviated in a style modified slightly from that used in the *Harvard Concordance to Shakespeare*. Other editions of Shakespeare are abbreviated under the editor's surname (Honigmann, Capell), or, in certain cases, under the series title (Cam., Oxford). When more than one edition by the same editor is cited, later editions are discriminated with a raised figure (Rowe²). All quotations from Shakespeare, except those from *King John*, use the text and lineation of *The Riverside Shakespeare*, under the general editorship of G. Blakemore Evans.

1. Shakespeare's plays

Ado	*Much Ado About Nothing*
Ant.	*Antony and Cleopatra*
AWW	*All's Well That Ends Well*
AYLI	*As You Like It*
Cor.	*Coriolanus*
Cym.	*Cymbeline*
Err.	*The Comedy of Errors*
Ham.	*Hamlet*
1H4	*The First Part of King Henry the Fourth*
2H4	*The Second Part of King Henry the Fourth*
H5	*King Henry the Fifth*
1H6	*The First Part of King Henry the Sixth*
2H6	*The Second Part of King Henry the Sixth*
3H6	*The Third Part of King Henry the Sixth*
H8	*King Henry the Eighth*
JC	*Julius Caesar*
John	*King John*
LLL	*Love's Labour's Lost*
Lear	*King Lear*
Mac.	*Macbeth*
MM	*Measure for Measure*
MND	*A Midsummer Night's Dream*
MV	*The Merchant of Venice*
Oth.	*Othello*
Per.	*Pericles*
R2	*King Richard the Second*
R3	*King Richard the Third*
Rom.	*Romeo and Juliet*
Shr.	*The Taming of the Shrew*
STM	*Sir Thomas More*
Temp.	*The Tempest*
TGV	*The Two Gentlemen of Verona*
Tim.	*Timon of Athens*
Tit.	*Titus Andronicus*
TN	*Twelfth Night*

TNK	*The Two Noble Kinsmen*
Tro.	*Troilus and Cressida*
Wiv.	*The Merry Wives of Windsor*
WT	*The Winter's Tale*

2. Editions and general references

Abbott	E. A. Abbott, *A Shakespearian Grammar*, rev. edn, 1870 (references are to numbered paragraphs)
Alexander	*William Shakespeare, The Complete Works*, ed. Peter Alexander, 1951
Baker	Herschel Baker, explanatory notes to *King John* in Riverside
Cam.	*The Works of William Shakespeare*, ed. W. G. Clark, John Glover, and W. A. Wright, 1863–6 (Cambridge Shakespeare)
Capell	*Mr William Shakespeare His Comedies, Histories, and Tragedies*, ed. Edward Capell, 1767–8
Collier	*The Works of William Shakespeare*, ed. J. P. Collier, 1842–4
Collier[2]	*The Plays of Shakespeare*, ed. J. P. Collier, 1853
Collier MS.	Manuscript emendations in Perkins's Second Folio (1632), Huntington Library
conj.	conjecture
Cotgrave	Randle Cotgrave, *A Dictionarie of the French and English Tongues*, 1611
Davies	Thomas Davies, *Dramatic Miscellanies*, 3 vols., 1784
Dent	R. W. Dent, *Shakespeare's Proverbial Language: An Index*, 1981 (references are to numbered proverbs)
Dyce	*The Works of William Shakespeare*, ed. Alexander Dyce, 1857
Dyce[2]	*Works*, 2nd edn, 1864–7
Edward III	*The Reign of King Edward III*, in *The Shakespeare Apocrypha*, ed. C. F. Tucker Brooke, 1908
EIC	*Essays in Criticism*
ELH	*ELH: A Journal of English Literary History*
ESC	*English Studies in Canada*
F	*Mr William Shakespeares Comedies, Histories, & Tragedies*, 1623 (First Folio)
F2	Second Folio, 1632
F3	Third Folio, 1664
F4	Fourth Folio, 1685
Farmer and Henley	John Farmer and W. E. Henley, *Slang and its Analogues*, 7 vols., 1890–1904
Fleay	*King John*, ed. F. G. Fleay, 1878 (Collins Classics)
Foxe	John Foxe, *Acts and Monuments*, 1583 edn
FQ	Edmund Spenser, *The Faerie Queene*, ed. A. C. Hamilton, 1977
Furness	*A New Variorum Edition of Shakespeare, The Life and Death of King John*, ed. H. H. Furness, 1919
Halliwell	*The Complete Works of William Shakespeare*, ed. J. O. Halliwell, 1853–65
Hanmer	*The Works of Shakespear*, ed. Thomas Hanmer, 1743–4
Heath	Benjamin Heath, *A Revisal of Shakespeare's Text*, 1765
Hibbard	G. R. Hibbard, *The Making of Shakespeare's Dramatic Poetry*, 1981
Hinman	Charlton Hinman, *The Printing and Proof-Reading of the First Folio of Shakespeare*, 2 vols., 1963
Holinshed	*Holinshed's Chronicles of England, Scotland, and Ireland* (1587), a photo-facsimile of Henry Ellis's edn, 6 vols., 1807–8, with an introduction by Vernon Snow, 1965

Honigmann	*King John*, ed. E. A. J. Honigmann, 1954 (Arden Shakespeare)
John	*King John*, ed. Ivor John, 1904 (Arden Shakespeare)
Johnson	*The Plays of William Shakespeare*, ed. Samuel Johnson, 1765
Jones, *Origins*	Emrys Jones, *The Origins of Shakespeare*, 1977
Keightley	*The Plays of Shakespeare*, ed. Thomas Keightley, 1864
Kemble	*Shakespeare's King John, A Historical Play*, revised by J. P. Kemble, 1804 (*John Philip Kemble Prompt Books*, vol. 5, ed. Charles Shattuck, 1974)
Kittredge	*The Complete Works of Shakespeare*, ed. George Lyman Kittredge, 1936
Knight	*The Pictorial Edition of the Works of Shakespere*, ed. Charles Knight, 1839–43
Kökeritz	Helge Kökeritz, *Shakespeare's Pronunciation*, 1953
Malone	*The Plays and Poems of William Shakespeare*, ed. Edmond Malone, 1790
Matchett	*King John*, ed. William H. Matchett, 1966
Maxwell	J. C. Maxwell's emendations of *King John*, *Notes & Queries* 195 (1950), 75–6; 473–4
Moore Smith	*King John*, ed. G. C. Moore Smith, 1900 (Heath's English Classics)
MSR	Malone Society Reprint
Neilson	*The Complete Dramatic and Poetic Works of William Shakespeare*, ed. William A. Neilson, 1906
ODEP	*The Oxford Dictionary of English Proverbs*, 3rd edn, rev. F. P. Wilson, 1970
OED	*Oxford English Dictionary*
Onions	C. T. Onions, *A Shakespeare Glossary*, 1911, rev. edn, 1953
Oxford	*William Shakespeare: The Complete Works*, ed. Stanley Wells and Gary Taylor, 1986
PBA	*Proceedings of the British Academy*
PBSA	*Papers of the Bibliographical Society of America*
Pope	*The Works of Shakespeare*, ed. Alexander Pope, 1723–5
RES	*Review of English Studies*
Riverside	*The Riverside Shakespeare*, ed. G. Blakemore Evans, Harry Levin *et al.*, 1974
Roderick	R. Roderick, *Remarks on Shakespeare*, in T. Edwards, *Canons of Criticism*, 7th edn, 1765
Rowe	*The Works of Mr William Shakespear*, ed. Nicholas Rowe, 1709
Rowe²	*Works*, 2nd edn, 1709
Rowe³	*Works*, 3rd edn, 1714
SB	*Studies in Bibliography*
Schmidt	Alexander Schmidt, *Shakespeare Lexicon*, 3rd edn, 2 vols., 1901
SD	stage direction
SEL	*Studies in English Literature*
SH	speech heading
Sider	*The Troublesome Raigne of John, King of England*, ed. J. W. Sider, 1979
Sisson	C. J. Sisson, *New Readings in Shakespeare*, 2 vols., 1956
SJH	*Shakespeare-Jahrbuch* (Heidelberg)
SJW	*Shakespeare-Jahrbuch* (Weimar)
Smallwood	*King John*, ed. R. L. Smallwood, 1974 (New Penguin)
SN	*Studia Neophilologica*
SP	*Studies in Philology*
SQ	*Shakespeare Quarterly*
S.St.	*Shakespeare Studies*
S.Sur.	*Shakespeare Survey*

Staunton	*The Plays of Shakespeare*, ed. H. Staunton, 1858–60
Steevens	*The Plays of William Shakespeare*, ed. George Steevens (with Johnson), 1773
Steevens²	*Plays*, 2nd edn, 1778
Steevens³	*Plays*, 4th edn, 1793
subst.	substantively
Theobald	*The Works of Shakespeare*, ed. Lewis Theobald, 1733
Theobald²	*Works*, 2nd edn, 1740
Tilley	M. P. Tilley, *A Dictionary of the Proverbs in England in the Sixteenth and Seventeenth Centuries*, 1950 (references are to numbered proverbs)
TLS	*The Times Literary Supplement*
TR	*The Troublesome Raigne of John, King of England*, 1591 (scene and line numbers are keyed to Sider's edn (*see above*))
Tyrwhitt	Thomas Tyrwhitt, *Observations and Conjectures upon Some Passages of Shakespeare*, 1766
Upton	John Upton, *Critical Observations on Shakespeare*, 1746
UTQ	*University of Toronto Quarterly*
Vaughan	H. H. Vaughan, *New Readings and New Renderings of Shakespeare's Tragedies*, vol. 1, 1878
Walker	William Sidney Walker, *A Critical Examination of the Text of Shakespeare*, 3 vols., 1860
Warburton	*The Works of Shakespear*, ed. William Warburton, 1747
White	*The Works of William Shakespeare*, ed. Richard Grant White, 1857–66
Whiting	Bartlett Jere Whiting, *Proverbs, Sentences, and Proverbial Phrases; from English Writings Mainly before 1500*, 1968 (references are to numbered proverbs)
Wilson	*King John*, ed. John Dover Wilson, 1936 (New Shakespeare)
Wright	*King John*, ed. W. Aldis Wright, 1886 (Clarendon Shakespeare)

Quotations from the Bible are from the Geneva version unless otherwise specified.

INTRODUCTION

King John has had a distinguished tradition on the stage in the eighteenth and nineteenth centuries, and critics have admired parts of the play, especially its dramatic poetry and the roles of Constance and the Bastard. But with notable exceptions the play has been undervalued. It is commonly said that *King John* is poorly constructed, that the Bastard is or should really be the hero, and that Shakespeare lacked interest in the script. Much of this depreciation may be attributed to a readiness to treat it as a piece of hack work, a hasty rewriting and toning down of the patriotic, anti-Catholic propaganda of *The Troublesome Reign of John, King of England* (1591). However, from another perspective – assuming, as I do, that Shakespeare was the only begetter of *King John* directly from the chronicles and that it was written before *The Troublesome Reign* – the play appears not to be derivative but original theatre of a high order, expressing historical and political ideas of continuing value. Its design is complex and its stagecraft varied and dynamic. It appears from its stage history that responses of actors and audiences have been more than usually volatile over changing theatrical and cultural conditions of several generations, and failures to appreciate the play in the twentieth century may tell us more about ourselves than about Shakespeare's art. The time may be ripe for a fresh appraisal. Since the design is at once theatrical and historical, depending greatly upon transactions in performance between players and audience, this account begins with stage history and then looks at the play's craftsmanship – its dramatic speech and symmetries – before attending to its political and moral implications. The problems of date and relationship with *The Troublesome Reign* are reserved for the Appendix.

Stage history

King John was in the past a favourite with actors and audiences because of its opportunities to depict passion in elaborate poetic and rhetorical speeches. Its complicated scenes and major roles require not only vocal power but intelligence to compass the changes of purposes and character. Yet the play's fortunes on the stage have fluctuated as much as that of any Shakespeare play. It must have attained some notoriety before it was published in the Folio, if it was known well enough to have been adapted by the author of *The Troublesome Reign* in 1591. Moreover, *The Troublesome Reign* was attributed to 'W. Sh.' on the title page of the 1611 reprint and to 'W. Shakespeare' in the 1622 quarto, as if the bookseller hoped to profit by the interest in the author and/or his well-known play. The part of Robert Falconbridge – legs like two riding-rods, arms like stuffed eel-skins, and a thin face – was apparently written for a ridiculously skinny actor, John Sincler (Sinclo, Sinklo), who played bit parts 1590–1604 for Strange's, Pembroke's, and the Chamberlain's Men. His name

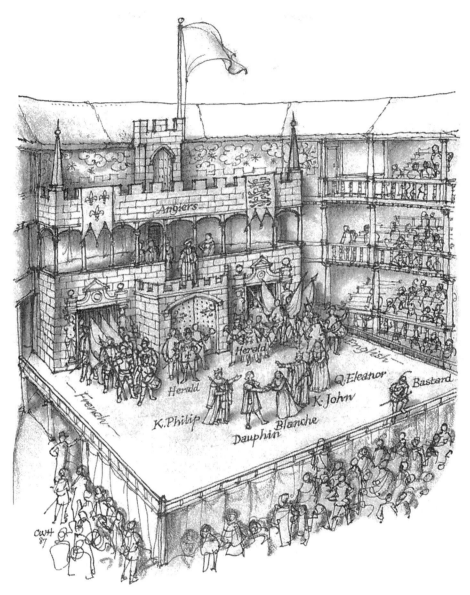

1 A possible staging of Act 2, Scene 1 in an early public playhouse (*c.* 1591), by C. Walter Hodges. This was the kind of stage in use before the introduction of a canopy supported on posts; see Glynne Wickham, '"Heavens", machinery, and pillars', in H. Berry (ed.), *The First Public Playhouse*, 1979

is mentioned in the plot of the *2 Seven Deadly Sins* (*c.* 1590), and in the stage directions of *3 Henry VI* 3.1.1, *The Taming of the Shrew* Induction 88, and *2 Henry IV* 5.4.1 for the part of Justice Shallow.[1] In addition to Francis Meres's listing it among Shakespeare's tragedies in 1598, there is a telling allusion to *King John* in Anthony Munday's *Death of Robert, Earl of Huntingdon* (acted about 1598, printed 1601): the characters John, Austria, Constance and Arthur appear in a dumb-show – and Hubert is addressed as 'Hubert, thou fatal keeper of poor babes' (sigs. D3ᵛ, F4).[2] Since *Troublesome Reign* and the chronicles have Arthur much older than a 'babe', the reference is to Shakespeare's Arthur and Hubert. *King John* is also listed in a document (12 January 1669) along with *Richard III* as among plays 'formerly acted at Blackfriars [i.e. by the King's Men 1608–42] and now allowed of to his Majesties Servants at the New Theatre', and those plays were apparently intended in the first place for public theatres.[3] Otherwise, no exact dates of performance survive until the 1737 revival at Covent Garden.

Then within a few decades *King John* became a popular play – in provincial theatres as well as in London. Although it was never among the greatest Shakespearean favourites, in the next 120 years it held the stage for about 58 seasons, and in some seasons (1760–1, 1766–7, and 1817–18) London theatregoers could compare rival productions.[4] (There were North American tours and many indigenous productions, too.)

Notable actors of the time took the roles of John, Constance, Hubert and the Bastard. At Drury Lane in 1745 Garrick and Mrs Cibber gave eight performances, her Constance being the main feature of this production, for her 'uncommon pathetic ardour in speaking', but Garrick was not wholly satisfied with his acting of John. He is said to have done well in the turbulent scene with Hubert (4.2) and in the death scene; however, it seems that he felt he could not generate sympathy for the king. Therefore in 1754 he shifted to the Bastard's role, and Mossop played John; in 1760–1 Sheridan was king to Garrick's Bastard, but Garrick lacked the physical stature.[5] Henceforth, he took neither role, but the play continued to be performed by

---

[1] His other roles may have been Pinch in *The Comedy of Errors* and the Apothecary in *Romeo and Juliet*. Edwin Nungezer, *A Dictionary of Actors . . . before 1642*, 1929; A. Gaw, 'John Sinclo as one of Shakespeare's actors', *Anglia* 49 (1926), 289.

[2] Malone Society Reprints, 1964; Honigmann, p. lxxiii.

[3] Irwin Smith, *Shakespeare's Blackfriars Playhouse*, 1966, pp. 503–4.

[4] Eugene Waith, '*King John* and the drama of history', *SQ* 29 (1978), 193–4, to which I am greatly indebted. C. B. Hogan supplies tables of performances in *Shakespeare in the Theatre 1701–1800*, 1952, I, 239–44; II, 319–33; these are supplemented by E. L. Avery *et. al.*, *The London Stage 1660–1800*, 1960–8, Index, 1979. H. Child outlines later performances in his succinct article in Wilson.

[5] Thomas Davies, *Dramatic Miscellanies*, 1784, I, 54, 113, and *Memoirs of the Life of David Garrick*, 1780, pp. 298–300. In a manuscript part-book for the role of King John belonging to Garrick (Folger Library MS.), Garrick composed a four-line speech on the last page, but not written into the part. It was perhaps tentatively meant to be placed among his final speeches, to generate that sympathy that Garrick strove for.

> The Lamp of Life is Dry, thy Prayers O Father!
> At Worcester let these Mortal Bones have rest
> My Eyes refuse the Light – the Stroke is giv'n,
> Oh I am call'd – I wander – Mercy Heav'n!

Cited by H. W. Pedicord, 'Garrick produces *King John*', *Theatre Journal* 34 (1982), 447.

Sheridan, Mrs Barry, Mrs Yates, and others. John Philip Kemble and his sister, Sarah Siddons, as John and Constance, began at Drury Lane in 1783 an intermittent series of performances, moving to Covent Garden in 1804. He continued until 1817, she until 1812; thereafter she gave public readings from Acts 3 and 4 of *John*. Among her most dazzling performances in Shakespearean roles were Constance, Lady Macbeth, Volumnia, and Queen Katherine. By most reports J. P. Kemble, unlike Garrick, got the necessary sympathy when he played a fine, kingly John, and it was thought that in the temptation scene (3.3) he evoked a 'noiseless horror', a 'muttered suggestion of slaughterous thought'.[1] It was Hazlitt's opinion, however, after admiring Kemble in the part for some years, that, compared to Edmund Kean, he was skilful but too studied, artificial, and solemn; he did not seem to feel the part.[2] Charles Kemble, a younger brother in the same family, joined the cast as a gentlemanly sort of Bastard in 1800. Charles Kemble is also noted for his later management of the troupe, when he ordered costumes and sets to be redesigned for historical 'accuracy', under the supervision of J. R. Planché for the November 1823 production. This was an important change in the staging of history plays, as we shall see.

William Charles Macready first played Hubert in Charles Kemble's company in 1822, and was promoted to the role of John in 1823 (in America 1827). By October 1842, with his own company at Drury Lane, he had became the most resourceful, if not the most gifted, actor and manager of the century, and a new production of *John* was the last of Macready's triumphs. Samuel Phelps, who once played Hubert with Macready's company, took up the leading role and followed Macready's revolutionary methods at Sadler's Wells in 1844 and 1851, and at Drury Lane in 1865 and 1866. Charles Kean made his mark as John, imitating Macready (less successfully) at the Princess's Theatre in 1852 and 1858 (American tours in 1846 and 1865). It is evident that by the 1830s *King John* was so familiar that it was honoured with a burlesque version, along with Macready's other famous productions – *Hamlet, Othello, Romeo, Macbeth*, and *Richard III*.[3] After about 1866, however, the play almost disappeared from the London and New York stages.

The leading actor-manager of the last quarter-century, Sir Henry Irving, never staged the play, but in 1899 Beerbohm Tree revived *John* at Her Majesty's Theatre in an elaborate production that ran for 114 performances – a swan-song for the grand old way. A similar revival was performed by R. B. Mantell in Chicago and New York, 1909. After that, the play was infrequently acted, mostly in the art theatres and in provincial repertory companies. Significantly, the Bastard's role, that was something of an embarrassment for most of the previous century, became the one

---

[1] James Boaden, *Memoirs of the Life of John Philip Kemble*, 1825, pp. 133–4.
[2] *A View of the English Stage*, 1906 edn, p. 271. Apparently Hazlitt fell under the spell of Edmund Kean's acting, but he probably did not mean that Kean's acting of John was superior to Kemble's, for Kean played John in only three performances in 1818 at Drury Lane, cut short by illness, and apparently he was not in his best form. See Child's 'Stage-history' in Wilson, p. lxxiv.
[3] *King John, (with the Benefit of the Act.) A Burlesque, in One Act*, by Gilbert Abbott A-Beckett. See *Nineteenth-Century Shakespeare Burlesques*, II, 1977. The burlesque follows the plot closely, giving the fullest treatment to the popular scenes 3.3 and 4.1.

most sought after. At the Old Vic, Balliol Holloway played the Bastard in 1926 (and at Stratford in 1940), Ralph Richardson in 1931, and Richard Burton in 1953; Paul Scofield took the part at the Birmingham Repertory Theatre in 1945, Anthony Quayle at Stratford in 1948, and Christopher Plummer at Stratford, Ontario, 1959.

King John did not fit into revivals of the cycles of Shakespeare's history plays, although Benson included it in his 'Week of Kings' at the Memorial Theatre in 1901. For forty years the play was generally treated as something of a stepsister, without a sufficient central character, according to reviewers, and by 1944 a theatre historian said that *King John* was 'now almost unknown as an acting play'.[1] Though there have been a few interesting productions since then, apparently *King Richard II*, virtually never shown on the eighteenth-century and seldom on the nineteenth-century stage, has taken *John*'s place among the histories as one of the favourite vehicles for actors.[2]

Since performances of Shakespeare's history plays as a whole have not fallen into disrepute, it is worth considering what were the causes of such favour for *King John*, followed by almost total neglect. Eugene Waith suggests that when *John* was highly regarded it dramatised personal values for a critical audience, whose experience was enhanced by grand historical sets and costumes.[3] Actors and audiences revelled in the passions of the characters; whereas nowadays the literary critics and directors have shaped the play to fit explicit political themes, turning it into ideological drama. Although Waith points out that the shift of emphasis did not necessarily cause the decline of *King John*, he rightly calls attention to the values of earlier performances that are now often neglected. Still, the search for specific explanations of the play's fortunes will tell us much about its staging.

Among the possible causes of favour and neglect, perhaps the most significant are (1) the appetite for political relevance, (2) the changes in style of acting, and (3) the rise of art theatres and the corresponding decline of the large patent theatres, which exaggerated stage sets and elaborated stage business. *King John* was potentially affected by these tendencies in the theatre.

First political relevance. Certain speeches in *John*, such as the king's defiance of the Pope's authority over a 'sacred king' (3.1.147–8), the Bastard's stirring attempt to encourage John to resist the Dauphin's invasion – 'Be great in act as you have been in thought' (5.1.45) – and the Bastard's final call for national unity have often been exploited on both sides of the curtain for their patriotic or political fervour. This was probably so from the very first performances in the 1590s, when audiences could cherish John's defiance of the Pope, and some probably recognised how closely John's anger with Hubert concerning his use of the king's warrant (4.2) resembles the great trouble that Secretary Davison suffered for his delivery of the queen's warrant for

---

[1] A. C. Sprague, *Shakespeare and the Actors*, 1944, p. 108.
[2] According to Sprague, *Shakespeare's Histories: Plays for the Stage*, 1964, p. 51, *Henry IV Part I* greatly declined in popularity in the nineteenth century; it apparently recovered slowly in the twentieth and is now the most frequently acted of the histories. *Richard III*, of course, has been a steady favourite since 1700.   [3] Waith, 'Drama of history', pp. 192–211.

the death of Mary Queen of Scots. Naturally, the adaptations like *Troublesome Reign* and Colley Cibber's *Papal Tyranny in the Reign of King John* were more calculated to kindle popular fears of Romanism and rebellion than the original play. Cibber's abortive attempt to stage his improvement of Shakespeare (*c.* 1736, acted in 1745 amidst threats of a Jacobite uprising) testifies that Shakespeare's script was for some people not sufficiently inflammatory. Nevertheless, the controversy over reports of Cibber's mutilations precipitated the first revival of the original play in 1737. Similarly, Richard Valpy cut the text grossly and added patriotic speeches for a production by the boys at Reading Grammar School (1800), which was performed once at Covent Garden (1803); J. P. Kemble's company quickly followed the debased version by one much closer to Shakespeare's text (1804). Indeed, Kemble deleted most of the 'indelicate' and bitter passages from the Bastard's speeches (though not so many as Valpy, who, like Cibber, omitted the whole first act), and, appropriately for the Napoleonic era, Kemble added a bit of jingoism at 5.1.74 that survived for many years on the stage:

> Sweep off these base invaders from the land:
> And above all; exterminate those slaves,
> Those British slaves, whose prostituted souls,
> Under French banners, move in vile rebellion,
> Against their king, their country, and their God.[1]

Beerbohm Tree's production was cut to make room for elaborate tableaux and a dumb-show of The Granting of the Magna Carta (4.1). One reviewer noted on the first night that the Bastard's final speech made heads turn to the box where sat Joseph Chamberlain, the embattled colonial secretary during the Boer War.[2]

Doubtless there is room in Shakespeare's histories, particularly in *John* and *Henry V*, for speeches and events that satisfy a thirst for political relevance, to which audiences in this century have not failed to respond. Thus, when *John* was staged at Stratford in the dark days of 1940 – the first time in 25 years – the reviewer for *The Times* on 9 May noticed that the Bastard stands 'truculently and . . . humorously for the English spirit against whoever seems to threaten its survival'. The play gained a 'new momentousness', for Balliol Holloway played the character of the Bastard 'with a lively sense of its present relevance'. At the other end of the political spectrum, public cynicism and disaffection with politics and war in the late 1960s and early 1970s may account for two more adaptations of *John*: Dürrenmatt's travesty in London in 1968, and John Barton's gallimaufry at Stratford in 1974.[3] Unlike these crude versions, however, the monumental staging of the play at the Weimar National Theatre, 1980, depicted graphically the horrors of war, with explosions and sirens,

---

[1] *John Philip Kemble Prompt Books*, ed. Charles Shattuck, 1974, vol. 5, p. 52; C. Shattuck, *William Charles Macready's 'King John'*, 1962, p. 10.

[2] *The Speaker*, 30 Sept. 1899, p. 346.

[3] *The Times*, 15 Nov. 1968, p. 9; R. L. Smallwood, 'Shakespeare unbalanced: the Royal Shakespeare Company's *King John*, 1974–5', *SJH* 112 (1976), 79–99. A performance closer to Shakespeare's script, at Stratford in 1970, made fun of the medieval power politics, in a Brechtian style (*The Times*, 16 June, p. 8).

without sacrificing the serious impact of the play.[1] The occasion of that production was probably the proposal in 1979 by the United States, with the assent of the North Atlantic Treaty Organisation, to deploy 572 Pershing missiles in West Germany.

Since political relevance as a basis for *King John*'s popularity is a spasmodic phenomenon, it is not likely to have directly caused the radical shifts of favour or disfavour. But such resonances are not insignificant, for the genuine patriotic and political interest of the script seems to have precipitated revivals, in which actors and spectators then discovered that it is an engaging drama: 'The history which makes such hard reading is surprisingly alive on the stage', said one reviewer in 1940, and it is 'an unexpectedly satisfying treatment of the play' to see John as a brilliant opportunist with an 'intensely political mind' (1953).[2]

The styles of acting in the late eighteenth and nineteenth centuries also account for much of *King John*'s appeal, for nearly every minor character has a passionate speech of some sort, with modulations of conflicting feelings suitable for exhibition in an age of sensibility. The major roles, John, Constance, the Bastard, and even Hubert, also offer actors the opportunity for development – what Stanislavsky later called 'perspective' – and within scenes an actor has many a chance to show his skill and judgement in big speeches fitted for a display of virtuoso acting.

Garrick certainly played John passionately, although his delivery was said to be more natural than that of his contemporaries.[3] For example, when he uttered 'O, when the last account 'twixt heaven and earth / Is to be made . . .' (4.2.216):

Garrick snatched the warrant from [Hubert's] hand, and grasping it hard, in an agony of despair and horror, he threw his eyes to heaven, as if self-convicted of murder, and standing before the great Judge of the quick and dead to answer for the infringement of the divine command.[4]

Mrs Cibber was remembered for Constance's last speech 'Oh Lord! my boy!' which she delivered 'with such an emphatical scream of agony as will never be forgotten by those who heard her'. Yet she depicted the variety of emotions, in her opening speeches of 3.1, 'with the utmost harmony and propriety, all the succeeding changes of grief, anger, resentment, rage, despondency, reviving courage, and animated defiance'.[5] Sarah Siddons tells how, off-stage, she worked up her emotions for Constance's opening lines to 3.1, 'Gone to be married!' Keeping her dressing-room door open, she could hear the goings-on upon the stage – 'the terrible effects' of the reconciliation of England and France and the marriage contract between the Dauphin and Blanche. The 'sickening sounds' of their march 'would usually cause the bitter tears of rage, disappointment, betrayed confidence, baffled ambition, and, above all, the agonizing feelings of maternal affection to gush into my eyes'.[6] The point of this oft-repeated story is not just her real tears but the mixture of feelings that caused them.

---

[1] Armin-Gerd Kuckhoff, 'Shakespeare auf den Bütten De DDR in Jahre 1980' *SJW* 118 (1982), 151–5.   [2] *The Times*, 28 Oct. 1953, p. 5.
[3] Perhaps this meant that Garrick did not intone the lines.
[4] Davies, *Miscellanies*, 1, 70.   [5] *Ibid.*, 1, 56, 35.
[6] T. Campbell, *Life of Mrs Siddons*, 1834, 1, 215.

2 The sorrowful countenance of Sarah Siddons, by an unknown artist

Francis Gentleman's 'Essay on Oratory' in Bell's edition of Shakespeare (1774) emphasises the importance of skilful acting that will evoke sympathy from an audience by careful exhibition of mixed feelings. Thus John's speech to Hubert (3.3) is a 'picture of deep diffident cruelty':

It is impossible for words to express, or imagination to paint, a finer representation of dubious cruelty, fearful to express itself, than this address of John's to Hubert exhibits; the hesitative circumlocution, with which he winds about his gloomy purpose, is highly natural, and the imagery exquisite. To do this scene justice, requires more judgment than powers . . .[1]

And J. P. Kemble, for all his grace, stateliness and solemnity, was said to be 'unsurpassable in John's scenes of cold-blooded villainy'.[2] It seems that Kemble consciously applied Hume's theory of tragedy to his acting of the role, mixing 'a leading passion of secret inquietude' with dignity and grace, so that the audience could overcome their disgust. 'A brooding, romantic, heroic dignity . . . made up the sublime quality of his King John. By making John's guilt a central aspect of his performance, he further ensured that no moral sensibilities would be offended.'[3]

But Macready outdid his predecessors in John's temptation scene with Hubert; his mixed emotions were described as 'a masterly exhibition of coward villainy'. One could see the fantastical thought of murder rising in his mind, but 'conscience-stricken fear and doubt of Hubert's compliance' delayed his utterance. There was a 'meanness alike in his cajolery and exultation'.[4] It is not surprising that Macbeth was Macready's greatest role, where he had more such opportunities for conflicting emotions – shame, fear and lust for power.

It is clear that Macready thought out the role of John intelligently, noting the opportunities for artful gradations of feeling and inner conflicts. Whereas earlier actors used John's defiance of Pandulph (3.1.147) merely as a way to get applause,

Macready threw into his manner and expression, the irritation of an aggrieved selfishness – his ire was birthed in a sense of encroachment on *his* privilege to tithe and tax – Shakespeare understood kings as well as he did Pandulphs, and knaves in humbler garb.[5]

Macready, moreover, thought he recognised more precisely than his predecessors the development of John's character. After years of trying various strategies, in 1842–3 he played the role 'almost as hero-king, yet incipiently vicious' in the first two acts and part of the third; then 'John as coward-king and villain thereafter' – in the temptation scene (3.3), in his remorseful confrontation with Hubert (4.2), and in the agonies of his death. 'He was careful not to give the character away, so to speak, by too many signs of weakness or meanness in the early scenes.'[6] The major change came in 3.3, when his confident manner gave way to hesitation and dissimulation, an example of his skilful transitions. According to one critic,

A gloom, which came in sudden contrast to the previous bustle of the drama, seemed to usher in the conversation between John and Hubert. A change had come over the play. It was a foreboding look that John cast on Arthur, the tongue faltered as the horrible mission was intrusted to Hubert. For a moment the countenance of the king beamed as he said 'Good

[1] Cited by Waith, 'Drama of history', p. 202, who believes that this suggests that the performance was 'thought of primarily in terms of emotional responses it evokes'. Perhaps so, but display of skill and judgement were prized, as the quotation indicates.
[2] Shattuck, *Kemble Prompt Books*, p. ii.
[3] Maarten van Dijk, 'John Philip Kemble as King John', *Theatre Notebook* 29 (1975), 23–4.
[4] *Spectator* and *Atlas* (1842–3), cited by Shattuck, *Macready's 'King John'*, p. 49.
[5] C. R. Pemberton, *The Monthly Repository*, Jan.–Feb. 1834, cited by Sprague, *Histories*, p. 16.
[6] Shattuck, *Macready's 'King John'*, pp. 48–9.

Hubert', but the gloom returned when he said 'Throw thine eye on yonder boy.' That he did not look Hubert in the face when he proposed 'death' was a fine conception.[1]

A reviewer for the *Spectator* thought it was 'conscience-stricken fear and doubt of Hubert's compliance' that delayed the utterance of the word. Nevertheless, like the critic in the *Atlas*, some did not care for Macready's 'gasping and spasmodic' utterance 'as though he had done the deed he desires to have done, and was spirit-stricken, pouring forth the baleful secrets of his agonized soul'.[2] This was part of the actor's other favourite device, borrowed from Mrs Siddons: the illusion of suppressed passion, achieved by dropping his voice and speaking in a harsh whisper that could be heard in the last row of the auditorium.

Aside from the mixture of tender and violent emotions the great actor-managers featured a heightened style of delivery to encourage the spectators' approbation. The leading actor set the tone and commanded the stage like a *prima donna*. Secondary characters had to keep their eyes on the star while he spoke to them, and he delivered most big speeches facing the audience, like arias, which invited applause, and were followed by the actor's obligatory bow. For example, the young James O'Neill (the playwright's father) was given friendly advice by the noted American actor Joseph Jefferson after O'Neill's first performance of a role in Jefferson's company: 'My boy, you got six rounds of applause tonight, and that is good. Very good. But there are eight rounds in the part and we must get them.'[3] Just so, Thomas Davies noted that the short battle scenes in Act 5 of *John* were 'often neglected by actors of some merit, because not attended with expected applause', but it is to Garrick's credit that he evoked applause even in these scenes. Mrs Cibber's stinging reproach of Austria beginning 'O Limoges, O Austria!' (3. 1. 114 ff.) 'was so happily modulated by a most accurate ear, that every material word in this uncommon burst of indignation was impressed so judiciously and harmoniously upon the audience that they could not refrain a loud and repeated testimony of their approbation' (*Miscellanies*, p. 38). In other words, they not only applauded but applauded again and again throughout the speech, and she bowed again and again.[4] Such rapport with the audience (familiar to us in grand opera) was appropriate for and reinforced by a self-conscious and explicitly artful style of acting. But when the pendulum swung from a tentative realism in the mid 1800s to an even more natural style of acting, in Irving's lifetime and later, the passionate speeches and the declamatory rhetoric of *King John* lost much of their appeal.

Signs of change were discernible by mid century, when actresses turned away from the complex of motherly love and a 'lofty and proud spirit' of Constance, as Mrs Siddons played her. Although Helen Faucit learned to conduct herself in a 'queenly' way, her voice lacked strength; she emphasised 'the feminine, the subtle, and the ideal rather than the bold and overwhelming'.[5] But with Mrs Kean there was no

---

[1] *The Times*, 25 Oct. 1842.
[2] Cited by Shattuck, *Macready's 'King John'*, p. 49.   [3] A. and B. Gelb, *O'Neill*, 1962, p. 24.
[4] See C. B. Hogan (ed.), *The London Stage*, part 5, vol. 1, pp. xcii–xciii.
[5] Carol J. Carlisle, 'Helen Faucit's acting style, *Theatre Survey* 17 (1976), 38–56. There was a disagreement about her acting of Constance, but apparently she managed the tender moments well (Shattuck, *Macready's 'King John'*, p. 51).

doubt, for she wholly domesticated the role, 'stripped of all elevation and grandeur of poetry'.[1] Then the critics diminished the role itself. H. N. Hudson thought Mrs Siddons was so gifted an actress that we tend to overpraise the role of Constance, whose speeches are full of 'redundancy or rhetoric and verbal ingenuity'. Barrett Wendell and Brander Matthews thought Constance was 'guilty of rant'.[2] In Macready's company, it was an omen of things to come that the actor James Anderson, who played the Bastard, was thought to be 'coarse' – 'too much of the bully and swaggerer', rude and 'devoid alike of respect and affection' to his mother. The reviewer in the *Spectator* declared that 'Charles Kemble was the only modern actor equal to represent the physical grandeur and moral dignity of this noble specimen of valorous manhood.' Only one reviewer thought the performance was closer to Shakespeare than Charles Kemble's was, for Anderson in the early scenes of the play seemed truly a bastard born. He even bastardised heroism, and 'His loudness and vehemence, occasionally a fault, is here an "observance."'[3] We should remember, too, that Anderson and other actors of the time were not allowed to speak many of the lines deemed offensive for a delicate taste. These changes, therefore, run deeper than a tendency toward natural acting, for they reflect the encroaching cultural values of Victorian England.

Compared to J. P. Kemble's style, Macready's was seen as realistic, for he extended Kemble's pauses so that they gave the illusion of a person thinking.[4] He also cultivated his favourite 'colloquialisms' or touches of nature that suggested a 'domestic' manner, fostering the values of family love, or he delivered a speech as if it were ordinary conversation. Early in his career he showed, according to Hazlitt, that he could deal out 'melodious declamation like a machine turning ivory balls', but he learned to modulate his delivery and to control the violence of his gestures, having noticed 'how sparingly . . . Mrs Siddons had recourse to gesticulation'.[5] Good taste, household piety, and restraint came to mean as much as histrionic exhibition.

After the turn of the century even Macready's imitators, especially Tree, seemed to be too artificial, and modern actors playing John, Constance and Arthur were often caught between a rock and a hard place, for they would be damned whether they played with the full expression that the lines invite or with muted understatement. A subdued introspective John may be as tasteless as a sentimental Arthur. Dame Sybil Thorndike continued in the 1920s, 1930s and 1940s to present a splendid and intense Constance, without much thanks from the critics. In the same way, Arthur's passionate speeches to save his eyes, formerly thought to be 'unmatched and unmatchable' for their pathos in a 'painful' scene, were described in the 1920s as 'impossible'.[6] A usually discerning critic, James Agate, called them 'affecting school boy stuff'.[7] This complete change in taste may be explained, in part, as due to mistakes of contemporary productions that sometimes cast a boy as Arthur instead of the traditional assignment to a young actress, for the virtuoso role requires a degree

---

[1] G. H. Lewes, *Dramatic Essays*, ed. Archer and Love, 1896, pp. 180–1.
[2] Sprague, *Histories*, p. 22.   [3] Shattuck, *Macready's 'King John'*, p. 52.
[4] Alan C. Downer, *The Eminent Tragedian: William Charles Macready*, 1966, p. 71.
[5] Downer, *Macready*, p. 32.
[6] Sprague, *Histories*, p. 22.   [7] *Sunday Times*, 16 Nov. 1924, p. 6.

of technical skill, with its shifts from sophisticated to childish expression.[1] (Certainly the BBC production in 1984 miscast Arthur with a boy who spoiled the scene.) In any case, actors in the roles of Arthur and Constance are seldom praised, and the role of John seems to be full of traps; hence the play has often failed or has only partially pleased on the modern stage – except for the Bastard.

According to Agate (1924) the Bastard is the one first-class character in the play, and Norman V. Norman played him with great gusto and humour. 'This was a miracle of casting, and the part can never have been better done.' John is not a king of England but 'some hangdog second murderer', and the actress who played Constance was 'a good enough railer'; she 'gave a first-class exposition of Constance's grief and snobbery'.[2] Ralph Richardson acted the Bastard with 'courageous bravura' and 'evident enjoyment of superfluous epithets'.[3] Alec Clunes's Bastard stepped out 'like a figure from a pageant of puppets', for the king was weak and treacherous, an unsympathetic personality, and the actress who played Constance spoke the lines 'realistically' which should have been declaimed.[4]

Yet Muriel St Clare Byrne, who saw the same production sixteen weeks later, thought that Joan Miller made Constance her best part in her first season, 'particularly . . . in that last most difficult scene of all, when half-crazed with grief for the loss of her son, she has to express it in some of the most elaborately rhetorical writing in Shakespeare'. She was not afraid of emotion, and she had 'both power and the pathos needed'. Although Miss Byrne noted that Alec Clunes had the humour and realism for the Bastard, he lacked a driving force, and he should not have been made up like a juvenile lead. She was most impressed by the achievement of the king's role, of which Robert Harris made an unconventional study. He refused to depict John as the villain, which in historical fact he was, but not in Shakespeare's script. Harris's 'profound fidelity' to the Elizabethan play that Shakespeare wrote encouraged him to resist 'the temptation to recompose [John's character] into a consistent portrait'. He left the three disjunct parts as they are in the script: first, the Reformation hero, built up as a symbol of Tudor nationalism; second, the evil, cruel, unscrupulous and unstable nature that was the historical John Lackland; and third, the nominal recovery of royal mystique, which is boosted emotionally by the Bastard's speeches in his behalf and by John's dying a victim of monkish vengeance. In her view, *King John* is 'a theme without heroes, but with spokesmen. The theme is the interdependence of Tudor nationalism and internal unity', but Shakespeare has to force a card on us to make the three instalments of the king seem to work. The anti-Catholic nationalist does not exactly turn into a murderer, for Shakespeare allows John to be only a murderer by intention. And once Arthur is dead, John becomes a semi-legitimate king, worthy of support from patriotic citizens. Altogether, Miss Byrne praised the production for its clarity and vigour, where she found her interpretation confirmed.[5]

[1] Sprague, *Histories*, p. 23.
[2] *Sunday Times*, 16 Nov. 1924, p. 6, review of the Fellowship Players' single performance on 9 Nov.
[3] *The Times*, 15 Sept. 1931.
[4] *The Times*, 17 April 1957, review of Stratford-upon-Avon production.
[5] M. St Clare Byrne, 'The Shakespeare season', *S.Sur.* 8 (1957), 482–5.

3   Richard Burton as the Bastard Falconbridge in the Old Vic production, 1953

Among other successful (with the reviewers at any rate) but quite different productions, that at the Old Vic, 1953, was an 'unexpectedly satisfying treatment of the play'. 'Mr Michael Hordern represents John as an opportunist of *near* genius . . . makes the movement of that intensely political mind an interesting spectacle, and . . . this helps us to understand why, through all his deviousness, he retains the loyalty of the Bastard.' Richard Burton 'gives the whimsically observant Bastard some of that silent momentousness which Sir Laurence Olivier once gave to Hotspur'.[1] On the other hand, Irving Wardle praised the production at Nottingham in 1961, where the theme was uppermost: 'That smooth-faced gentleman, tickling Commodity' is the real hero of the play. When the Dauphin declares his love for Blanche (2.1.496 ff.), the two kings come forward at the same time 'to carve up the territory on the basis of this new alliance'. Wardle found this 'extremely witty and entirely in keeping with the bitter mood' of the script, but he complained that the actress who played 'quibbling Constance' was not enough of an 'emblem of a politically victimized humanity'. 'The really original performance is Barry Foster's King John', who presented 'a derisive laughing boy who rides his crest of success as if at a drunken party, and even subsides into infantile giggles on his death bed'.[2]

These reviews help us distinguish two kinds of dramatic values in our time. Both look for coherence, but the first discovers it in convincing acting that enables a spectator to believe in the transactions on the stage – how Falconbridge can remain loyal to a king such as John. Each actor has certain qualities that enhance this relationship even as the characters are kept distinct. Hordern's John is worthy of our interest in so far as he displays his 'intensely political mind', necessary for the difficulties that he faces. Burton's Falconbridge has conviction too in his momentously silent observation of the king and others along with his bemused engagement and detachment that enhance his political commitments regardless of his master's personal faults. No doubt Commodity is a tool for both politically minded characters in the Old Vic production, but fifteen years later the second reviewer finds it not primarily in the actor's art but in a bit of witty stage business or in characters who should be emblems and implicit comments on the theme. For him the play is essentially a dialectical process, leading to a portable meaning. The real hero is an abstraction and the characters are prized as they are political victims or infantile wantons. The second kind of production and the values it implies are in danger of degrading the drama. But that need not be so. The visual and other non-verbal experiences of a play must always have their place in the whole, because action, costume, and scenic effects give substance to the actor's words and feelings. In a fully satisfying production perceptive audiences will expect something of both.

The history of stage effects in *King John* is perhaps as important as anything mentioned so far. From about 1780 the visual appeal of performance gradually departed from minimal or conventional use of sets, costume, and incidental stage business. In the early nineteenth century bold experiment speeded up the process, which led to a splendid exfoliation of scenes and stage business in the 1840s. Later in the century there followed a period of imitation and decadence. Then, after years

[1] *The Times*, 28 Oct. 1953, p. 5.   [2] *The Times*, 25 Sept. 1968, p. 15.

of relative neglect (1900–40), the play received slightly more attention as it was fitted out and interpreted in line with the tendencies of recent theatre.

Productions of *King John*, as much as any other play, inaugurated a new era of Shakespearean theatre with the interest in what was taken for historical accuracy of costumes, often called the archaeology of staging. The movement began with the refitting for Charles Kemble's company in 1823 at Covent Garden. Before that time it was common for the actors in history plays to appear in contemporary fancy dress, or in vaguely Elizabethan or Roman costumes, but not medieval, although J. P. Kemble had attempted a general sort of archaism for 'old English plays' at the new Covent Garden in 1809. This historical realism was eventually accompanied by interest in 'correct' scenery. Usually there had been various drops and wings depicting a street or a palace or the Tower of London (for *Richard III*) which were used indiscriminately for old plays. So an actor performed against a set, not in it.[1] Apparently Charles Kemble, who took over the management of Covent Garden from his brother, was interested in antiquities, and with the aid of James Robinson Planché he had new costumes designed suggestive of the thirteenth century. Thus, in the second act John's battle dress was decorated with an emblem of rampant lions taken from his great seal. Queen Eleanor's costume was adapted from her effigy in the Abbey of Fontevrault. If no specific association could be found, as with a fictional or little-known person, Planché settled for an image of a thirteenth-century knight, cardinal, or herald found in analogous 'authorities'. Exactly when scenery too was created for the picturesque effect is not certain, but it must have occurred at about the same time, for this is part of the transformation of the arts in England, along with medievalisation of taste. In the theatre historical accuracy offered an opportunity for splendour with picturesque groups of actors, deployed to create beautiful effects. The visual patina of history and the assurance in the programme notes that everything about the performance and sets was absolutely authentic obviously enhanced the audience's pleasure. On the first night at Covent Garden, 24 November 1823:

When the curtain rose, and discovered King John dressed as his effigy appears in Worcester Cathedral, surrounded by his barons sheathed in mail, with cylindrical helmets and correct armorial shields, and his courtiers in the long tunics and mantles of the thirteenth century, there was a roar of approbation, accompanied by four distinct rounds of applause . . .[2]

Indeed, history had in the nineteenth century taken the place of epic poetry in the scale of literary forms; and historical dramas like Schiller's *Wallenstein* and historical paintings like David's *Oath of the Horatii* seemed to magnify heroic moments in human experience.[3] The next step was to make history palpable, in concrete detail, even as the audience was aware of the art by which it was done.

When Macready took over the management of Drury Lane in 1841, he more than his predecessors combined the sets and costumes and acting of the major productions into harmonious spectacles, and significantly his first season started with a finely outfitted opera – Gay and Handel's *Acis and Galatea*, along with a well-researched

[1] Downer, *Macready*, p. 23.
[2] Planché, *Recollections and Reflections*, 1872, 1, 56–7; cited by Sprague, *Histories*, p. 4.
[3] Herbert Lindenburger, *Historical Drama*, 1975, ch. 3; also Waith, pp. 209–11.

Merchant of Venice and other revivals. In the second season he made extraordinary efforts to restore *King John* as 'an animated picture of those Gothic times which are so splendidly illustrated by the drama'. Prior to Macready's revolution the supernumeraries were generally limited to three or four, but to be realistic in this *King John* he had to crowd the stage, and one reporter counted 300 supers, all of whom had to be trained and rehearsed.[1]

Although Macready cared for detail in costumes, it was not just a matter of correct design, for the actors spent countless hours learning how to wear their armour correctly and to get the feel of costumes in a particular setting. The sets were brilliantly executed by William Telbin, as shown in Charles Shattuck's reproductions of the watercolour designs, and the total effect was a 'celebration of English History and English Poetry' – 'the gothic and chivalric grandeur of the Middle Age'. Each character was 'marked [by his costume] with picturesque exactness', and the scenes all had 'the air of truth, the character of simple and strong fidelity' – particularly the Orchard designed for Swinstead Abbey and the 'picture' of Northampton Castle. John Forster, who wrote this appreciation of the revival, emphasised that above all 'in every movement of the tragedy, there is Mind at work, without which wealth of material is nothing'.[2] From other comments of the same kind, we can gather that this production was a masterpiece of ensemble playing, design, and harmonious conception, probably the 'finest work that Macready had ever put together'.[3]

According to Macready's own principles of stagecraft, enunciated three years earlier, he claimed that whereas J. P. Kemble's drama was 'stationary', and in stage arrangements 'remained traditional', his purpose was innovative, to bring alive Shakespeare's dramas 'with the truth of illustration they merit'. Instead of concentrating on the leading actor exclusively, he tried to follow Sir Thomas Lawrence's observation that 'every part of a picture required equal care and pains', so he sought in his company's staging to 'give purpose and passion to the various figures of [his] group'. Hence the detailed diagrams in his prompt-books, marking where every character should stand or sit in certain scenes. The ideal was 'to transfer his picture from the poet's mind to the stage, complete in its parts and harmoniously arranged as to figure, scene, and action'.[4]

The stage business worked within the set, each movement carefully planned for co-ordinated action. The management of the prison scene (4.1), for example, is typical of his precision. The audience first saw an 'ominous vaulted chamber . . . painted in gloomy olive grays' with two practicable doors – one on the left before which hung a dark green tapestry, and one at the back locked with a key in it. When the latter door was opened a 'chamber piece' was visible behind. Light that seemed to come from the window, in which stood a crucifix, was set between arches at stage right. As Shattuck remarks (p. 28), 'this was obviously not real light, but only bright paint on flat canvas', but the actual stage lights were dimmed 'to enhance the melodrama

[1] Downer, *Macready*, p. 217. The Macready-Kean prompt-book indicates 88 supers in Act 2.
[2] John Forster, *The Examiner*, 29 October 1842; cited by Shattuck, *Macready's 'King John'*, p. 1.
[3] Shattuck, *Macready's 'King John'*, p. 2.
[4] Macready, *Diaries*, II, 17–18, cited by Downer, *Macready*, p. 225.

4 Act 4, Scene 1: vaulted apartment in Northampton Castle, for Macready's production in 1842. Designed by William Telbin

gloom of the scene'. A heavy antique table and chair stood at right centre, and off-stage left there were ready a pan of imitation fire, a set of blinding-irons painted red hot, and some cords to tie Prince Arthur to the chair; off-stage rear there was a bow and arrow ready for Arthur to carry in.

According to the detailed directions in the prompt-book, when Hubert says to the two attendants 'Heat me these irons hot', he gives them to the second attendant; while both attendants go to the left, the first stops and says 'I hope your warrant will . . .' etc., and they go out. Hubert unlocks the other door and calls to Arthur, then he *sits in the chair and leans on table*. Arthur, *who has been playing with his bow, on left, suddenly turns, observes Hubert intently, and goes to him* saying 'You are sad.' At Hubert's aside, 'His words do take possession of my bosom', he *rises and paces a few steps in agitation, then gives him the warrant*, and *on seeing Arthur's emotion he turns away*. Arthur, at 'Must you with hot irons burn out . . .' etc., *drops the warrant*. After some other business, Hubert stamps his foot and the attendants re-enter with cord, irons, and pan of fire:

Arthur runs shrieking to cling round Hubert, right – The second Attendant puts down the pan of fire, and gives the iron across to Hubert, as he commands [i.e. 'Give me the iron'], – First Attendant has the rope, and seizes Arthur,–they both strive to disengage his arms and legs from Hubert, during his speech [Arthur's 'Alas, what need you be so boist'rous'] and drag him away, to left, – as he says 'Nay hear me, Hubert' etc.

5 Act 4, Scene 1: Arthur, Hubert and Executioners, by James Northcote, 1789. Hubert is thought to be a portrait of J. P. Kemble, but may possibly be Robert Bensley, who played Hubert frequently between 1767 and 1795

6   Act 4, Scene 1: Arthur, Hubert and Executioners, by Henry Fuseli

After Hubert relents, he throws away the irons, kneels and embraces Arthur.[1]

A few details concerning the attendants' actions originated in J. P. Kemble's prompt-book, and Charles Kean much later added a few of Arthur's tender gestures to Hubert. But the mass of stage business and the scene designs originated in Macready's production. Shattuck discovered that Kean's prompt-books were copied for him from Macready's lost prompt-book, and the sets were imitations of Telbin's paintings for the celebrated 1842 performances.

As stage business increased and more money was spent on sets and costumes, the burden of producing the play became onerous, and there were failures, like Kean's unfortunate American tour of 1852. Then Beerbohm Tree's fancy staging in 1899 at Her Majesty's Theatre in its very excess may have killed the play. By outdoing what had been successful in earlier productions, Tree set out to please the eye or amuse the audience at any cost to the drama, no matter how intrusive. For example, the first act begins in a 'nobly vaulted chamber of Northampton Castle' with two thrones on a dais, before which stands 'the portly chamberlain, wandbearing, red-robed' at the very top of a 'great staircase. An organ sounds, and he stalks majestically down. After him skips a little jester.' Later that jester speeds Robert Falconbridge off the stage with a whack of his bladder. Another typical bit of visual wit intrudes in 3.3: in 'a glade of slim beeches John communes with the faithful, grim Hubert', and while Arthur plucks daisies, the king 'smiles down at him as he passes, and the child starts

---

[1] Shattuck, *Macready's 'King John'*. Sprague, in *Shakespeare and the Actors*, pp. 113–14, cites some of this business, but he thought these details were Charles Kean's invention.

7 Act 5, Scene 1: John brooding about his surrender of the crown on Ascension Day, by E. A. Abbey, 1902. Abbey was probably influenced in this picture by Herbert Beerbohm Tree's 1899 production at Her Majesty's Theatre

away. There are some daisies growing near the spot where the king has been whispering his behest [to Hubert]. Lightly, he cuts the heads off them with his sword . . .'

Max Beerbohm, the reviewer who records these and dozens of other theatrical touches, admits that he found the play insufferably tedious to read, but he claims that a good production 'makes one forget what is bad in sheer surprise at finding so much that is good . . . I have never seen a production in which the note of beauty was so incessantly struck as in this production of *King John*.' Beerbohm grants that Shakespeare's masterpieces are well worth seeing even if skimpily produced, but the public will not go to the inferior plays unless they are set out elaborately.[1]

The entire review has a strangely guarded tone and a narrow focus on stage business and effects, but regardless of what Max Beerbohm really thought about his brother's art, other reports verify that Tree's production of *King John* was distinctly old-fashioned. Tree included sixteen tableaux, which the public expected, for pageantry was 'inevitable' in a history play, and this production presented 'a picture of life under the Angevin kings as correct and splendid as is ever likely to be realized'.[2] Another reviewer agreed that the stage spectacle was 'superb – giving the impression of tumultuous life, essential to a chronicle play'. He admitted that Tree was not an impressive actor, but that his was 'plausible, well-conducted acting'.[3]

Nearly everything about Tree's staging violated the emerging ideas of modern theatre – it was busy without significance, distrustful of the script and of the value of conviction in acting. The play became just a sweetmeat. Of course, Tree did this with most of his productions, but in spite of his success at the box-office, his *King John* seems to us a failure, perhaps because we are aware (as Max Beerbohm was) of other trends in the theatre at the turn of the century: the decline of the taste for the gothic and the picturesque; the new importance of small repertory companies, on the model of the Meiningen players – inspired by Macready's example, by way of Phelps[4] – which emphasised the unity and harmony of a performance; and realism in sets as well as in acting. The days of the extravaganza were numbered, and *King John*, indelibly marked with a sumptuous theatrical style, almost disappeared from the stage.

Although the play has lately received more attention, the directors seem to be struggling to find the right combination of effects to harmonise acting and script. According to James Agate, one such experiment, a production staged by Tyrone Guthrie for the Old Vic at the New Theatre in 1941, was beautiful to look at. With no concessions to realism, the set was mainly 'heraldic curtains and sweeping banners, with a great display of armour and gonfalons' and 'whimsical . . . bouncing hobby horses before the walls of Angiers'. The play was primarily an occasion for the decadent John, 'a fine intellect poisoned' – played by Ernest Milton, 'pallid, subtle, marsh-lit, in a stylised red wig'.[5] Still, Agate found most of the actors and the play

[1] Max Beerbohm, *More Theatres 1898–1903*, 1969, pp. 191–3, 347. Furness, *Variorum*, attributed the review to G. B. Shaw.   [2] *The Athenaeum*, 23 Sept. 1899, p. 427.
[3] *The Speaker*, 30 Sept. 1899, p. 346.   [4] Downer, *Macready*, p. 352.
[5] J. C. Trewin, *Shakespeare on the English Stage 1900–1964*, 1964, p. 188. Trewin also notes that Peter Brook's production for the Birmingham Repertory Theatre (1945) 'began with what looked like a court bacchanal [and] never drifted into a monotony of blustering barons', p. 197.

8 The Bastard's anger: 'Here's a stay / That shakes the rotten carcass of old Death / Out of his rags' (2.1.455). Ernst Schmidt as King Philip, Dietrich Mechow as King John and Hans Radloff as the Bastard in the Weimar National Theatre production, 1980

disappointing, and 'What a bad play this is! All about a war in which it is not possible to take the slightest interest.'[1]

Since the director has taken the place of the dictatorial actor-manager, he reigns over a company, and like his predecessor he too does ingenious things with sets, costumes and stage business, to bring out distinct implications of the drama. The director at best moulds the performance into a coherent experience, or at least attempts connections between the parts. Sometimes that linkage is symbolic or abstract; for example, the stylised sets for the BBC television production (1984) seemed to match the atmosphere of 'dubious wheelings and dealings' and the 'cynical veerings of power-figures given over to pursuit of advantage'. In keeping with this atmosphere, interiors were accented by 'heavy arches and massy pillars bedizened with zigzags, lozenges and hieratic-looking patterns'; exteriors flaunted 'an archaic panoply – pavilions and pennants under a silky blue sky', and costumes had a fancy embroidered and 'faintly barbaric sumptuousness'. In the same spirit, the acting of Richard Wordsworth's 'formidably lethal' Pandulph was 'wizened and unwinking' as he 'snakes his way through his speeches' twisty arguments'. Some of the best scenes in the production were those where he 'loops coils of equivocation around Charles Kay's bemused King Philip and Jonathan Coy's ambitious, callow Dauphin'.[2] On the other hand, the scenery for the Weimar production (see illustration 8) was stark and minimal, suggesting a devastated land, and while the two kings bowed to the Citizen of Angiers, the actor playing the Bastard added meaning to his exclamation: 'Here's a stay / That shakes the rotten carcass of old Death / Out of his rags' (2.1.455) – kneeling before the body of a dead young soldier. This was one of several touches that kept him, in spite of his warrior-swagger, on the human side of the play's moral and political life.[3]

The 1957 stage effects for the Stratford-upon-Avon production directed by Douglas Seale were created mainly by lights. Thus the scenes of war and violence were translated into a 'sinister, brooding atmosphere by setting the action against a background darkness or else an ominous leaden sky, shot with livid flame' which suggested the 'wrathful heavens'. In the more intimate scenes there was 'a fine spill of light against the darkness, in which the players and the splashes of color made by their costumes stood out in sharp relief'. Miss Byrne would rather have disposed of the 'Norman-Nondescript' backgrounds, and replaced the medieval costumes with Elizabethan dress on an open stage without lighting effects, because *King John* is more Tudor than medieval. Although that kind of fidelity is not likely to become a trend in the theatre of our time, it is encouraging to see the artful simplicity of recent staging of history plays at Stratford, Ontario, as well as at Stratford-upon-Avon.

Dramatic speech

The declamatory style in its most blustering form has a special place in *King John*. Nearly every character uses it from time to time, except for Melun, who is heard at

[1] *Sunday Times*, 13 July 1941, p. 2.   [2] Peter Kemp, *TLS*, 7 Dec. 1984, p. 1416.
[3] Courtesy of Philip Brockbank, who saw the performance.

the moment of death, when all men should speak the plain truth. Even the Bastard practises it when he must represent the king: 'Now hear our English king, / For thus his royalty doth speak in me.' There follows a farrago of ridicule, defiance, boasting, and sneering at the Dauphin's invading army, as if it is a mere courtly masque:

> This apish and unmannerly approach,
> This harnessed masque and unadvisèd revel,
> This unhaired sauciness and boyish troops . . .

5.2.131–3

But the audience knows that John is emotionally and militarily unfit to resist the French invasion, which is far more dangerous than a 'dwarfish war'. The Bastard here simply follows his own advice to John, putting on the dauntless spirit of resolution and covering up his fear and distrust, an impression reinforced by the heavy-handed parallelism, polysyllabic diction, the inevitable epithets before nearly every noun, alliteration, and the elaborate conceit.

But in spite of the nominal decorum of the speech, with its obligatory defiance before a battle, by this time in the play such a show does not carry much conviction. The relative subtlety and flexibility of the dramatic poetry in Acts 3 and 4 and in parts of Act 5 make it seem too artificial. The same kind of style, though not as extreme, can be discerned in Salisbury's overblown protestations of regret that he must betray his king and country (5.2.8–39). Here, too, the Dauphin treats the speech with a note of mockery, calling it an 'earthquake of nobility' (42), and in effect he asks the English defectors to grow up, leave those 'baby eyes' (56) to those who do not recognise their real interests. He promises the nobles that they will thrust their hands deep into 'the purse of rich prosperity' (61) for shifting loyalty to him. Therefore, by cynical mockery Shakespeare has to some extent distanced the audience from the overblown passage.

In contrast to his fifth-act bluster, the Bastard's more authentic personal voice carries conviction when he whole-heartedly thanks his mother for giving him a great father:

> Who lives and dares but say thou didst not well
> When I was got, I'll send his soul to hell.
> Come, lady, I will show thee to my kin,
>   And they shall say, when Richard me begot,
> If thou hadst said him nay, it had been sin.
> Who says it was, he lies; I say 'twas not.

1.1.271–6

Defending his mother's sin as venial, he declares that he will be her champion, for he knows in his bones that her fault was not her folly. It was her glory that she had to lay her heart at the disposal of Richard's commanding love. Although the six lines are rhymed they seem unpremeditated – in natural word order, mostly monosyllabic. In his high spirits the Bastard talks as he feels, so we believe that he is willing to back up his words with action. The not/naught pun at the end is a witty grace-note that emphasises frank acceptance of himself as well as of his mother. Shakespeare's plain style creates conviction here, as in many private utterances in the play, when it is the vehicle for straight talk. Its generic affinities are with comedies like *The Two*

Gentlemen of Verona where the hyperbolic style masks affectation or insincerity –
usually in the men – and the plain style denotes sincerity in the women.[1] There is
also a distinction between Petruchio's heroic boasting in public and his frank, terse
speech in intimate moments with Kate, which resembles that between the Bastard's
two styles.

In *John* the distinction is evident from the first two acts and the first scene of Act 3.
The kings of England and France are not such deep-dyed dissimulators as
Pandulph, who always speaks with calculation, but when they undertake to defend
their interests before the gates of Angiers, they declaim vigorously (2.1.204–66). With
a mixture of high-mindedness and violent threats they put their cases to the citizens
on the walls above, and they speak in Marlowe's mighty lines:

> And but for our approach, those sleeping stones,
> That as a waist doth girdle you about,
> By the compulsion of their ordinance
> . . . on the sight of us your lawful king,
> Who painfully with much expedient march
> Have brought a countercheck before your gates . . .   2.1.216–24

Moreover, John adapts Tamburlaine's 'bullets like Jove's dreadful thunderbolts /
Enrolled in flames and fiery smouldering mists' (*1 Tamburlaine* 2.3.19–20):

> And now, instead of bullets wrapped in fire
> To make a shaking fever in your walls,
> They shoot but calm words folded up in smoke   2.1.227–30

The two kings make equally plausible arguments and are equally unconvincing, for
their speeches seem confected. After the battle the English and French heralds claim
victory for their respective armies, in symmetrical communiqués purporting to be
straight from the field, but their pompous, ceremonial language and over-confident
declarations of victory cancel each other out. It is hard to believe anyone who decorates
nearly every noun with an epithet: 'bleeding ground', 'dancing banners', 'silver-
bright', 'purpled hands', and so on. In reply the Citizen avoids the rhetorical tricks
of the heralds and restricts himself to a pattern of equal phrases:

> Blood hath bought blood, and blows have answered blows;
> Strength matched with strength, and power confronted power;
> Both are alike, and both alike we like.
> One must prove greatest. While they weigh so even,
> We hold our town for neither, yet for both.   2.1.329–33

By contrast with the hyperbolic style, the relative plainness has a ring of truth,
confirming that neither army has won a decisive battle, as the audience suspected. But
when the Citizen finds it necessary to save the city from almost certain destruction
by the combined armies, he dissimulates as much as the kings and in the same style.
He flatters France's son and England's niece, as 'lusty love' in 'quest of beauty'; in
Blanche the Dauphin is 'a blessèd man' and she a 'fair divided excellence' (2.1.426

---

[1] Hibbard, pp. 99–103.

ff.). In short, he proposes a dynastic marriage between two people who have never spoken to each other, for whom he will open the 'fast-closèd gates' with 'swifter spleen than powder can enforce'. After offering such bait the Citizen proves that he can be as seemingly intransigent as the kings who stand below: 'without this match, / The sea enragèd is not half so deaf, / Lions more confident, mountains and rocks / More free from motion' (2.1.450–3). The shabby colours of rhetoric and the thundering oratory do not seem to trouble the royal opponents and their entourage, for they are too busy thinking about the mutual advantages of such a marriage. Except for the Bastard, who ridicules the style in a way that would do honour to Hotspur:

> Here's a large mouth indeed,
> That spits forth death and mountains, rocks and seas,
> Talks as familiarly of roaring lions
> As maids of thirteen do of puppy-dogs! . . .
> Zounds! I was never so bethumped with words
> Since I first called my brother's father Dad.   2.1.457–67

This soldier's disdain for a civilian imitation of the language of smoke, cannon-fire and bounce reduces the citizens to 'scroyles of Angiers', who stand on their battlements like spectators in a theatre, gaping and pointing at the armies' 'industrious scenes and acts of death', contemptuously demeaning the honourable art of war. The brilliant reduction of roaring lions to puppy-dogs calls attention to the parody, and the joke about calling 'my brother's father Dad' assures everyone that he ought to know false words when he hears them. The Bastard's own proposal, which is forgotten once Angiers interjects its tempting compromise, has the virtue of cutting through pretence. There is no glory in fighting for the approval of 'these jades', 'this peevish town'. Better to level the city then, let the armies turn 'face to face' and show the kings' mettle in a clean conflict that Fortune will decide. In effect the Bastard wants the kings to avoid negotiation or compromise and to make their virtues speak in a battle of 'equal potents, fiery-kindled spirits' (2.1.358). His otherwise zany proposal, therefore, would wipe out stains of bad theatre and leave a possibility that at least one army might come away with victory, but the honey-tongued promises of Commodity so beguile the leaders that they ignore the Bastard's honourable but hare-brained proposal.

Consequently, this is a functional use of style that prepares for his Commodity soliloquy. And, in general, the variety of styles and their juxtaposition make the play, as Hibbard observes, 'something of a poetic workshop, a place in which [Shakespeare] reassesses old techniques and tries to find out new ones'. The lack of smooth connections and the 'tentative' quality of the styles and the inclination toward parody suggest perhaps the 'experimental nature' of the script.

Aside from the declamatory rhetoric and the critical attitudes toward it, Shakespeare fashioned a more intensely dramatic style for John and Constance. For example, John's temptation of Hubert (3.3.19–69) is a step toward the supple contextualised dialogue of *Julius Caesar* and *Macbeth*. As Hibbard suggests, 'John is the first of Shakespeare's tragic criminals, the man of power who gives way to temptation that the successful exercise of power brings with it' (p. 39). For this purpose John's speech creates the illusion of his inner feelings while he consciously

9 Act 3, Scene 3: King John and Hubert whispering, by C. Walter Hodges. 'He is a very serpent in my way . . . Dost thou understand me?'

manipulates Hubert with his words. To prepare for the encounter he sends the Bastard safely off-stage, back to England where the one honest man will be kept too busy to interfere until it is too late. Eleanor draws Arthur to one side, as if by previous agreement with her son, and she and Arthur whisper unheard by the audience, while the king and Hubert talk confidentially. This is a visual image of conspiracy that recurs in the play (1.1.40–3, 2.1.468, 4.2.68). At first John flatters 'gentle Hubert' (3.3.19), to whom he owes much – 'good friend', what 'good respect I have of thee' (24, 28). The dialogue is framed by his implied promises that he will 'pay' for Hubert's love 'with advantage' (22); 'Hubert, I love thee. / Well, I'll not say what I intend for thee' (67–8). Such vagueness characterises his talk, as he circles the subject insinuatingly to create what government officials now call *deniability* and Francis Bacon says was called 'The turning of the cat in the pan' – to speak so obscurely about what one wants done until one's subordinate advocates it.[1] Bacon knew of a public official who 'when he came to have speech, he would pass over that

[1] 'Of Cunning', *Essays*, ed. J. Pitcher, 1985, pp. 127–8.

he intended most, and go forth, and come back again and speak of it as of a thing that he had almost forgot' (p. 127). John's apparent false starts – 'I had a thing to say, / But I will fit it with some better time' (25), 'I had a thing to say, but let it go' (33) – seem spontaneous, but Bacon recommends that tactic too: 'The breaking off in the midst of that one was about to say, as if [the speaker] took himself up, breeds greater appetite in him with whom you confer, to know more' (p. 127). Hubert rises to that bait willingly, with affirmations that exceed the king's tentative remarks: 'I am much beholden to your majesty' (29) and 'what you bid me undertake, / Though that my death were adjunct to my act, / By heaven, I would do it' (56–8). Machiavelli mentions the prince's need for servants like Hubert who want to be deceived, for princes must be great dissemblers.[1]

In a staccato climax the two voices are as one, and it is not possible to determine exactly who has the greater culpability:

JOHN Death.
HUBERT   My lord.
JOHN   A grave.
HUBERT   He shall not live.
JOHN   Enough.   (3.3.66)

Hubert is the willing tool as much as John is the apparent operator; neither is exactly pleased with his role. The intensity of John's struggle to handle the situation comes out of his language in hints of his disordered and involuntary thoughts. He gives the impression that he really does not want to say the thing he must say. Speaking of his 'good respect' for Hubert, he lets fall that he is 'almost ashamed' of it (27–8). Amidst this dissimulation he openly wishes that his confidant could take in his request without his eyes, or that he could hear without ear, and 'make reply / Without a tongue, using conceit alone', as if there were an inexpressible horror in his mind that he cannot utter in broad daylight (48–50). In the proper setting for his dreadful command, his tongue would be in the midnight bell, whose 'brazen mouth' sounds in the 'ear of night'. He wishes that Hubert were 'possessèd with a thousand wrongs'. Only the spirit of melancholy should run through Hubert's veins; merriment is a 'passion hateful to my purposes'. What is evasive in the rest of John's speech becomes in these deranged words and images an involuntary fear. The images are not composed as in the big set speeches of 2.1 and 3.1; they spill out and grow in a way all their own while John speaks. Although he does not discover his feelings yet to himself, he at least betrays them to the audience.[2]

In the rest of the play John's dialogue depicts his increasing helplessness. He reserves the old hyperbolic style for scattered bursts of hope, but as he feels the reins of power slip from his hands, he sounds plaintive: 'Why do you bend such solemn brows on me?' (4.2.90); 'O, where hath our intelligence been drunk?' (116); 'Withhold thy speed, dreadful Occasion!' (125). Formerly he was proved to be self-sufficient; now he is dependent upon others: 'This inundation of mistempered

[1] *The Prince*, trans. Ricci, rev. E. R. P. Vincent, pp. 64–5; cited by Greenblatt, *Renaissance Self-Fashioning*, 1980, p. 24.
[2] Hibbard, pp. 36–8, thinks the king discovers his purpose while he talks.

humour / Rests by you only to be qualified' (5.1.12). When the invasion reaches a
critical point, he turns over to the Bastard 'the ordering of this present time' (5.1.77).
Finally, on his deathbed, totally impotent, he complains pitifully,

> I do not ask you much,
> I beg cold comfort; and you are so strait
> And so ungrateful, you deny me that.
>
> 5.7.41–3

The temptation scene that we examined above has a companion at the end of 4.2,
when John's defensive speeches gain an authenticity while he loses assurance, under
Hubert's steady pressure. Hubert is now the active rather than the reactive character,
and he tries the king's soul, scourging his conscience and picking at the scabs of
hypocrisy until John needs to be told that Arthur lives. So Hubert searches for signs
of repentance and pushes the king to the edge of despair before the regretful words
come out of his mouth:

> My nobles leave me, and my state is braved,
> Even at my gates, with ranks of foreign powers.
> Nay, in the body of this fleshly land,
> This kingdom, this confine of blood and breath,
> Hostility and civil tumult reigns
> Between my conscience and my cousin's death.
>
> 4.2.243–8

Now that John drops his bluster and begins to assess his position frankly, Hubert is
willing to 'make a peace between your soul and you'. His method of eliciting that
plain admission from the king is not as devious as the way John worked on him in
Act 3. Instead of flattering, he possesses the king with fears by depicting the state of
mind of the common people, who whisper in each other's ears of Arthur's death: one
grips the hearer's wrist, others wrinkle their brows and roll their eyes or stand open-
mouthed. Hubert repeats the images of bodily parts that the peers used earlier in the
scene to call attention to the signs of concealed guilt in John's breast: a 'heinous fault'
in his eyes, a 'close aspect', and a tell-tale blush while whispering with Hubert
(4.2.71–7).

Hubert and John's dispute about a warrant for the execution of the murder is
conducted in the same bodily terms. And after the announcement that Arthur lives,
the style of John's apology to Hubert again suggests that his perceptions are troubled
and involuntary, as in the temptation scene. Once more the images of eyes, blood, and
face disturb him:

> Forgive the comment that my passion made
> Upon thy feature, for my rage was blind,
> And foul imaginary eyes of blood
> Presented thee more hideous than thou art.
>
> 4.2.263–6

Constance too suffers disordered perceptions which govern her rage and enhance
her declamatory style when she feels utterly impotent. In Act 2 she and Eleanor
sound like a pair of brawling women, hurling imprecations in their 'ill-tunèd
repetitions' (2.1.197), but the splendour of her baffled outrage in Act 3 has an energy
that surpasses anything of the kind in the play. Her articulate power, which modern

audiences may find tiresome, seldom failed to affect eighteenth- and nineteenth-century theatre audiences. Her whole being is her pride in her son's rights, and her anger at anyone who deprives him of his birthright is so all-consuming that she becomes splendidly awful in her suffering. Unlike the iron-jawed queens in *Richard III*, Constance is not just a nemesis with a loud voice; her tongue stings the conscience of King Philip, and she wins sympathy in the desolation of her grief. In this upside-down world she is a walking reminder of the perfidy of kings, a helpless widow who calls upon God to protect her and her fatherless child.[1] Moreover, with the baleful assistance of Pandulph, her curse takes effect within 200 lines.

> Arm, arm, you heavens, against these perjured kings!
> A widow cries; be husband to me, God!
> Let not the hours of this ungodly day
> Wear out the day in peace; but ere sun set,
> Set armèd discord 'twixt these perjured kings.   3.1.107–11

She begins the scene with Salisbury when he has just told her the news of the marriage treaty, and her reply immediately suggests disordered thoughts. Her figures of repetition become excessive; she shoots her questions in a fusillade of four, her fearful denials in three. 'It is not so; thou hast misspoke, misheard' (3.1.4). She insults kindly Salisbury in short bursts:

> Fellow, be gone: I cannot brook thy sight;
> This news hath made thee a most ugly man.   3.1.36–7

Her response to Arthur's hope that she will be 'content' also suggests that she is distraught. She could be content if Arthur were grim and ugly,

> sland'rous to thy mother's womb . . .
> Lame, foolish, crooked, swart, prodigious,
> Patched with foul moles and eye-offending marks,   3.1.44–7

for then she would not love him! Obviously there is a certain truth in what Eleanor said of Constance: she is ambitious and wants to be queen so she can 'check the world' (1.1.32, 2.1.123). Her pride and hopes are inextricably entangled in her son's future, a natural inclination for any parent, but how much greater a temptation for the mother of a prince. Her vehemence increases when she thinks of the injustice done to his natural beauty and the fortune of his birth, for Fortune now is 'corrupted, changed, and won from thee'; she 'adulterates hourly' with John, and France is a 'bawd to Fortune and King John' (3.1.54–61). This moral outrage does to Salisbury what Constance wants him to do to France: 'Envenom him with words' (63). If she cannot have a crown for her son, she will act out her sovereign grief in an inspired defiance that lifts her to imperiousness. She will not go to the kings; let the kings come to her and do homage to her sorrow. As King Richard II saw himself in a dramatic light, sitting on the ground like the King of Woe,[2] so Constance is the

---

[1] Jones, *Origins*, p. 242. She is not a widow in the chronicles, nor is Arthur a fatherless child.
[2] See illustration 10, from Dürer's *Little Passion*, for a woodcut of Christ in this role, sitting on a stone, with a crown of thorns and the stigmata (E. Panofsky, *Albrecht Dürer*, 1948, no. 236).

10   Man of Sorrows: a model for Constance's grief (3.1.73). A woodcut by Albrecht Dürer from *The Little Passion, c.* 1511

Queen of Sorrows, a timeless figure, without future or past. Her plain words now dignify the occasion, and she sits on her throne, the ground.

> I will instruct my sorrows to be proud,
> For Grief is proud and makes his owner stoop.
> To me and to the state of my great grief
> Let kings assemble . . .

3.1.68–71

The signs of Constance's incipient madness are clearest in her increased use of repetition. There is an early example when she rings the changes on *plague* and *sin* (2.1.179–90), but in the third act she picks up a word from the previous speaker and racks it compulsively – for example, in the litanies on *day* (3.1.83–95), *law* (185–90), and *need* (212–16), and in the climactic series of verbs and nouns accompanied by *me* and *my* (3.4.92–105). The most telling speech is her repeated denial that she is mad: 'I am not mad: this hair I tear is mine . . . I am not mad. I would to God I were . . . Preach some philosophy to make me mad . . . being not mad . . . If I were mad . . . I am not mad . . .' (3.4.45–59). Her inspired fury gains authority when she speaks like an Old Testament prophet. In response to Austria's 'Lady Constance, peace' she cries 'War, war, no peace! Peace is to me a war' (3.1.113). It is a dishonest peace because of the corruption that engendered it, as Erasmus comments on Jeremiah 6.13, 8.10, and Isaiah 48.22: there is a warfare in every person, and it is as if 'this

11 'I will not keep this form upon my head, / When there is such disorder in my wit': Sarah Siddons as Constance, tearing her hair (3.4.101–2), by C. Warren, after a drawing by J. Thurston, 1804

peace of ours were . . . actually the most shameful kind of war . . . You lunatic! You cry "Peace! Peace!" when you have God as your enemy.'[1]

The fell anatomy that Constance wishes to call up is Death, the pale horse, pale rider, who is followed by Hell, and who, for Constance, would replace God as her husband. Therefore, the language of her final speeches suggests her utter desperation – a tragic madness that anticipates the rages of Lear, who senses his own injustice, although he is more sinned against than sinning. Constance and her perfidious allies share the guilt for their exploitation of Arthur. As the Bastard has told us, France came to Arthur's cause as God's own soldier, and the peace that he made is a 'mad composition' suitable to a 'Mad world, mad kings' (2.1.561).

---

[1] *Enchiridion*, trans. R. Himelick, 1963, pp. 39–40. See supplementary note to 3.1.113.

Unlike Constance and John, the Bastard keeps his sanity and remains more or less a whole man in a mad world, perhaps because he manages to be both in and out of every complex situation. He can throw himself into action one moment and in the next he can contemplate the moral and political constraints of his position. His sense of humour and his light touch alternate with his earnestness and practicality. In these various modes he is still primarily a social animal, conscious of himself in relation to other people. Once he is recognised by Eleanor and the king as the living image of Cœur-de-lion, by the trick of his face and the 'large composition of his body', he begins to find his identity, and they treat him as a member of the family. The truth about ourselves as others see us inevitably interests a dramatist; thus, in the words of Ulysses, a man

> Cannot make boast to have that which he hath,
> Nor feels not what he owes, but by reflection;
> As when his virtues, aiming upon others,
> Heat them, and they retort that heat again
> To the first giver.   *Troilus and Cressida* 3.3.98–102

As private a character as Brutus admits that the 'eye sees not itself / But by reflection, by some other things' (*Julius Caesar* 1.2.52). So, Eleanor recognises the Bastard's similarity to his natural father in the 'accent of his tongue', and his speech, and that is the face he presents to the world.

Aside from his parody of the declamatory style and his authentic plainness in a crisis, the Bastard has an earthy, racy style that establishes him clearly as the leader of the volunteers who will go abroad to fight for the king. He represents what Chatillon calls the 'unsettled humours of the land' that have been spilled out, not unlike English volunteers led by the peppery Sir Roger Williams, who went to the Low Countries under Leicester.[1] Their traits, as described in Act 2, confirm much of our impression of the Bastard in Act 1; he is rash, reckless and fiery, willing to give up his property at home and to carry his birthright proudly on his back, seeking fortune abroad with his new-found grandam and uncle. He indicates his pride in his body, when he gives thanks that he does not look like his half-brother, with legs like riding-rods, arms like stuffed eel-skins, and a face so thin that he must not stick a rose behind his ear, lest men should say 'Look where three-farthings goes!' (1.1.143). He speaks to the king straight off with a jaunty colloquialism unlike the formal speech of others: 'I put you o'er to heaven, and to my mother' (1.1.62), and he corrects the old queen unceremoniously, informing her that he does not wound his mother's honour:

> No, I have no reason for it.
> That is my brother's plea, and none of mine,
> The which if he can prove, a pops me out
> At least from fair five hundred pound a year.
> Heaven guard my mother's honour, and my land!   1.1.66–70

The anticlimax, 'and my land', adds just the impudent touch, as does his bold confession to the king, in the same madcap tone, 'O old Sir Robert, father, on my

---

[1] See 2.1.69–71 and Commentary.

knee / I give heaven thanks I was not like to thee!' (1.1.82–3). The rest of his talk is a string of quips with light irony, but when Eleanor offers him the great opportunity she brings out a dauntless spirit, and he switches tone in mid speech.

> Brother, take you my land, I'll take my chance.
> Your face hath got five hundred pound a year,
> Yet sell your face for five pence and 'tis dear.
> Madam, I'll follow you unto the death.   1.1.151–4

It is as blunt and unqualified a commitment as possible, after such diffidence, and in action and word he sticks to it, even when he knows she and the king are wrong.

His speeches to his mother later in the first act go through the same pattern, beginning with impudence and wit, especially in his quick replies:

> LADY FALCONBRIDGE Hast thou denied thyself a Falconbridge?
> BASTARD As faithfully as I deny the devil.   1.1.251–2

The rejoinder suggests a sort of rebaptism with his new name. But he ends the scene with a vital commitment, beyond good and evil, to his mother and to what he calls simply 'my kin':

> Come, lady, I will show thee to my kin,
>   And they shall say, when Richard me begot,
> If thou hadst said him nay, it had been sin.   1.1.273–5

However, it is in the vitality of his two early soliloquies that he creates the illusion of a whole dramatic character as expressive as nearly anyone in the early plays. Berowne and Petruchio are, perhaps, his only peers. Like the comic Vices in late Morality plays, who run with the hare and hunt with the hounds – Ambidexter in *Cambises*, Politic Persuasion in *Patient Grissell*, for example – he is 'a mad wag on extremely good terms with the audience'.[1] But these soliloquies present difficult problems of tone and dramatic significance. How seriously does he mean it when he says that he will deliver 'sweet, sweet poison for the age's tooth' (1.1.213) or that 'Gain, be my lord, for I will worship thee' (2.1.598)? Should we believe him when he intimates a future venality? Looking ahead, he sees that it is fit for 'the mounting spirit' like himself, who is the child of his time, to strew the footsteps of his advancement in the world with a certain amount of flattery. In the same vein he caps the speech on Commodity with a bit of self-criticism. In effect, 'Who am I to rail on this Commodity, since my hand has not yet been tempted?' When he is in a position of power and wealth, he can be expected to worship Gain, like the kings who now break faith upon Commodity.

The usual opinion about these speeches is that nowhere in the rest of the play does he do what he says he will do. He does not exactly flatter, and he seems to be an opponent of bad bargains; therefore, we should assume, so the argument goes, that in his soliloquies his moral awareness is still latent; or perhaps the concluding affirmations of the two soliloquies are meant just as a joke, a part of his Erasmian wit. But it is not like Shakespeare to mislead the audience in something so important. He

---

[1] F. P. Wilson, *The English Drama 1485–1585*, 1969, p. 61.

devotes two long artful speeches to these matters early in the play, where they are likely to fix the spectator's estimate of an important character. The Bastard's prospective resolves look like signposts of things to come. And since even Erasmus's Folly becomes serious the longer he speaks, he may be the model for the Bastard's pattern of thought.

I think the difficulty with these soliloquies has been increased by twentieth-century critics who have an exaggerated estimate of the Bastard's integrity. His moral and patriotic grandeur have been elevated so far above the shabbiness of others that some critics wish to turn him into the very hero of the drama.[1] However, if we conceive the Bastard in a somewhat lower register – as an ebullient, loyal soldier with his head screwed on right and with wonderful perceptions in a crisis, a person with uncanny resources for a public man, as we shall see – he fits the early soliloquies reasonably well. It is true that he does not exactly flatter, but he advises the distempered lords to cover up their wrath against the king; 'Whate'er you think, good words I think were best' (4.3.28). He prudently curbs his tongue and follows the king's orders when he suspects the worst of John, and he lets the 'spirit of the time' teach him speed in his majesty's service (4.2.176). He attends to a 'thousand businesses' of the monarchy even though he knows it is just 'the decay of wrested pomp' that he defends (4.3.158, 154). We may praise him for these necessary acts and words; nevertheless, they are simulations. He admits, in an aside, that although he is going to speak defiantly to the Dauphin, 'Our party may well meet a prouder foe' (5.1.79). Although he is not shown sequestering money for his personal use, he zestfully does the king's bidding to shake the bags of hoarding abbots, and he testifies that nothing can hold him back 'When gold and silver becks me to come on' (3.3.13). He certainly knows the weakness of the king's position, for in the Commodity speech he admits that to back Arthur's cause is a matter of conscience and charity. As we have seen, for France it is an honourable war, whereas John behaves like a tyrant, serving his own ends rather than the kingdom's, in a dishonourable treaty.[2] The point is, therefore, that the Bastard does accommodate tactfully when he is in a tight spot; he is not so much a hero as a pragmatist. At the king's death, for example, he does not always speak what he feels but says what he ought to say. Moreover, unless one listens very carefully at the beginning of the Commodity speech, it is possible to miss entirely the two lines devoted to King John's duplicitous part in the treaty, and to imagine that France is the only offender.

The form of the Commodity speech has been compared with Berowne's soliloquy on Love, which has the same driving energy and the accumulation of degrading attributes and personifications, and it ends with a similar turn. After excoriating himself, Dan Cupid, and the dark-eyed Rosaline, Berowne's railing collapses into seeming acceptance of his dotage.

---

[1] See pp. 41–3 below.
[2] 'In concluding treaties, as in everything else, the good prince should look to nothing but the advantages of his people. But when the opposite is done, when the prince considers it more to his advantage that the interests of the people have been reduced, then it is not a treaty, but a conspiracy.' Erasmus, *The Education of a Christian Prince*, (1516), trans. L. K. Born, 1938, p. 238.

> Well, I will love, write, sigh, pray, sue, groan:
> Some men must love my lady, and some Joan.   *Love's Labour's Lost* 3.1.204–5

He expects to be a corporal to General Cupid, a cuckold to his wanton mistress, and worst of all a perjurer, a vow-breaker, hence the object of ridicule by his fellows; yet he accepts it bemusedly.

The Bastard's soliloquy differs from Berowne's in one important respect, for the first 25 lines centre on his astonished recognition of the venality of kings, especially the French king. The Bastard distances himself from the 'base and vile-concluded peace' which illustrates a hateful but universal tendency in nature. It is the vile-drawing bias of the world that bends every human purpose, course, and intention away from charity and good faith. Although Commodity is a daily break-vow that wins all 'kings . . . beggars, old men, young men, maids', we are led by the speaker's high indignation to assume that he stands to one side, unaffected like an observer. Whereas Berowne's speech is intensely self-lacerating until the last two lines, the Bastard's is at first directed toward others; then he turns the ambiguous light on himself, to admit ruefully that now he can afford to be sanctimonious, but if he is to be the servant of the king afterwards and to profit by it, he might as well say 'Gain, be my lord', which is the equivalent of 'John be my lord'. He emphasises the point by a shift from the hyperbolic style – with its parallelism, serial adjectives and nouns, and intensifiers, giving the one great sentence an oratorical roundness – to a measured simplicity at the blunt question 'And why rail I on this Commodity?' If he is to be implicated with his master, he may feel rather like the poet in Sonnets 33, 34, and 35. If the 'heaven's sun' 'permit the basest clouds to ride / With ugly rack on his celestial face', the poet not a 'whit disdaineth' his friend's faults, for 'Suns of the world may stain, when heaven's sun staineth.' The poet even feels responsible for seeming to authorise his friend's trespass, 'Myself corrupting, salving thy amiss'. In the same way, the Bastard may expect to become an accessory to his master, for the dyer's hand is subdued to what it works in.

In the same spirit, I take the first soliloquy's ambiguities seriously at the end when he affirms that he, as a bastard of the time, will learn the ways of the world, administering the 'Sweet, sweet, sweet poison' that the age requires, not necessarily to deceive, but to survive and avoid the deceit of others. The same playful seriousness can be found at the end of his zany proposal at the gates of Angiers that the opposed armies unite and destroy the city and then fight it out between themselves:

> How like you this wild counsel, mighty states?
> Smacks it not something of the policy?   2.1.395–6

He can play the game of policy if it will lead to an eventually clean fight, after they have taken care of these 'scroyles of Angiers' that flout the kings. The word *smacks* may be used advisedly here, to remind us of the first soliloquy, that he would be just a bastard of the time if he does not 'smack of observation – / And so am I – whether I smack or no'. Not just outwardly but 'from the inward motion', he will dissimulate. It is an unexpected irony typical of the drama that the Bastard's wild proposal of a temporary alliance between France and England should precipitate the citizens' treaty, an eventuality that begins the vortex which will swallow King John and almost destroy the kingdom.

Symmetries and design

Like Shakespeare's other histories and tragedies, the play falls into two unequal parts, roughly equivalent to Acts 1–3 and 4–5.[1] The first part concerns two challenges to John's authority, one of which he finesses, the other he overcomes: the second part concerns the French invasion, which the kingdom survives but John does not. Part I is dominated by three massive scenes with Tamburlaine-like debates, used as weapons with intent to beat down an opponent. Part II still contains some big speeches, but the scenes are scaled down and they move ahead breathlessly from one catastrophe to the next. Part I creates the conditions for John's tragedy in a series of dubious and difficult choices, vows and broken vows, that foreshadow worse times to come. In the second part the characters still must choose, but in their compounded troubles events seem to slip from their control. As a result the world becomes so treacherous and unpredictable that oath-breaking seems more meritorious than oath-keeping.[2]

Therefore, in the world of the play most decisions are necessarily impure: an idea that Shakespeare also dramatises in the dilemmas of York in *Richard II*, and he devotes four plays – *Julius Caesar, Troilus and Cressida, Measure for Measure* and *Coriolanus* – to the futility of moral absolutism in politics. Although some of the characters make their difficult choices quickly, without agonising over them very much, John goes through a series of personal trials in 3.3 and 4.2, Hubert in 4.1 and 4.2, Salisbury in his passionate, hand-wringing speech at 5.2.12–39, and Blanche in 3.1.326–8. The audience is helped to piece out the implied human significance of events by the Bastard's two soliloquies and his occasional asides. The larger patterns of the play, especially its symmetries, also help define the issues and knit the two parts of the play together.

On the one hand are three power-brokers – Eleanor, the Citizen of Angiers, and Pandulph – who promote bargains between antagonists. They have mastered the arts of policy: a talent for knowing when to talk sweetly or to threaten, when to offer inducements and to compromise, and when to stand on high principles. What the Bastard calls Commodity, the vile-drawing bias of the world, a form of self-interest, is the main purpose of their statecraft, whereby a prince's or pope's personal interest is thought to be coextensive with national and church interest.[3] Their results are generally mixed, but in one case the bargain is relatively happy and long-lasting. In the dispute between the Falconbridge brothers Eleanor offers the Bastard a different kind of inheritance if he wants to join the Plantagenet family and will give up his land to Robert. Everyone is satisfied, nor does the Bastard give up all commodity, as is often claimed, for his is an achievement of self and of social standing to be recognised

---

[1] See Emrys Jones, *Scenic Form in Shakespeare*, 1971, ch. 3.
[2] Sigurd Burckhardt, '*King John*: the ordering of this present time', *ELH* 33 (1966), 150.
[3] See 2.1.367 and supplementary note.

as the son of Cœur-de-lion. This is the only bargain that holds to the end of the play. Other bargains with a shorter life generally harm someone. The Citizen of Angiers's proposal of a dynastic marriage between Blanche and the Dauphin saves the city from destruction, recognises John's right, and enriches the provinces of France. His bargain receives Eleanor's crafty approval and amendment, as she whispers to John (2.1.467 ff.). But to one of the other mother–son pairs it leaves only a token satisfaction; Arthur, created Duke of Brittany, is given just the city of Angiers as his bitter inheritance.

The arch-politician of them all enters in Act 3, Scene 1 as if in answer to a widow's cry for help, but Pandulph is not heaven's avenger, for he soon shows that he has no interest whatsoever in Constance's need. He represents the power of the church militant and uses its curses of interdiction and excommunication to discipline rebellious kings. If France's vow of friendship impairs the interests of papal authority, the vow must be broken at any cost. Thus he drives a wedge between the two kings, and he promotes armed discord all right, but it is part of a cruel game in which Arthur once more becomes a pawn, this time a fatal pawn of French and papal aspirations. Since the Citizen disappears from the play after Act 2 and Eleanor soon fades away, Pandulph, the quintessential power-broker, has the stage clear for his kind of shuttle diplomacy. Henceforth, he instructs the Dauphin in military opportunism, raising his hopes to become King of England by exploitation of Arthur's inevitable murder and by the consequent civil disorder. Then, when England is pressed by the invasion, he negotiates John's submission to the church, confident that the breath that blew up this storm of war can make fair weather in the blustering land (5.1.21). But by the logic of events Pandulph's pupil has grown up and refuses to be controlled. Like John in defiance of the Pope in Act 3, the Dauphin will not be Rome's slave (5.2.97), and the war must run its eccentric course. With a final twist Pandulph is by chance true to his bargain with John when he returns with the Dauphin's peace offer (5.7.82). The zigzagging fortunes of war allow the return of the English lords upon Melun's persuasion, and the treachery of the Goodwin Sands allows Pandulph to keep one promise in the end.

Like figures in a Morality play, the power-brokers are matched with three innocents – Arthur, Lewis, and the Bastard – who encounter public life and are changed by it.[1] Arthur, being the youngest and most helpless of the three, is largely passive in his political role; for example, he must tolerate the distasteful assistance of Austria. But in private he begins to mature. He starts as a precocious child, a 'green boy' who 'promiseth a mighty fruit' (2.1.472–3), sensitive to the feelings of adults and protective of his mother. When separated from Constance, he looks for a father in Hubert, but under threat of losing his eyes he finds his tongue and seems to save himself (4.1). Just before he dies while escaping, Arthur faces his personal dilemma as squarely as the most mature characters: 'As good to die and go, as die and stay' (4.3.8).

The Dauphin begins nearly as 'green' and 'fresh in this old world' as Arthur

---

[1] Jones, *Origins*, pp. 235–46.

(3.4.145), suggested by his naïve use of the clichés of love-making (2.1.496 ff.), and his shame and disillusion at the loss of glory when the French have been defeated (3.4.107–11). However, under Pandulph's instruction he grows into an adventurer, who knows his own interests and pursues them without scruple. His urbane corruption is represented in his reply to Salisbury's regrets that the infection of the time forces him and the other lords to march after a foreign leader in their land. The Dauphin mocks this 'noble temper' and recommends that the peers

> Commend these waters to those baby eyes
> That never saw the giant world enraged,
> Nor met with Fortune other than at feasts . . .
> Come, come; for thou shalt thrust thy hand as deep
> Into the purse of rich prosperity
> As Lewis himself . . .
>
> 5.2.56–62

Perhaps the corruption of Lewis's values reflects that 'falling away from social unity' that is 'constantly present in every generation' of historical tragedies, following the murder of a prince.[1] Moreover, the Dauphin thinks of his change as a healthy maturation; let babies shed tears, not hearty men of the world like himself, who know how to make the most of opportunity.

Finally, like Arthur, he must recognise the facts as distinct from illusions about his military position. At sunset on the day of battle, he declares that he has forced the English to retire weakly; he thinks the French have come off 'bravely' when they furl their tattered colours, sure that they are 'Last in the field and almost lords of it' (5.5.8). Still, undeniably bad news destroys his confidence. Count Melun is slain, the English lords have defected back to John, and Lewis's supply ships are sunk. The best he can say now about the day's battle is 'The stumbling night did part our weary pow'rs', and he looks for some comfort in the thought that John himself left the field two hours before sunset. The whole enterprise of his invasion is so like a stumbling night that the Dauphin sounds world-weary and deflated when he orders the next morning's trial of 'fair adventure'.

The Bastard's mock-innocence at the start of the play animates his original, many-sided character, and his movement to a wider experience of the world constitutes a major theme in the tragedy. In his bemused simplicity he already seems larger than life. Whether he is true-begot or not, he scarcely conceals his pleasure in being well-begot, and his unmixed zest for his lineage colours everything he says to Eleanor and his mother in the first act. Without the slightest guile, he is a 'good blunt fellow' and a 'perfect Richard' in spirit and appearance (1.1.71, 91). He seems not to care a whit whether his whimsical diffidence about his parentage harms his chances for £500 a year, and it is entirely in character that he should renounce his safe inheritance in favour of the risky pursuit of honour. His wit casts an intelligent light upon his disarming remarks, and his capacity for self-mockery reveals his native sensitivity to the very conditions of life. The distinction is familiar in the Senecan tradition, restated by Ben Jonson in praise of a man who

[1] Northrop Frye, *Fools of Time: Studies in Shakespearean Tragedy*, 1967, p. 36.

12   King Richard I robs the lion of his heart, in the manner of Samson and Hercules killing a lion bare-handed. A woodcut from John Rastell, *The Pastyme of People* (1530)

> Dar'st breathe in any air, and with safe skill,
>   Till thou canst find the best, choose the least ill;
> That to the vulgar canst thyself apply,
>   Treading a better path not contrary . . .[1]

[1] *Epigrams*, 119.

Thus Falconbridge is 'one who sees the worst, seems to approve of it, and chooses the best'.[1]

On the battlefield at Angiers he achieves personal revenge upon the murderer of his father, earning the right to wear the lion skin to match his heart. At first hand he learns the dangers of Commodity, even though he has not yet been tempted. Under the pressure of difficult public choices that test him harrowingly in the pivotal scenes of Act 4, he reaches his full stature. There and in the final scenes he remains deeply engaged, presenting the audience with an ideal self. He is a profoundly realised character who guides the audience and himself through the maze of the world.

He remains a loyal servant in spite of what he grievously suspects about John and Hubert. Earlier in the play he recognises his ambition and the attractions of personal gain, and inevitably he becomes implicated in the king's business, for he recommends as well as practises dissimulation. He remains detached enough, nevertheless, and different from others. On the whole he is ethically and politically in the world but not of it. Like Shakespeare's later creations (Hamlet, Lear, Coriolanus), the Bastard begins as a type and ends as an archetype, representing a deeper and broader humanity.[2] England needs him as much as the play needs him; yet for all his great qualities and integrity, he plays a subordinate role in the action.

Since several critics have taken an exaggerated view of his political role and persistently magnified his place in the second movement of the action, we must re-examine the case. A rough contrast of the Bastard and King John was made by G. G. Gervinus more than a hundred years ago:

[The Bastard's] course through the tragic events ... is the very reverse to that of King John. The latter begins with power and kingly thoughts and ends in weakness, the Bastard bounds light of heart into the wider sphere that opens before him, and advances steadily in seriousness and strength even to a tragic greatness.[3]

H. H. Furness sharpened the contrast by asserting that 'the titular hero is not the protagonist' and Shakespeare must have seen that 'John's was not a character which lent itself to dramatic treatment': he was 'utterly perfidious, a poltroon, and a moral coward'.[4] Dover Wilson was equally misleading to say that John's 'character is evidently drawn as a foil to that of the real hero, the Bastard' (p. IX). In a sustained defence of this interpretation Adrien Bonjour asserted that John's role diminishes as the Bastard's grows in a series of moral tests which confer on him 'the depth . . . of a dramatic hero'. Hence, the design of the play is determined by the character – the man of integrity – with whom the audience feels the most sympathy. 'And just because the Bastard never [loses] sight of the higher interest of the nation, while preserving his loyalty and personal integrity intact, he is now able to prevent the total collapse of the English forces, and succeeds in restoring national unity.'[5]

[1] F. P. Wilson, 'The English history play', in *Shakespearean and Other Studies*, 1969, p. 31.
[2] For this special meaning of an archetypal character see Eric Bentley, *The Life of the Drama*, 1967, pp. 40–51.
[3] Gervinus, *Shakespeare Commentaries*, 1849–50, trans. Bunnètt, 1875 edn, pp. 366–7.
[4] Furness, pp. x–xi.
[5] A. Bonjour, 'The road to Swinstead Abbey,' *ELH* 18 (1951), 269–71.

There can be no doubt that the Bastard takes on greater responsibility late in the action, for John in his decay leaves to him 'the ordering of this present time' – to negotiate with the Dauphin and to repel the French army (5.1.77). In the name of John he addresses the Dauphin in the style that he urged John to use (5.2.127 ff.). We are told that he asked the king, now suffering with fever, to leave the field, presumably for his safety when the battle seems to go against the English (5.3.5), and 'In spite of spite, [Falconbridge] alone upholds the day' according to Salisbury (5.4.5). In the last scene he leads the peers in swearing allegiance to Prince Henry, and he delivers the final speech, assessing the state of the kingdom and its political future, 'If England to itself do rest but true'. He means that they are safe if England – including king, nobles, and commons – does not behave again as John, the barons, and citizenry did, helping to wound themselves. In his role as commentator he calls our attention to the political meaning of this cautionary tale; moreover, the closing speech is an important statement for Shakespeare's contemporaries, considering the threats and fears of England's internal enemies in the late 1580s and early 1590s.[1]

We should also keep in mind that other characters grow in stature and importance as John fades: Hubert and Salisbury, for example. And the accumulated impressions that the Bastard gives on stage do not create a central character nor a dramatic hero in the usual sense. Although the audience is invited to sympathise with him throughout, he is not at the centre of the political action. After leading the volunteers behind Eleanor, his mainly private quest is for revenge upon Austria in the first part; in the second part he brings news, carries messages, saves Hubert from the angry peers, and he stays with John in spite of his worst suspicions. He tries to buck up the king, unsuccessfully, and he loses the best part of his army in the Wash – certainly a monumental blunder. He is an inchoate leader in the final scenes, lurching from one crisis to the next. Above all, he does not save England in any historical or dramatic sense that the audience can tell.[2] The battle between the French and English forces depicted in 5.3, 5.4, and 5.5 appears to be a stand-off, and the two armies are rendered impotent by unrelated disasters. Contrary to the exaggerated view of the Bastard, it is Melun's confession and the subsequent return of the peers to John (but, in effect, to Prince Henry) that change the tide of events, along with the Dauphin's loss of his fleet, enabling Pandulph to intercede. If anything saves England, it is Fortune and the awakened consciences of several characters.

In the last scene Falconbridge is somewhat confused and out of touch. Ignorant of the peace offer, he brings news that the Dauphin is raging at their heels and that he has lost his army, a message that he shouts into the dying king's ear. Apparently that false report breaks the last string of John's heart, one more cause of anguish piled upon anguish that contributes to the king's bad death. In a formal expression of grief, the Bastard pledges to follow the king 'to heaven': good words that put the best face on an ugly situation, rather like Prince Henry's pious hope that his father's soul and body will go to an everlasting rest. As Smallwood points out, the audience is shown clearly enough that John dies with 'no sign of repentance, no indication of hope of

[1] Honigmann, pp. lxxii–lxxiii.   [2] Honigmann, pp. lxxi–lxxii.

salvation; only that unobserved, despairing death'. His 'unreprievable condemnèd blood' burns like a living hell-fire within.[1] Consequently this is something of an embarrassing moment that no one wants to mark in its naked desolation. The Bastard breaks the ice by rallying the peers to repel the enemy attack, but is told that there is no external enemy. As Salisbury says earlier in the same scene, it is going to be up to Prince Henry, not the Bastard, to set a form upon the chaos which John has left behind. Although the Bastard gestures to take charge of the funeral arrangements, Henry has them already in hand. Altogether, this is hardly a heroic climax for Falconbridge, who has to be disabused of his errors and presumption. He is not the one who holds in his hands the 'destiny of the nation'.[2]

The Bastard has splendid instincts, and he maintains a loyalty to the ancient and accepted laws of the monarchy, but he seldom takes the centre of the stage. He is in and out of the action, engaged and detached, a commentator with special rapport with the audience, a tester of other characters' mettle, a loyal servant, and a resolute soldier: in short, the most interesting and complex character in the play. But it tells us much about his role that he typically comes late to a bad situation (4.2, 4.3, 5.1, 5.2, 5.7). He is well-meaning but relatively ineffectual. Still, he is one of the few characters in Shakespearean tragedy who is capable of an impersonal loyalty, like Brutus or perhaps York in *Richard II*.[3] Although he starts as an adventurer, the Bastard finally gives of himself to the welfare of the kingdom without asking much in return. John, however, has brought the body politic to such chaos that one good man can do very little.

The vicissitudes of John and his kingdom remain, therefore, at the centre of the play, for Shakespeare's larger plan incorporates the Bastard along with others – Hubert, Arthur, Constance, the Dauphin, and the power-brokers – in the most articulated network of mirroring devices of his early plays. In part I John and his supporters go to France with an army to defend his ambiguous right to the throne, and the war for the city of Angiers ends in a draw, followed by a dishonourable bargain. In part II Lewis goes to England with an army to establish his slender right to the throne, and that war ends in a draw, with a presumably honourable treaty.[4] Both leaders vociferously declare their independence of Rome (3.1.162–71; 5.2.78–116), and both make a bargain with Pandulph. Both are betrayed by a conscientious subordinate – Hubert and Melun – with whom they have conspired to commit murder. One gratuitous detail, not in the historical sources, calls attention to this mirroring device when Melun credits his change of heart partly to his friendship with Hubert (5.4.40–1). Moreover, their honourable disobedience to authority reflects badly upon their masters, and in effect they save John and Lewis from blood-guilt. But their intention to murder for political gain cannot be forgotten. The defection and return of Salisbury and the other peers also suggests that from the English point of view Lewis deserves less respect than John. At any rate Salisbury feels relieved when, given the opportunity to recant, he and the other peers decide

---

[1] Smallwood, p. 43.
[2] Bonjour, pp. 271–2. See supplementary note to 5.6.38, on the supposed temptation of the Bastard.
[3] Frye, *Fools of Time*, p. 26.   [4] Honigmann, pp. lxix-lxx.

they will 'calmly run on in obedience / Even to our ocean, to our great King John' (5.4.56–7).

The contrast of Lewis and John reinforces this preference if we notice that the Dauphin is absolutely unscrupulous and cynical in part II of the play, whereas from Act 3 to the end, John consistently exposes his troublesome conscience. Although, like Macbeth, he overrules his conscience frequently, John only once hardens his heart. He is closer, perhaps, to Clarence or Buckingham than to Richard III, in his moral sensitivity and remorse after the fact. Still he feels immensely guilty when he proposes the ghastly deed to Hubert, and some of Shakespeare's best writing in the play is found in depiction of this guilty awareness, as we have seen in the discussion of style and expression.

If the Dauphin casts an oblique light upon John's character and draws attention to his better and worse qualities, the symmetrical positioning of Constance and John juxtaposes her helpless, proud, frenzied outrage and his final, half-mad delirium. What happens to Constance at the end of part I happens to John at the end of part II, a device that Emrys Jones calls structural rhyming.[1] Constance grieves magnificently at the expected loss of her son, and John, who began with rage, degenerates into a helpless and hellish fever for the seeming loss of his kingdom. Constance moves step by step toward her great mad scene and her impending death; John is drawn into a vortex of receding hopes, hastened by the death of Eleanor but also as a consequence of Arthur's supposed death and its repercussions. In her last scene Constance wishes death would come to her like a lover cramming her 'gap of breath with fulsome dust' (3.4.32), and she will kiss him as her husband. Although she protests that she is 'not mad, but sensible of grief' (53), she wishes that Pandulph would preach to her some philosophy to make her really mad. She implies that behind apparent madness her reason teaches her to find a way to destroy herself (25–6). When she leaves the stage King Philip follows her for fear of 'some outrage' (106) and later she is said to have died in a frenzy, three days before Eleanor, her natural antagonist and John's mentor.

In his last scene John raves in much the same way but with reduced grandeur. His blood is thoroughly corrupted by poison, but his brain still works enough to foretell his death. At times he is 'insensible' to pain,[2] as Henry reports, but when he is carried on stage he indicates that he feels the fire of hell. As vividly as Constance calls for 'amiable lovely Death' to cram her 'gap of breath', he bids winter to 'thrust his icy fingers in [his] maw', and the 'bleak winds' to 'kiss [his] parchèd lips' (5.7.36–40). Both characters die a bad death, the expression of their tremendous rages, and both die thinking, perhaps, that they have lost what they treasure most. Yet, typically in this play, the audience sees that it is not quite so. Constance grieves in anticipation of her son's death, but Arthur survives the king's plan to have him murdered, only to die by accident. Similarly, the last news the Bastard shouts into the king's ear is half true and half false, and it may or may not have broken the king's heart string.

[1] Jones, *Scenic Form*, pp. 76–8. The device first appears in *2* and *3 Henry VI* and is repeated in *Julius Caesar* and *Hamlet*, where in each case the two parts conclude on the same note.
[2] Hanmer and Capell's emendation; the Folio reads 'invisible'.

Salisbury assumes, too comfortably, that the Bastard breathes 'dead news in as dead an ear' (5.7.65).

The symmetry of Constance and John's despair invites us to think about other resemblances that call attention to their tragic waste. They share an anxious instability, combined with towering assurance of their rights; therefore, their moral outrage is always ready to break out. Constance is 'sick and capable of fears' (3.1.12), and her rages come upon her when she complains of any injustice to Arthur and her ambitions for him. She lives and dies in her son's fortunes so violently that her grief becomes larger than life; like Seneca's Medea, she has apocalyptic premonitions,[1] wishing that her outcries could shake the earth and bring on the end of the world:

> O that my tongue were in the thunder's mouth;
> Then with a passion would I shake the world,
> And rouse from sleep that fell anatomy . . .   3.4.38–40

Since, as Gordon Braden points out, anger is a dangerous emotion even for a wise man, she needs that inner control which Arthur and King Philip urge upon her: 'be content' (3.1.42), 'Patience, good lady' (3.4.22), 'you utter madness and not sorrow' (43). But her rages become obsessive, for she is 'as fond of grief as of [her] child' (192). In her proleptic mourning she compels all outward signs to correspond to her inward disorder: 'Grief fills the room up of my absent child, / Lies in his bed, walks up and down with me . . .' Her hair must come down, for she cannot keep any form upon her head when 'there is such disorder in my wit' (93–102).

John goes through much the same cycle in a different order, because he is trying to defend his power, not to obtain it. At first he is indignant when his authority is challenged; he thunders righteously to Chatillon in Act 1, at Pandulph in 3.1.147–71, and at King Philip:

> France, I am burned up with inflaming wrath,
> A rage whose heat hath this condition,
> That nothing can allay, nothing but blood . . .   3.1.340–2

Once he has possession of Arthur, his fear of the boy struggles with his inhibitions, suggesting an incipient derangement when he orders the murder (3.3.20–55). At the beginning of 4.2 his anxious need to placate the English lords reveals rather than conceals his guilt, causing him to misstep. Then, like Constance, he complains that Hubert is trying to possess him with his fears (4.2.203). Although John kindles flickering hopes from time to time in the second movement of the play, they die at the next and the next bit of bad news. As Arthur and King Philip spoke to Constance, the Bastard attempts to stiffen John's self-control by putting him in mind of his earlier resoluteness: 'Be great in act, as you have been in thought. / Let not the world see fear and sad distrust . . .' (5.1.45). But it is of no avail, for John droops and dwindles. Fever and poison may be another manifestation of a sick heart (5.3.4). The king, whose heroic wrath had no bounds in the first movement of the play, falls

---

[1] *Medea*, 464–5, 374–79. See Gordon Braden, *Renaissance Tragedy and the Senecan Tradition*, 1985, ch. 2; Jones, *Origins*, pp. 269–70.

in the second movement under the tide but rises temporarily 'aloft the flood' with each new hope to salvage his authority (4.2.138–9). He is finally inundated (5.1.12), and he wishes that all his kingdom's rivers could 'take their course / Through [his] burned bosom' (5.7.38).

The difference, however, between John and Constance is that she dies in a half-mad fit of grief for the injustice done upon her and her son. John dies in the madness of a criminal conscience. His hell within is peopled with 'a fiend, confined to tyrannise / On unreprievable, condemnèd blood' (5.7.47–8); his bowels 'crumble up to dust' (31), and he shrinks against 'this fire'. In the end he is just a 'clod / And module of confounded royalty' (57), like the kingdom he leaves behind – a chaos shapeless and rude, to which others must give a new form.

John's success turns into despair at the end, like that of Macbeth, whose ambitions are gradually displaced by fears and by compulsive and self-defeating attempts to shore up his diminishing power. Like Macbeth when he stops listening to his wife, John seems to lack insight, particularly after the death of his mother. Montaigne puts it well: 'there is nothing that throws us so much into dangers as an unthinking eagerness to get clear of them', for 'Fear sometimes arises from want of judgement as well as from want of courage.'[1]

Politics and conscience

The foundation of *King John* is political, for, like all Shakespeare's history plays, it deals with questions of law and power. And as in many of the early histories the trappings of divine providence and mystique of kingship figure only provisionally in the England and France of this drama.[2] The state is for the most part demythologised. Portents, tongues of heaven, and other cosmic signs have had the wonder taken out of them and are reduced to natural causes by the hard-headed representative of the church, Pandulph. Although fanatically devoted to a higher cause, his 'prophetic spirit' envisions little more than the pressures of *realpolitik*, for behind the screen of divine authority he sees the shedding of Arthur's 'true blood' as merely an opportunity for his French allies to exploit: it is 'wonderful / What may be wrought out of [the] discontent' of the rebellious English people when they hear of Arthur's murder (3.4.178). Even Prince Arthur does not appeal to the sacred blood of kings when he pleads for his life and eyes.

Before the gates of Angiers John declares that he is the lawful king under God simply because he wears the crown, and he brings 30,000 soldiers to witness for the fact (2.1.273). King Philip is 'divinely' sworn to defend Arthur's lineal right before the same city, as if it were just a matter of equity (2.1.241), and the chief spokesman for the citizens says that, although God knows who is the true King of England, his identity has not been revealed to mankind so far (368–72). Nor does the trial by

---

[1] 'Of Coaches', *The Complete Essays of Montaigne*, trans. Donald M. Frame, 1958, pp. 685–6.
[2] See Henry Ansgar Kelly, *Divine Providence in the England of Shakespeare's Histories*, 1970, and John Wilders, *The Lost Garden*, 1978, for mixed evidence about providential history in the two cycles. Kelly and Wilders say little about *John*, however.

combat of the two armies in Act 2 prove anything. In Act 3 when John denies the
Pope's authority over him and insists that he rules under God directly (3.1.147–8),
that statement may be taken as accepted doctrine as well as a self-serving defence
against the encroachment of Rome. If he believes what he says, his vociferous
assertion of divine authority calls attention to the ineffectualness of such claims. Since
God does not speak in His own person, He must speak only through someone whom
the political order has authorised to speak. 'The crucial thing – except as a question
of plain power – is not whether that someone is the Pope, the Emperor, or King; the
crucial thing is that there *be* one, and only one, such voice.'[1] Disputes between
supposed spokesmen for God cancel each other out with cries of 'thou dost usurp
authority' and 'Excuse it is to beat usurping down' (2.1.118 ff.). Therefore, the
cosmic structure of divine providence, sacred authority, and the rest of 'Tudor
Doctrine' is in doubt, and the notion of absolute obedience is not a sure guide
through a play like *King John*. When there is a *de facto* and a *de jure* king, whom does
a subject obey, especially if the ruling monarch is powerful and the rightful king is
young and weak?

The one glancing reference to cosmic order in the play is ironic, as E. M. W.
Tillyard acknowledged.[2] The created world, that naturally 'of itself is peisèd well'
to 'run even upon even ground', has been changed by Commodity, the Bastard points
out, and now it is made to run on a bias (2.1.574–86). So this old world operates not
on divine order but on skewed principles of gain, advantage, and broken faith. The
Lady Constance is one of the few characters who 'directs our gaze above the low
ceiling of the play's worldly setting to the all-witnessing heavens', and her widow's
curse (3.1.107–11) seems to have real effects, for her wish is granted when the
perjured kings come to 'armèd discord' before sunset.[3]

Later in the play a natural providence may be said to take over with only a vague
supernatural aura. For example, Peter Pomfret's foreknowledge that John will deliver
up his crown 'ere the next Ascension Day at noon' is handled like the discredited
soothsayer of classical drama. John tempts Fate by locking Peter up and setting his
execution for that day and hour (4.2.155 ff.). Later, when John gives up his crown
to Pandulph, he recalls the prophecy but rationalises his action as a meaningless
ceremony: after all he gave up the crown voluntarily for reasons of state, not by
compulsion (5.1.25–8). Naturally that ploy does not work any better than the king's
unfortunate attempts to bring the rebellious nobles back. Similarly, at the death of
Arthur and the defection of the peers, it seems to the Bastard that heaven frowns
upon the kingdom (4.3.159), and later he asks God not to burden him and other
loyalists with more than they can bear. But the usual pattern in *King John* is that
occasionally found in early chronicles: 'success is attributed to God, but misfortune
is blamed on some personification' like Time, Occasion, or Fortune.[4] Fortune is
nothing but a whore (3.1.54–61), a capricious lady (119). Occasion is a flood or a
roaring tempest (4.2.139, 341) or a speedy lady (4.2.125) whose forelock must be

[1] Burckhardt, 'Present time', p. 143.
[2] *Shakespeare's History Plays*, 1944, repr. 1962, p. 250.
[3] Jones, *Origins*, pp. 240–2.   [4] Kelly, *Divine Providence*, p. 207.

grasped, for she is bald behind. The impression is that this is a fallen world, from which God is removed and alien; His ways are mysterious. The most telling image of that condition is in the Bastard's moving speech over the body of Arthur, that begins

> I am amazed, methinks, and lose my way
> Among the thorns and dangers of this world.   4.3.140–1

Like natural man in a fallen world, he finds himself in a labyrinth, beset by uncertainty and temptation.

According to the politics of this old world, government rests upon power and law, cemented by loyalty; that is, it requires the ability to rule effectively within a certain consensus of the king, the courts, and the people.[1] The king must have at least an appearance of lineal right, but what counts is the recognition of his authority by his people. A *de facto* king can come to his throne unlawfully and yet keep it by ruling well, eventually passing it on to a fully legitimate successor, as Henry IV did. This is possible if he can hold off foreign invaders and control subversive movements against him, and if he has the tacit backing of his subjects.

The first forty lines of Act 1, for example, raise the question of John's doubtful right in such a way that it seems to be a worrisome but not a disabling fact. John's 'strong possession much more than [his] right', Eleanor whispers, will have to carry them through the conflict with France over Arthur's claim. But the dominant impression of John at this time is favourable, for he behaves like a king, dignified and courteous to the French ambassador. And he breathes defiance at the French armies (1.1.27) in terms that cannot have seemed to an Elizabethan audience as hypocritical or weak. He moves with speedy assurance to set forth the expedition, and he knows where to get the money to finance it. Eleanor reminds him that power will have to be his main strength because he has neglected to use 'easy arguments of love' in his handling of Constance and Arthur. Obviously she thinks that prudent negotiation and simulated love beforehand would have been more profitable and less risky than war. Nevertheless, like the people, whose support he has, she is behind him, a soldier ready to go to France with the troops. Together John and Eleanor are a dauntless pair, more than a match for the mother and son who seek to take their place. Their effectiveness is further dramatised in the same scene when they respond quickly to the Bastard's 'very spirit of Plantagenet', and they welcome him enthusiastically into the family. The Bastard then becomes a leader of the fiery volunteers who go to fight for the king and risk all their resources in quest of a new fortune. Amidst these and other interlocking dependencies of loyalty and self-interest there is much to be said for the person in strong possession of the crown.

In sixteenth-century England – the nursery of Shakespeare's political values – royal power was real but limited. Although absolute authority was an important

[1] Sir Thomas Smith, *De Republica Anglorum* (1583), ed. Mary Dewar, 1982, is the clearest contemporary account of these matters, especially Bk. 1.7, 9, 10; Bk. 11.1, 3, 4. See E. Talbert, *The Problem of Order*, 1962; W. Sanders, *The Dramatist and the Received Idea*, 1968, ch. 9; and Edna Z. Boris, *Shakespeare's English Kings, the People and the Law*, 1978, chs. 1–3. On the theme of loyalty, see Honigmann, p. lix, n. 3.

feature of the French monarchy, an English king shared power to some extent among various elements of the commonwealth. The king or queen ruled in Parliament, an arrangement that implied the need for advice from others. Significantly, it was Parliament that ratified Queen Elizabeth's right of succession by the will of Henry VIII.[1] And the importance of shared authority is measured by the disastrous consequences of attempts by James I and his successor to assert divine right and to rule without Parliament, as if the king was entirely self-sufficient and above the law. John, too, recognises the corporate limitations of the English commonwealth when he justifies his position as protector of Angiers against its enemy, and he asks that the city reciprocate by due recognition of his kingship (2.1.222). He also solicits the peers' approval and counsel in 4.2, because he wants them to reaffirm their vows of loyalty, even before there is news of the French invasion. This is in itself not a sign of weakness but a proper way for an English king to handle himself. John succeeds in the early episodes of the play when he has the apparent support of Salisbury, Essex, Pembroke, and those volunteers led by the Bastard. He also dispenses the law strictly in the opening scene, then tempers a hard decision with equity. The nobility remain loyal, though they may sympathise with Constance and Arthur's cause (as Salisbury implies by his sorrowful gestures while he looks upon Arthur, 3.1.19–24). But if the king seems only to pretend to follow their counsel, he undermines his position, and when, by all the evidence the nobles have, he appears to be responsible for Arthur's death, they rebel (4.2.95–122). Power and authority begin to slip through John's fingers not because he is a usurper, but because he has become a tyrant – in the eyes of the lords he has broken the law – and he has lost the support of many of his subjects. The lords defect to the enemy, London welcomes the invader with rejoicing, and the Dauphin marches almost to England's throne. But at the end of the play it is the irony of fortune that John's son comes to power by lineal right, for his rival is dead and young Henry will rule by consent, now that the barons are 'come home again' (5.7.102, 115).[2]

These political assumptions are the foundation but not the superstructure of the drama, because Shakespeare's political imagination is particular whereas most of the theorists are general.[3] His characters are forced to make personal choices in a society torn with strife, and they act in response to specific pressures that bring them to dramatic life. John's overgenerous dowry for Blanche is a costly necessity, typical of this mad world, but it does not seem to bother John as much as it does King Philip for accepting that bribe and abandoning Arthur's claim, for Philip has personally betrayed Constance (3.4.15–22 ff.). Although only a few characters – the Citizen and Pandulph – are almost wholly constituted by public values, most seem to possess an individual consciousness (good, bad, or indifferent) that flickers into life at moments that could change the course of history. Since they cannot avoid the ethical imperative

---

[1]   See the reference to Richard Cœur-de-lion's deathbed will that left the crown to his youngest brother John (2.1.191–4).
[2]   Sir Thomas Smith applied the doctrine of shared authority by pointing out that King John's surrender of sovereignty to the Pope was 'forthwith and ever sithens taken for nothing' because it was 'never approved by his people, nor accorded by act of parliament' (*De Republica Anglorum*, p. 56).
[3]   Sanders, *Dramatist and the Received Idea*, p. 70.

of their situations, public loyalty has for them an inevitably personal resonance. It is not that public values, like the saving of a city or a kingdom, do not matter, but that in this play especially private conscience often counts at the dramatic moment.

The force of private values in the kingdom is made clear to the audience in the central scenes of the drama (4.1., 4.2, 4.3) that depict the beginning of John's decline. When the king and his subjects are swept by the flood of events, their personal values come into play with political loyalty and the necessity to survive. The private nature of human consciousness enhances a character, who sees the kingdom and his situation through the prism of his experience. It is as an individual that each must contemplate God's judgement, an eventuality that John so dreads that he wants to include Hubert as a partner:

> O, when the last account 'twixt heaven and earth
> Is to be made, then shall this hand and seal
> Witness against us to damnation!   4.2.216–18

The political consequences of his guilt bring nearly total chaos in the body politic and in the king's mind:

> Hostility and civil tumult reigns
> Between my conscience and my cousin's death.   4.2.247–8

However, it is the conscience of the king's subjects that makes the real trouble for John and England, for conscience is, by its very nature, not open to public scrutiny or control. That was one of the awkward political dangers of the Reformation, as Wilbur Sanders observes.

Post-Reformation political theory is founded on an inherent contradiction. The extirpation of popery was achieved partly by appealing to private conscience as final arbiter in matters of religion; but, the Reformation once accomplished, conscience must necessarily be commanded to discontinue its revolutionary activity. The trouble was that conscience the dog, once roused, would not to kennel, and it remained to plague its masters with its unpredictable vagaries throughout the next two centuries (p. 150).

It became an open question whether it was lawful for citizens to resist a prince who transgresses the law of God, and whether they were bound by oaths to an unjust monarch. St Augustine declared that 'Where there is no justice, there is no commonwealth.'[1] Erasmus hedged that definition when he came to the duties of citizens, who 'are bidden to endure worthless magistrates, so as not to disrupt the order of the state, provided that they perform their duties and do not give orders that are opposed to God'.[2] Moreover, the homily on 'Obedience to Rulers and Magistrates' says absolutely that 'we may not obey king's magistrates, or any other, (though they be our own fathers) if they would command us to do anything contrary to God's commandments'.[3] But it was common opinion among thoughtful people

---

[1] *Of the City of God*, 4.4. and 19.21. See Harold Laski's introduction to the 1924 edn (reprinted 1972) of *A Defence of Liberty against Tyrants*, trans. of *Vindiciae Contra Tyrannos*, attr. to Hubert Languet, 'Edinburgh' [Basle?], 1579, 1580.   [2] *Education of a Christian Prince*, p. 178.
[3] *Certain Sermons or Homilies* (1547), 1582 edn, vol. 1, sig. ʀ8. The more stringent 'Homily against Disobedience and Wilful Rebellion' published after the northern rebellion, 1571, omits that important proviso.

of the age that, as Montaigne believed, one should avoid changing the government and overturning rulers, even if they are tyrants.

The reasons for such caution are manifold, for, as Shakespeare implies in *King John*, knowledge is never complete in a fallen world, and values are subtly modified by the way one senses the ambient air. The outcome of choice is determined by too many unknowns, as the cluster of three scenes shows.[1] They concern the implications of Hubert's dilemma whether he should obey the king's order to execute Arthur or obey his conscience and renounce royal favour. For prudential and moral reasons he chooses to disobey the king and tell a white lie. Since he agreed to kill the boy,[2] and he intended to do it (4.1.123–4), he must sacrifice one kind of loyalty for another, personal loyalty to Arthur and conscience. The only solution to his dilemma is to mislead the king for a while by pretending that Arthur is dead. This is one of many 'dear' offences or good faults in this play, like Lady Falconbridge's submission to King Richard's 'commanding love' (1.1.261–7), Count Melun's deathbed confession (5.4) and the Bastard's unswerving loyalty to John even when he becomes a tyrant. But to make the situation more precarious, an overarching dramatic irony affects the audience's view of Hubert's choice, for we know that the success of the impending French invasion hangs upon Arthur's fate, as does nearly everything else in the play.[3] Pandulph predicted that if Arthur is not dead already, when news spreads of the Dauphin's approach to England,

> Even at that news he dies, and then the hearts
> Of all his people shall revolt from [John],
> And kiss the lips of unacquainted change,
> And pick strong matter of revolt and wrath
> Out of the bloody fingers' ends of John.   3.4.164–8

Hubert, therefore, plays a more dangerous game than he knows, and the audience may very well fear that the mere opinion that Arthur is dead could have the same force as an execution, just as Arthur's later accidental death prevents a reconciliation between the king and his nobles, until John himself is dying.

The whole of the prison scene is suffused with personal intimacy, and Hubert's asides early in the dialogue suggest that he has imperfectly suppressed his natural inclination toward mercy. From the beginning he fears that the boy's words will take possession of his bosom against his will (4.1.33). He tries to harden his heart, but he weeps involuntarily. The aim of Arthur's appeal is to reproach his keeper, who has by now become his friend but is still his executioner: 'I would to God / I were your son, so you would love me' (23–4). Every speech becomes so personal that it burns into Hubert's conscience, and his defences crumble before the boy's pretty but potent moral argument from the inherent nature of things: even the hot iron seems to die

---

[1] Wilders, *The Lost Garden*, pp. 79–101, explains the contingent pressures and moral dilemmas in other history plays.

[2] Blinding is presumably taken as the equivalent of killing or castration. John orders 'Death' (3.3.66), the warrant calls for burning out both eyes (4.1.39), Hubert concedes that Arthur may 'live' (4.1.121), and the king should believe him 'dead' (4.1.127).

[3] See Appendix on the handling of sources, pp. 194–210 below.

of grief rather than put out his eyes; only Hubert would force the fire to blush with shame; and the fire 'like a dog that is compelled to fight' will snap at its own master.

> All things that you should use to do me wrong
> Deny their office. Only you do lack
> That mercy which fierce fire and iron extends . . .   4.1.117–19

Although some critics have dismissed Arthur's rhetoric as unconvincing, the childish illogicality of his argument and its wishful thinking are what make it reach Hubert. This is particularly so if we notice that Hubert from the beginning tries to conceal his true feelings from himself. The dialogue carries a certain psychological truth, and, given what he knows and feels in his newly activated conscience, Hubert naturally chooses the lesser of two evils. It is a difficult choice too, since he disobeys the king's orders and he undergoes 'much danger' for Arthur. He has no way of knowing, unfortunately, that the situation at court will change before he arrives to tell his white lie.

As Arthur's appeal saves Hubert from a bad conscience, so John's misfortunes in the next scene virtually condemn him for the crime that he ordered and that Hubert means to save him from. The merciless irony of Fortune forces him to answer for a crime he believes he committed, and, as Smallwood points out, we are not asked to share his fears and stresses 'but to judge his response to their challenge' (p. 35). John has a conscience too, but his political fears overcome his best impulses.

The pivotal scene (4.2) begins ominously with John's evident anxiety and the lords' dripping sarcasm about the need for a second coronation. Although he wants to be looked at 'with cheerful eyes', the lords mock him with flattering language, and John's attempt to quiet his fear breeds more fear. In the first three acts he has distinguished himself by mixing diplomacy with heroic furor, and by the ability to put his words into action. He defeats his foreign enemies and scatters them as if they were an armada struck by a roaring tempest at sea (3.4.1–3), an image that is calculated to enhance John's standing with an Elizabethan audience. But after the capture of Arthur his self-assurance is replaced by royal paranoia. Soon it will be the English lords' turn to be furious. For fear of their displeasure John grants them custody of Arthur before he knows that he can deliver the boy alive. He tries feebly to evade responsibility one moment, and the next he confesses his guilt, as Fortune whips him back and forth between desperate hope and legitimate fear. When Hubert finally recognises that it is time to clear the king's conscience – crying 'Arthur is alive' – John is so distraught that he thinks simply of his own safety. 'O, haste thee to the peers, / . . . And make them tame to their obedience!' (4.2.260–2).

Each a prisoner of his fears, the king and Hubert act upon imperfect knowledge in response to conflicting pressures – Hubert showing his moral strength, John his weakness. In much the same way the English lords are victims of their very decency, because they see the situation from another limited perspective. They have their own well-substantiated fears, based on secret information, for Hubert showed the warrant to a friend of Pembroke's – apparently one of the 'dogged spies' among the executioners (4.1.128). The lords' request for custody of Arthur is justified by the

threat to the peace of the kingdom from 'murmuring lips', and they warn John of the
harm to the boy's education if the king should 'choke his days' in confinement
(4.2.55–8). The audience well knows that the lords are right when they warn the king
that he creates a danger to his safety from the 'time's enemies' (61), who would take
advantage of his injustice and use it for their purposes. But it is the king's darker
purpose that the lords have in mind, if the imprisonment of the boy is evidence of
a greater fear that attends the 'steps of wrong' (57), a phrase that recalls John's earlier
words describing Arthur:

> He is a very serpent in my way,
> And wheresoe'er this foot of mine doth tread,
> He lies before me.   3.3.61–3

While Hubert whispers the dreaded news, the lords see John's 'colour come and go'
– a sign of the conflict between his 'purpose and his conscience'. So they expect a
hypocritical announcement, and having been convinced in advance of the king's
deception and criminality, they walk out in high dudgeon. By their lights it is natural
that they do not recognise their defection as treason. Since the 'king hath
dispossessed himself of us', the equivalent of a deposition, they assume that they are
released from their vows, and as former counsellors they withdraw their support:

> We will not line his thin bestainèd cloak
> With our pure honours, nor attend the foot
> That leaves the print of blood where'er it walks.   4.3.24–6

Such is the art of making the audience understand the tragic blindness of human
choices.

At the beginning of the next scene the situation has worsened, for not only has the
French invasion begun but the lords have now been in touch with Pandulph and
Melun on behalf of the Dauphin. Again it seems to the lords that the least evil choice
in these perilous times is to accept the Dauphin's 'gentle offer' (4.3.11–13); hence
their entry and departure are marked by their resolve to meet him at Saint
Edmundsbury. Assuming that they 'know the worst' (27), they are ready to misread
the discovery of Arthur's body lying openly on the ground as another sign. It calls
for vengeance (4.3.37–8), and implicitly validates their plans to join the only other
available claimant to the throne. Once again, Hubert comes at an inopportune time,
when the lords are on their knees, swearing solemn vows of revenge (65 ff.). His
announcement – 'Arthur doth live' – that would have been good news to them in the
last scene if promptly delivered, now seems a bold-faced lie. At court the false news
seemed too true; now the true news proves false. The scene is managed so that the
peers cannot believe in the sincerity of Hubert's tears when he sees the boy's body,
nor can they share the Bastard's open-mindedness. The circumstances have so stifled
the lords with the 'smell of sin' that they are driven away by their own misapplied
sense of honour.

If God weeps for such human blindness, He does not intervene. The dilemmas in
these scenes, crafted for maximum differentiation of choices, allow only the god-like
audience to see the causes of political and moral chaos, rooted in conscience and need,

13 Act 4, Scene 3: a possible Elizabethan staging, by C. Walter Hodges
    a Arthur on the walls (4.3.1–2)
    b The Bastard and the nobles discover the body (4.3.34)

and nurtured by misfortune. The effect is a partial indeterminacy of the rights and wrongs of anyone's actions. Although John ordered the execution, he is in action just an *ex post facto* murderer.[1] The English lords' misjudgement of signs leads them to make the wrong decision for the right reasons. Hubert's desire for the rewards of obedience is at war with his moral nature. Hence the fading of Hubert's sense of guilt. He begins with an unqualified promise to the king ('He shall not live', 3.3.66), which he remembers even while he relents to Arthur ('see to live . . . Yet am I sworn, and I did purpose . . . to burn them out', 4.1.121–4), but later he insists on his purity of intention despite his outward deformity ('Within this bosom never entered yet / The dreadful motion of a murderous thought', 4.2.254–5), and to Falconbridge he declares his complete innocence ('If I in act, consent, or sin of thought, / Be guilty of the stealing that sweet breath . . . / Let hell want pains enough to torture me!' 4.3.135–8).

Despite Falconbridge's late entry to the turmoil of these scenes, he soon plays a significant part. Earlier in the drama he maintains a lightly detached air, while he learns the ways of the world, but now, fresh from the country, with few preconceptions about the imbroglio at court, he keeps a cool head and grows in stature. In contrast to the others, he seems for a while to be the one statesman left in the kingdom. When necessary he indifferently rebukes his superiors, equals, and inferiors. Formerly he ridiculed the Duke of Austria, the Citizen of Angiers, and the Dauphin; now his blunt speeches are directed to his erring countrymen. He dashes cold water in the king's face when John does not want to hear bad news:

> if you be afeared to hear the worst,
> Then let the worst, unheard, fall on your head.   4.2.135–6

With open defiance he stops the lords from butchering Hubert:

> Thou wert better gall the devil, Salisbury.
> If thou but frown on me, or stir thy foot . . .   4.3.95–6

In private he gives Hubert a similar tongue-lashing (4.3.116 ff.). But it is in his silences, in his quiet comments, in his new-found tact that he assumes the role of mediator. In an effort to keep the peace and to promote a semblance of harmony, he tries to be honest but still to avoid needless friction. For example, he tests the king privately with the report that he met the angry lords seeking Arthur's grave 'whom they say is killed tonight / On your suggestion' (4.2.165–6). John ignores this invitation to vindicate himself, and the Bastard says no more about it. He agrees that in the 'spirit of the time' he will try to bring the peers back to court so John can win their loves again. Then, alone with the distempered lords, Falconbridge tacitly acknowledges that their grievances may be justified, and he never loses their respect, who still refer to him at the peak of their anger as 'renownèd Falconbridge' (4.3.101). He advises them that it does not matter what they think; under the circumstances 'good words I think were best' (28). Though he seems to agree that the murder

---

[1] Dover Wilson says John is 'a murderer in intention, if not in fact' (Wilson, p. lix). See Muriel St Clare Byrne on Shakespeare's 'forcing a card', p. 12 above.

of Arthur is a 'damnèd and a bloody work', his proviso – if it be 'the work of any hand' (57–9) – rings true for the audience. Similarly, when in private he expresses his grievous suspicions of Hubert, he couches them in the subjunctive: 'if thou didst this deed of death . . . if thou didst kill this child . . . If thou didst but consent / To this most cruel act . . .' The speech has all the strong feeling and the potential outrage that the peers felt a few moments before, except that he withholds judgement, allowing Hubert to defend himself. With a simple command the Bastard neither accepts nor rejects Hubert's declaration of total innocence: 'Go, bear him in thine arms', and he reflects quietly on the image of a suspected murderer lifting the body gently: 'How easy dost thou take all England up!' (4.3.142). The Bastard knows enough not to enquire too closely about his master's or Hubert's culpability, but Hubert appears to pass a test, presenting an impression of a grieving father: 'I honoured him, I loved him and will weep / My date of life out for his sweet life's loss' (4.3.105). It suggests the figure of woeful Talbot with his dead son in his arms (*1 Henry VI* 4.7.29) as well as the father who unknowingly killed his son (*3 Henry VI* 2.5.79 ff.), and a figure that Shakespeare will use again in the last scene of *Lear*.

Amidst the labyrinthine uncertainties of the kingdom, Falconbridge is sure of one thing: 'The life, the right, and truth of all this realm' has fled to heaven. This is a quiet assertion of what he has known since his Commodity soliloquy. It is not a moment of discovery, nor a sudden blinding truth he never realised.[1] In Act 2 he recognises that France's sponsorship of Arthur's claim is 'honourable' (2.1.585) and that usurping John stops Arthur's legitimate 'title in the whole' by means of a shady deal with France (2.1.562). Falconbridge naturally allies himself with Constance in 3.1 against the Duke of Austria. And once Arthur is dead he knows better than the peers that the miserable remains of England left behind must somehow be salvaged. This is the Bastard's test, more significant than the ones he gives to others, and he moves quickly from his personal grief to an assessment of the dangers to the realm. Like Hubert in the prison scene, he makes a quick decision as he defines his responsibility. It is an achievement of self-possession, as Smallwood says:

There is no talk about 'pure honour' such as we have just heard from the lords (4.3.25). The situation does not allow of judgments in such black and white terms. There is not one with an untarnished claim to loyalty, but a choice must be made: 'vast confusion waits.' The death of Arthur has become irrelevant because a new situation is created by it.[2]

The war now seems to be little more than a filthy dog-fight over the 'bare-picked bone of majesty', and personally the Bastard envies the happy man who can draw his cloak around him to hold out this storm, but he must, as a public man, attend to a thousand businesses (4.3.155–9). He makes the same kind of decision a few moments before when he saves Hubert's life and when he suppresses his suspicions of the king. This is his role as a royal servant, and when he calls attention to his mental reservations, he shows the mature awareness of an honest man in public life. His insight is much like Montaigne's:

---

[1] Compare Tillyard, *Shakespeare's History Plays*, p. 257, and Hibbard, p. 137.
[2] Smallwood, p. 39.

The virtue assigned to the affairs of the world is a virtue with many bends, angles, and elbows, so as to join and adapt itself to human weakness; mixed and artificial, not straight, clean, constant, or purely innocent . . . Civic innocence is measured according to the places and the times . . . We may regret better times, but not escape the present; we may wish for different magistrates, but we must nevertheless obey those that are here. And perhaps there is more merit in obeying the bad than the good. As long as the image of the ancient and accepted laws of this monarchy shines in some corner, there will I be planted. If by bad fortune they come to contradict and interfere with each other, and produce two sides dubious and difficult to choose between, my choice is likely to be to steal away and escape from that tempest; in the meantime nature may lend me a hand, or the hazards of war.[1]

These might well be the mature reflections of the Bastard's divided but sound mind. He enters public life with a mock innocence, but his pragmatic view of it makes him a worthy guide for the audience through the maze of this play. As a practical man he elbows his way amidst the bends and angles of policy, willing to adapt or even to dissimulate if necessary. Although in private he often speaks plainly, in public he learns to adjust his style for appearance' sake, and in spite of his Montaigne-like scepticism he maintains a statesman-like loyalty to an increasingly bad king. But in the Bastard's situation late in the drama, the death of Arthur removes one of those dubious and difficult choices among conflicting loyalties; so, although he would like to, he does not steal away and escape from the tempest. The image of the ancient and accepted laws of this monarchy shines dimly indeed; yet he puts the best face upon the king's affairs and hopes that the hazards of war and nature will lend a hand.

[1]   Montaigne, 'Of Vanity', trans. Frame, pp. 758–60.

NOTE ON THE TEXT

King John was first printed in the 1623 Folio, where it was placed at the head of the histories, and since that text is the only authority for the play, all modern editions are based upon it. It contains a fair number of misreadings, omissions, muddles, and inconsistencies, suggesting that it was printed from a manuscript prepared by two scribes, who in turn copied probably from the author's foul papers (see Textual Analysis, pp. 184–93 below).

The collations at the foot of the page record all substantial departures from the copy text, but the editor has silently modernised the spelling and punctuation. When altered punctuation and spelling have significance, those changes are recorded. If the old spelling conceals a pun or innuendo, it is normally noted in the Commentary. Additions to stage directions are placed in the text within square brackets. Each textual note begins with the lemma (a word or phrase from the text), a square bracket, and the source of the reading; subsequent readings follow in chronological order with the name of each editor who first included it in the text. Selected emendations favoured by former editors are recorded whether or not they have been accepted in this edition. Occasionally, a proposed emendation is recorded as a conjecture (*conj.*), if it was later admitted to the text or if it seems worthy of serious consideration. *This edn* indicates the present editor's new readings.

An asterisk in the lemma of a note in the Commentary is used to call attention to a word or phrase that has been emended in the text; the collation should be consulted for further information.

King John

LIST OF CHARACTERS

KING JOHN *of England*
ELEANOR, *Queen Mother*
PRINCE HENRY, *son of John, later Henry III*
BLANCHE *of Spain, niece of John*

PEMBROKE ⎱
SALISBURY ⎰ *English lords*
ESSEX ⎰
BIGOT ⎰

HUBERT, *confidant of John*
ROBERT FALCONBRIDGE, *son of Sir Robert Falconbridge*
Philip, the BASTARD *Falconbridge, his half-brother*
LADY FALCONBRIDGE, *widow of Sir Robert*
JAMES GURNEY, *servant to Lady Falconbridge*
PETER OF POMFRET, *a prophet*
HERALD, MESSENGER, EXECUTIONER, *Lords, a Sheriff, English soldiers, trumpet, another executioner, and attendants*

KING PHILIP *of France*
Lewis the DAUPHIN
ARTHUR, *Duke of Brittany, son of King John's elder brother Geoffrey*
CONSTANCE, *mother of Arthur*
Duke of AUSTRIA, *Viscount of Limoges*
MELUN, *a French lord*
CHATILLON, *ambassador from France to King John*
HERALD, MESSENGER, *other French soldiers, trumpets, and attendants*

CITIZEN *of Angiers*
Cardinal PANDULPH, *legate from the Pope*
Other citizens and attendants

Notes

The list of characters is based mainly on that of Rowe, the first to appear in print, and on Capell and Smallwood.

KING JOHN The youngest son of Henry II and Eleanor. His reign (1199–1216) was noted for at least three major crises: his disputed right to the throne, his defiance of Pope Innocent III about the appointment of the Archbishop of Canterbury, and his later wars with France. (See Appendix, p. 199 below.)

ELEANOR Eleanor of Aquitaine, successively Queen of France and England; she married King Louis VII of France in 1137, divorced him in 1152, and in the same year married Henry, Count of Anjou, who became King Henry II of England in 1154. She bore him five children. She led armies into battle, and was a canny politician. John was her favourite until her death in 1204.

PRINCE HENRY Born 1207 by John's second wife, succeeded to the throne 1216 and died

1272. His role in the play is frequently doubled with that of Arthur, but he should not seem as immature as Arthur.

BLANCHE Blanche of Spain, the granddaughter of Eleanor of Aquitaine, by the marriage of Eleanor's daughter (by Henry II) to Alfonso King of Castile; therefore, John was her uncle in the modern sense.

PEMBROKE William Marshall, Earl of Pembroke, served loyally Henry II, John, and Henry III. Holinshed says his son joined the Dauphin's invading army, which may account for Shakespeare's making him a rebel.

SALISBURY Historically William Longsword, bastard son of Henry II. His role in the play is as an early sympathiser with Constance and a reluctant leader of the revolting lords after news of Arthur's death.

ESSEX *and* BIGOT Each of these is a mostly silent third lord in various scenes. Geoffrey Fitzpeter was Earl of Essex at the beginning of John's reign, and Holinshed identifies him as chief justiciar, which may account for his association with a legal dispute in 1.1.44, his only appearance in the play. He died in 1213, after mediating some of the differences between the king and his angry peers. His name or title is never mentioned in the dialogue. Bigot, Earl of Norfolk, is named at 4.2.162 as one of the disgruntled lords looking for Arthur's body, and he speaks in 4.3. One actor could play both roles and that of King Philip.

HUBERT Hubert de Burgh was a distinguished servant of the crown under Richard I and, beginning in 1215, was chief justiciar under John and Henry III. He was a gallant soldier, known as a popular hero who drove the French from England. His part could be doubled with the Citizen of Angiers.

ROBERT FALCONBRIDGE An unhistorical character, played by a tall, thin-faced actor named Sinclo. See pp. 1–3 above.

Philip the BASTARD *Falconbridge* Largely unhistorical, but suggested by a mention in Holinshed of 'Philip, bastard son to King Richard, to whom his father had given the castle and honour of Coinack'. In 1199, he 'killed the Viscount Limoges, in revenge of his father's death'.

KING PHILIP Philip II of France, called Augustus (1165–1223), who succeeded to the throne in 1180, and accompanied King Richard I on a crusade to the Holy Land.

DAUPHIN The title is an anachronism, not having been used by the French royal family until 1349, and signifies the first son of the king. Although Lewis was the same age as Arthur, the title gives him a status as second in command.

ARTHUR Historically (and in *TR*) Arthur was about 15 years old at the time of the conflict between King John and King Philip over John's right to England's continental territories, but Shakespeare makes him seem just a child, ruled by his mother. His part could be doubled with that of Prince Henry.

CONSTANCE She is presented as a helpless widow of Geoffrey, but in fact she left her second husband, the Earl of Chester, in 1199 and married the lord Guy de Thouars. Shakespeare shapes her role as a mirror to Eleanor, even in the news of both their deaths 4.2.120–3. Her part could be doubled with that of Lady Falconbridge.

AUSTRIA The Duke of Austria imprisoned King Richard Cœur-de-lion and held him for ransom, and Shakespeare conflates Austria with the Viscount Limoges, who fatally wounded Richard with a bolt from a cross-bow during a siege. This consolidation enhances the Bastard's honourable revenge, by killing two of his father's enemies at one blow. The same actor could play Austria, Robert Falconbridge, an Executioner, and Peter of Pomfret.

MELUN Melun is one of the great conscience figures in the play, taken from Holinshed and Foxe, who say that he was sworn to kill the English lords, but his conscience prevented him. His part could be doubled with that of Eleanor.

PANDULPH Shakespeare combines several papal emissaries into one character: among them a Roman lawyer Pandulph, who exhorted John 'to leave his stubborn disobedience to the Church', interceded with John for the appointment of Stephen Langton as Archbishop of Canterbury, encouraged King Philip's abortive invasion of England, and brought John to repentance. Another legate, Cardinal Gualo, tried unsuccessfully to stop the Dauphin's later invasion of England, after John capitulated to the Pope. Pandulph's part could be doubled with that of Chatillon, and one of the Heralds.

THE TRAGEDY OF KING JOHN

1.1 *Enter* KING JOHN, QUEEN ELEANOR, PEMBROKE, ESSEX, SALISBURY, [*and attendants,*] *with the* CHATILLON *of France*

KING JOHN Now say, Chatillon, what would France with us?
CHATILLON Thus, after greeting, speaks the King of France
  In my behaviour to the majesty,
  The borrowed majesty of England here.
ELEANOR A strange beginning: 'borrowed majesty'?   5
KING JOHN Silence, good mother, hear the embassy.
CHATILLON Philip of France, in right and true behalf
  Of thy deceasèd brother Geoffrey's son,
  Arthur Plantagenet, lays most lawful claim
  To this fair island and the territories,   10
  To Ireland, Poitiers, Anjou, Touraine, Maine,
  Desiring thee to lay aside the sword
  Which sways usurpingly these several titles,
  And put the same into young Arthur's hand,
  Thy nephew and right royal sovereign.   15
KING JOHN What follows if we disallow of this?

Title] *This edn;* The life and death of King John F   Act 1, Scene 1   1.1] *Actus Primus, Scæna Prima.* F
0 SD SALISBURY] *and Salisbury* F   0 SD *with the*] F; *with / Rowe; with them / Honigmann*   0 SD CHATILLON]
Johnson; Chattylion F *(subst. throughout)*   8 brother] F4; brother, F   11 Poitiers, Anjou, Touraine] *Poyctiers,
Aniowe, Torayne* F

---

*Title See supplementary note.

Act 1, Scene 1
  1.1 F divides acts and scenes throughout.
  0 SD Taking their cue from *TR*, some productions have staged a dumb-show coronation. In any case, an Elizabethan production would require a platform with a chair and footstool for the king under a canopy, what was often called for in contemporary scripts as 'a state set out'.
  0 SD *attendants* Hubert may be included here and in Acts 2 and 3, as a confidant of the king.
  0 SD *the* CHATILLON *of France* The phrase implies an official title, although in the dialogue 'Chatillon' is used alone as a name.
  1 **Now say** The sense of a continuing conversation can be suggested if Chatillon enters with John, but productions usually delay his entry until the king sits.

3 **In my behaviour** In my own person. Compare the Bastard's speech, 5.2.128–9, for the same use of 'in': 'Now hear our English king, / For thus his royalty doth speak in me.'
  4 **borrowed** false, put on.
  6 **embassy** message.
  9 **Arthur** Since Richard Cœur-de-lion left no direct descendant, he had designated his nephew Arthur as next in line to the throne, but Eleanor persuaded him on his deathbed to alter his will, passing over Arthur in favour of John, her youngest son (see 1.1.109 and 2.1.192 nn.).
  10 **territories** lands within or adjacent to England.
  11 **Poitiers, Anjou, Touraine, Maine** See supplementary note for the importance of these provinces in western France.

CHATILLON The proud control of fierce and bloody war,
　　　　To enforce these rights so forcibly withheld.
KING JOHN Here have we war for war and blood for blood,
　　　　Controlment for control. So answer France.　　　　　　　　　20
CHATILLON Then take my king's defiance from my mouth,
　　　　The farthest limit of my embassy.
KING JOHN Bear mine to him, and so depart in peace.
　　　　Be thou as lightning in the eyes of France;
　　　　For ere thou canst report, I will be there:　　　　　　　　　25
　　　　The thunder of my cannon shall be heard.
　　　　So hence. Be thou the trumpet of our wrath,
　　　　And sullen presage of your own decay.
　　　　An honourable conduct let him have.
　　　　Pembroke, look to't. Farewell, Chatillon.　　　　　　　　　30
　　　　　　　　　　　　　Exeunt Chatillon and Pembroke
ELEANOR [*Whispers*] What now, my son, have I not ever said
　　　　How that ambitious Constance would not cease
　　　　Till she had kindled France and all the world
　　　　Upon the right and party of her son?
　　　　This might have been prevented and made whole　　　　　35
　　　　With very easy arguments of love,
　　　　Which now the manage of two kingdoms must
　　　　With fearful-bloody issue arbitrate.
KING JOHN Our strong possession and our right for us.
ELEANOR Your strong possession much more than your right,　　40
　　　　Or else it must go wrong with you and me;

---

20 Controlment for control] *Wilson, conj. Vaughan;* Controlement for controlement F　25 report,] F; report *Capell*
25 there:] F; there, *Rowe*　30 SD *Exeunt] Warburton; Exit* F　41 me;] *Pope;* me, F

17 control compulsion, mastery.

19 blood for blood Compare Gen. 9.6: 'Whoso sheddeth man's blood, by man shall his blood be shed' and the proverb 'Blood will have blood' (Tilley B458).

20 *Controlment for control Dover Wilson's emendation restores the metre and brings out a distinction between a check and a compulsion.

25 report The pun on 'report' bridges the conceit of 'lightning' (24) closely followed by 'thunder' (26) (Dent L281). Dr Johnson thought that the image did not suit well, for 'lightning is destructive, thunder is innocent', but Jove's thunderbolts give the image of its terror. Compare *H5* 2.4.99–100: 'in fierce tempest is |the King of England| coming, / In thunder and in earthquake, like a Jove'.

27 trumpet i.e. the herald.

28 sullen presage . . . decay a foreboding, like the dismal passing bell that announces your own death.

29 conduct escort.

34 Upon In support of. See 2.1.237 n.

36 arguments of love expressions of friendship.

37 manage (1) action or conduct of government, (2) skilful handling, as in managing a weapon. The meaning is rooted in the training and control of horses; compare 17, 'proud control'.

38 issue outcome; a discharge of blood, as from a wound or sore. See *OED* Issue *sb* 4a.

41 i.e. no matter what your right, your possession and your right will have to defend us.

So much my conscience whispers in your ear,
Which none but heaven and you and I shall hear.

Enter a sheriff [and whispers Essex in the ear]

ESSEX   My liege, here is the strangest controversy
  Come from the country to be judged by you   45
  That e'er I heard. Shall I produce the men?
KING JOHN Let them approach.

                                               [Exit sheriff]

  Our abbeys and our priories shall pay
  This expedition's charge.

Enter ROBERT FALCONBRIDGE *and Philip [the* BASTARD *with sheriff]*

                        What men are you?
BASTARD Your faithful subject I, a gentleman,   50
  Born in Northamptonshire, and eldest son,
  As I suppose, to Robert Falconbridge,
  A soldier, by the honour-giving hand
  Of Cœur-de-lion, knighted in the field.
KING JOHN What are thou?   55
ROBERT The son and heir to that same Falconbridge.
KING JOHN Is that the elder, and art thou the heir?
  You came not of one mother then, it seems.
BASTARD Most certain of one mother, mighty king –
  That is well known – and as I think one father.   60
  But for certain knowledge of that truth
  I put you o'er to heaven, and to my mother.
  Of that I doubt, as all men's children may.
ELEANOR Out on thee, rude man! Thou dost shame thy mother,

---

43 SD *and . . . ear*] Riverside; *and whispers Essex* / Capell; not in F   47 SD *Exit sheriff*] Capell; not in F   49 expedition's] F2; expeditious F   49 SD] *Follows* you? *at 49 in* F   50 SH BASTARD] *Philip* F (or / Phil. / to 132)   50 subject I,] Capell; subject, I F   54 Cœur-de-lion] Pope; Cordelion F (throughout)

43 SD *Enter . . . ear* If the sheriff enters at about 38, as in many productions, we see two pairs of whisperers simultaneously. (See 2.1.468 ff., 3.3.18 ff., and 4.2.68 ff.) The bracketed phrase 'and . . . ear' is adapted from *TR: and whispers the Earle of Sals in the eare*.

45 **judged by you** The king and his council constituted the highest court, a royal power that the Magna Carta abridged a few years later.

54 **Cœur-de-lion** Accent on the first and third syllables as in modern French. F's anglicised form 'Cordelion' may suggest the familiarity of Richard's heroic reputation (Smallwood).

54 **knighted in the field** knighthood conferred just before or after battle; the usual and most honourable occasion.

61–3 **certain knowledge . . . children may** Recalling proverbial wisdom as in John Heywood's *Epigrams* (1562), 50: 'Who is thy father child, axt his mother's husband. Axe my mother (quoth he) that to understand' (Tilley M1193), and perhaps glancing at 'It is a wise child that knows his own father' (Tilley C309).

62 **put you o'er** refer you to.

64 **rude** uncivilised, coarse.

And wound her honour with this diffidence.   65
BASTARD I, madam? No, I have no reason for it.
That is my brother's plea, and none of mine,
The which if he can prove, a pops me out
At least from fair five hundred pound a year.
Heaven guard my mother's honour, and my land!   70
KING JOHN A good blunt fellow. Why being younger born
Doth he lay claim to thine inheritance?
BASTARD I know not why, except to get the land,
But once he slandered me with bastardy.
Now whe'er I be as true begot or no,   75
That still I lay upon my mother's head,
But that I am as well begot, my liege –
Fair fall the bones that took the pains for me –
Compare our faces and be judge yourself.
If old Sir Robert did beget us both   80
And were our father and this son like him,
O old Sir Robert, father, on my knee
I give heaven thanks I was not like to thee!
KING JOHN Why, what a mad-cap hath heaven lent us here!
ELEANOR He hath a trick of Cœur-de-lion's face,   85
The accent of his tongue affecteth him.
Do you not read some tokens of my son
In the large composition of this man?
KING JOHN Mine eye hath well examinèd his parts
And finds them perfect Richard. [*To Robert*] Sirrah, speak,   90
What doth move you to claim your brother's land?

---

75 Now] *Wilson, conj. Wright;* But F   79 yourself] *Warburton;* your selfe F   81 him,] *Collier;* him: F

65 **diffidence** distrust, lack of faith.
68 **a** he; the unaccented form of the pronoun, typical of the Bastard's vernacular. Compare 2.1.136; 'and a may catch your hide'.
74 **once** at one time; in short.
75 *****Now** 'But', the Folio reading, is probably an error, for the Bastard prefers the Marlovian 'Now', especially to emphasise a noteworthy point. See 1.1.165 and 1.1.259, both passages concerned, as here, with the all-important question of his begetting. (Among heroes of the history plays, only Prince Hal uses 'now' so often.)
76 **still** always.
76 **lay . . . head** leave it to my mother to say; she will have to answer for it. See *OED* Head *sb* 35a *on one's head*; and Lay *v* 28.

78 **Fair fall** May good befall, fair hap befall. Berowne also puns on the sexual meaning of 'fall' in *LLL* 2.1.124–5: '*Kath.* Fair fall the face it covers! *Ber.* And send you many lovers!'
80 **old Sir Robert** 'Old Faukenbridge', a character in the play *Look About You* (1600), suspects that Prince Richard is in love with his wife, but the lady never loses her honour.
84 **map-cap** A 'wild head', as the Bastard is called in *TR* 2.70.
86 **affecteth** resembles, imitates.
88 **composition** physique.
90 **perfect Richard** Compare *Temp* 1.1.29–30: 'his complexion is perfect gallows'.
90 **Sirrah** The customary address to an inferior.

BASTARD Because he hath a half-face like my father!
         With half that face would he have all my land –
         A half-faced groat five hundred pound a year!
ROBERT   My gracious liege, when that my father lived,   95
         Your brother did employ my father much –
BASTARD [*Aside*] Well sir, by this you cannot get my land:
         Your tale must be how he employed my mother.
ROBERT   And once dispatched him in an embassy
         To Germany, there with the emperor   100
         To treat of high affairs touching that time.
         Th'advantage of his absence took the king,
         And in the meantime sojourned at my father's,
         Where how he did prevail I shame to speak.
         But truth is truth. Large lengths of seas and shores   105
         Between my father and my mother lay,
         As I have heard my father speak himself,
         When this same lusty gentleman was got.
         Upon his deathbed he by will bequeathed
         His lands to me, and took it on his death   110
         That this my mother's son was none of his;
         And if he were, he came into the world
         Full fourteen weeks before the course of time.
         Then, good my liege, let me have what is mine,
         My father's land, as was my father's will.   115
KING JOHN Sirrah, your brother is legitimate:
         Your father's wife did after wedlock bear him,
         And if she did play false, the fault was hers,

---

93 half that face | F; that half-face *Theobald*

92 **half-face** profile; thin face. Like Sir Andrew Aguecheek (*TN* 5.1.207), he is a 'thin-faced knave, a gull' and, therefore, less than a full man. Hotspur disdains anything less than manly honour (*1H4* 1.3.208): 'out upon this half-faced fellowship!'
93 ***half that face** even less of a human specimen than his father. The phrase should not be emended to 'that half-face', because it would lose the intensifying force of the original. Compare *1H4* 4.3.23–4: 'Their courage [is] with hard labour tame and dull, / That not a horse is half the half of himself.' There is probably a pun on 'face' = impudence or cheek.
94 **half-faced groat** A very thin silver coin, with the monarch's face in profile.
104 **shame** am ashamed.

105 **truth is truth** Proverbial (Tilley T581).
105–8 **lengths of seas ... got** A futile argument, legally, because Sir Robert returned well before the birth of the child. A child born in wedlock could not be bastardised unless the father was overseas for the entire time of the wife's pregnancy.
108 **lusty** vigorous, merry.
109 **will** Sir Robert's deathbed will, disinheriting the eldest son, is emphasised here and at 115, 130, and 133, and the king rules strictly according to law. But the parallel with John's doubtful inheritance of the crown, via a deathbed will, is left for the audience to discover in Act 2.
110 **took ... death** swore an oath not just on his deathbed, but on his chances of salvation; an affirmation that carries conviction; see 5.4.28–9.

Which fault lies on the hazards of all husbands
That marry wives. Tell me, how if my brother,   120
Who as you say took pains to get this son,
Had of your father claimed this son for his?
In sooth, good friend, your father might have kept
This calf, bred from his cow, from all the world;
In sooth he might. Then if he were my brother's,   125
My brother might not claim him, nor your father,
Being none of his, refuse him. This concludes:
My mother's son did get your father's heir,
Your father's heir must have your father's land.

ROBERT   Shall then my father's will be of no force   130
        To dispossess that child which is not his?

BASTARD   Of no more force to dispossess me, sir,
        Than was his will to get me, as I think.

ELEANOR   Whether hadst thou rather be: a Falconbridge,
        And like thy brother to enjoy thy land,   135
        Or the reputed son of Cœur-de-lion,
        Lord of thy presence and no land beside?

BASTARD   Madam, and if my brother had my shape
        And I had his, Sir Robert's his, like him,
        And if my legs were two such riding-rods,   140
        My arms such eel-skins stuffed, my face so thin
        That in mine ear I durst not stick a rose
        Lest men should say 'Look where three-farthings goes!'
        And to his shape were heir to all this land,

---

122 his?] *Theobald;* his, F   134 rather be:] *Smallwood;* rather be F; rather, – be *Capell*   137 beside?] F4; beside. F
139 Robert's his,] *Rowe;* Robert's his F

119 **lies on the hazards** is one of the risks.
124 **calf . . . cow** 'he which married the woman, shall be said to be the father of the child, and not he which did beget the same . . . for whose the cow is, as it is commonly said, his is the calf also', H. Swinburne, *Brief Treatise of Testaments* (1599), sig. y6 (Honigmann). Tilley C765: 'Who bulls the cow must keep the calf.'
127 **refuse** disclaim, disown.
127 **concludes** is decisive, settles the case.
132–3 **force . . . will** The Bastard thinks of the greater force of will (i.e. lust) that begot him. (See below, 264–5.) That 'will' often meant lust is clear from *AWW* 4.3.16: 'this night he fleshes his will in the spoil of her honour'.
134 **Whether** One syllable.
135–6 **like . . . Cœur-de-lion** After the Bastard

has shown his likeness to King Richard in body, this is the test of his spirit.
137 **Lord of thy presence** i.e. be in possession and master of your true person as son of Richard.
137 **no land** Contrary to the rule that every knight must own land worth at least £120.
139 **Robert's his** i.e. 'his shape, which is also his father's'. Schmidt considers this passage a double possessive, 'his' often being used to show possession, as 'Ben Jonson his best piece of poetry' (*Epigrams*, 45, 'On His First Son').
140 **riding-rods** switches.
143 **three-farthings** Several coins of low value had a rose stamped behind the queen's head in profile, the three-farthing piece being very thin.
144 **to his shape** in addition to his figure.

Would I might never stir from off this place,   145
I would give it every foot to have this face.
I would not be Sir Nob in any case.
ELEANOR I like thee well. Wilt thou forsake thy fortune,
Bequeath thy land to him, and follow me?
I am a soldier and now bound to France.   150
BASTARD Brother, take you my land, I'll take my chance.
Your face hath got five hundred pound a year,
Yet sell your face for five pence and 'tis dear.
Madam, I'll follow you unto the death.
ELEANOR Nay, I would have you go before me thither.   155
BASTARD Our country manners give our betters way.
KING JOHN What is thy name?
BASTARD Philip, my liege, so is my name begun,
Philip, good old Sir Robert's wife's eldest son.
KING JOHN From henceforth bear his name whose form thou
                bearest: 160
Kneel thou down Philip, but rise more great,
Arise Sir Richard and Plantagenet.
BASTARD Brother by th'mother's side, give me your hand;
My father gave me honour, yours gave land.
Now blessèd be the hour by night or day   165
When I was got, Sir Robert was away.
ELEANOR The very spirit of Plantagenet.
I am thy grandam, Richard, call me so.
BASTARD Madam, by chance but not by truth; what though?

---

147 I would] F2; It would F   159 wife's] *Rowe*; wiues F   160] *One line in Pope; divided at* From . . . name / . . . bearest F

145 Would . . . place May God strike me dead if I lie. Tilley s861, the earliest recorded use.

147 Nob A nickname for Robert, with a pun on 'head' = the head of a stick. T. Harman, *A Caveat* (1567), sig. G2ᵛ, in a glossary of beggars' cant, defines 'nab' as 'a head'. 'Nob in any case' has bawdy connotations, as in *Wiv.* 4.1.57–62 and *Ado* 1.1.182.

148–9 forsake . . . follow me See the Appendix, p. 200 below, n. 1, for similarities with the Bastard of Orleans.

153 Dear because a groat is worth fourpence.

154–6 follow . . . way The joke is adapted from a proverb (Tilley p89): 'At an ill passage honour thy companion.' Compare Gascoigne, *Suppose* (1573), 5.5, p. 234: 'Hence to the gallows knave. – What

soft and fair sir, I pray you, I pray sequar, you are my elder' ('sequar' = I follow).

159 wife's eldest son Possibly recalling the saying about bastards, 'My lady's eldest sons' (Dent l.30.1 and *Ado* 2.1.9).

162 Sir Richard . . . Plantagenet Eleanor, John, and Hubert call him by his new name once, Salisbury uses his title once, and the Bastard jokes about it (185). Otherwise he continues to be known as Falconbridge or Philip (as in *TR*), perhaps because his original name was already fixed in the popular mind.

165 hour With a pun on 'whore'. See 3.1.56 n.

169 truth honesty, virtue; with a play on 'troth' = 'marriage'.

169 what though? what of that?

Something above a little from the right,   170
   In at the window, or else o'er the hatch.
Who dares not stir by day must walk by night,
   And have is have, however men do catch.
Near or far off, well won is still well shot,
   And I am I, howe'er I was begot.   175
KING JOHN Go, Falconbridge, now hast thou thy desire;
A landless knight makes thee a landed squire.
Come madam, and come Richard, we must speed
For France, for France, for it is more than need.
BASTARD Brother adieu, good fortune come to thee,   180
For thou wast got i'th'way of honesty.

                  Exeunt all but Bastard

A foot of honour better than I was,
But many a many foot of land the worse.
Well, now can I make any Joan a lady.
'Good den, Sir Richard.' – 'Godamercy fellow.'   185
And if his name be George, I'll call him Peter;
For new-made honour doth forget men's names:

---

170 above] *This edn;* about F; about, F4   182 A foot] *Rowe; Bast.* A foot F

170–5 Something . . . begot Playful application of conventional phrases and proverbs, as here, was admired by Elizabethans of all classes, not just country folk. See F. P. Wilson, 'Shakespeare and the diction of common life', *PBA* 42 (1941), 167–97. The Bastard turns *window, hatch, stir, catch,* and *shot* toward his well-begotten conceit. In *Cor.* 1.1.205–8 a similar list of sayings without the innuendos represents the speech of simple folk.

170 *Something above Rather more than. See supplementary note.

170 from the right Suggesting the 'bar sinister' in a coat-of-arms for a bastard, and a pun on 'right' (truth).

171 In . . . hatch Improper entry, implying bastardy. Compare Middleton's *Family of Love* (1608), sig. F4: 'Woe worth the time that ever I gave suck to a child that came in at the window'; and Dekker and Webster's *Northward Hoe* (1607) 1.1.130–1: 'kindred that comes in o'er the hatch'. See Tilley and Dent W450.

171 hatch The lower half of a door.

172 walk by night prowl, do nightwork. See *2H4* 3.2.199–209, on Jane Nightwork, the bona roba.

173 have is have A catchphrase also used in *AYLI* 5.1.40, possibly related to 'Own is own' (Tilley H215 and O100).

174 shot As in archery, traditionally analogous to love-making. See *LLL* 4.1.10–12, 108–35, for the greasy talk of shooting one's deer: 'Let the mark have a prick in it', 'A mark marvellous well shot'.

177 landless knight i.e. Sir Richard Plantagenet, not 'John Lackland' the king, but the analogy may be suggested.

181 i'th'way of honesty Proverbial (Tilley and Dent W115).

182 foot footing, status. See *OED* sv *sb* 24.

183 many a many many and many. See *OED* Many *adj* 1b.

183 foot of land A familiar phrase. Compare the old metrical romance *Cuer du Lyon* (1528 edn), sig. G4: 'He shall not have a foot of lond / Never more but of my hond' (Honigmann).

184 make . . . lady marry any common woman (who will thus be titled 'lady'); probably related to the saying 'Joan is as good as my lady (in the dark)' (Tilley J57).

185 Good den God give you good evening.

185 Godamercy God give you mercy.

185 fellow i.e. the plain countryman calls me 'sir' and I reply 'fellow'.

187 new . . . names Adapted from the proverb 'Honours changes manners' (Tilley H583).

'Tis too respective and too sociable
For your conversion. Now your traveller,
He and his toothpick at my worship's mess,   190
And when my knightly stomach is sufficed,
Why then I suck my teeth and catechise
My pickèd man of countries: 'My dear sir',
Thus leaning on mine elbow I begin,
'I shall beseech you' – that is Question now,   195
And then comes Answer like an Absey book:
'O sir', says Answer, 'at your best command,
At your employment, at your service, sir.'
'No sir', says Question, 'I, sweet sir, at yours.'
And so e'er Answer knows what Question would,   200
Saving in dialogue of compliment,
And talking of the Alps and Apennines,
The Pyrenean and the river Po,
It draws toward supper in conclusion so.
But this is worshipful society,   205
And fits the mounting spirit like myself;
For he is but a bastard to the time
That doth not smack of observation,
And so am I – whether I smack or no,

---

189 conversion.] *Capell*; conuersion, F; conversing. *Pope*   203 Pyrenean] F2 (*Pyrennean*); *Perennean* F   208–9 smack
. . . smack] *Theobald*; smoake . . . smacke F; smack . . . smoke *Pope*

188–9 'Tis . . . conversion i.e. one who has just
risen in rank does not show too much regard and
courtesy for others below him. 'Conversion'
probably means (1) change to something better or
higher; (2) conversation or converse (compare
Englishman for my Money 1.1, p. 477: 'Inpudent
villain and lascivious gorls, I have o'erheard your
vild conversions').

189 your . . . your The colloquial use, vaguely
implying 'as you know'; see *Ham.* 5.1.189 and
OED Your 5b.

189 traveller Compare *AWW* 2.5.28: 'A good
traveller is something at the latter end of a dinner'
– i.e. to amuse the table with tall stories.

190 toothpick The affectation of a traveller,
courtier or gallant.

190 my worship's mess my table (where like a
great magnate I dispense hospitality to those who
'feed and fawn' upon me in my prosperity (as Lord
Burghley observed in *Certain precepts* (*c.* 1584), in
Advice to a Son, ed. Wright (1962), p. 11)). Strictly
speaking, a mess was a table for four, so the Bastard
may imply that the traveller has been allowed to sit
with persons of quality.

193 pickèd spruce, refined. Compare *LLL*

5.1.12–14: 'He is too picked, too spruce, too
affected, too odd as it were, too perigrinate, as I
may call it.'

195–6 Question . . . Absey book The primer in
an elementary school was the shorter catechism
with the ABC in front, and instruction went by
question and answer.

201 dialogue of compliment formal address;
like Osric's speeches in *Ham.* 5.2, and what Jacques
calls 'th'encounter of two dog-apes' (*AYLI* 2.5.26).

205–16 But . . . rising The Bastard will be *in* this
new political world, but he will not be *of* it. See p.
41 above.

206 mounting aspiring, ambitious.

207 bastard to the time no true son of the
age.

208 *smack taste; associated with 'tooth' and
'sweet poison' at 213.

208 observation (1) paying close attention to
others with observant care, i.e. imitating, (2)
obsequiousness, paying court. Compare Hamlet,
who was 'Th'observed of all observers' (*Ham.*
3.1.154).

209 so am I i.e. not a true child of the time.

And not alone in habit and device,   210
Exterior form, outward accoutrement,
But from the inward motion – to deliver
Sweet, sweet, sweet poison for the age's tooth,
Which, though I will not practise to deceive,
Yet to avoid deceit, I mean to learn,   215
For it shall strew the footsteps of my rising.
But who comes in such haste in riding-robes?
What woman-post is this? Hath she no husband
That will take pains to blow a horn before her?

Enter LADY FALCONBRIDGE *and* JAMES GURNEY

O me, 'tis my mother. How now, good lady?   220
What brings you here to court so hastily?
LADY FALCONBRIDGE Where is that slave, thy brother? Where is he
That holds in chase mine honour up and down?
BASTARD My brother Robert, old Sir Robert's son?
Colbrand the Giant, that same mighty man?   225
Is it Sir Robert's son that you seek so?
LADY FALCONBRIDGE Sir Robert's son. Ay, thou unreverend boy,
Sir Robert's son! Why scorn'st thou at Sir Robert?
He is Sir Robert's son, and so art thou.
BASTARD James Gurney, wilt thou give us leave a while?   230
GURNEY Good leave, good Philip.
BASTARD   Philip? – sparrow! James,
There's toys abroad; anon I'll tell thee more.
                                            Exit James [Gurney]

218| woman-post| F4; *no hyphen in* F   219 SD| *Capell; after 221* F   231 Philip? – sparrow!| *Steevens², conj. Upton*
(subst.); Philip, sparrow, F; *Philip! – spare me, Theobald; Philip! sparrow: Capell*

210 habit and device clothing and knightly insignia.
212 inward motion inclination, secret desire, prompting. See *OED* Motion *sb* 9.
213 sweet poison flattery. A commonplace (Dent F349.1).
213 tooth taste.
216 it . . . rising as I rise flattery will be strewn before me like flowers before a great man's footsteps.
218 woman-post Instead of the usual male post-rider.
219 blow a horn The post, always in haste, therefore blew a horn. There is probably a joke here about cuckolds who advertised their horns and women who travelled about and cuckolded their husbands. Dent thinks the speech is related to the

saying 'Wear a horn and blow it not' (Tilley H618).
223 holds in chase hunts, pursues by way of harassment. Compare *Cor.* 1.6.18–19: 'Spies of the Volsces / Held me in chase.'
225 Colbrand the Giant A champion of the Danes, fought by the hero in the popular romance *Guy of Warwick*.
230 give us leave A courtly way of asking to be alone (Dent L167.1).
231 *Philip? – sparrow!* Gurney has spoken familiarly ('good Philip') and the Bastard pretends to bridle at the common name, now worth no more to him than something to call a sparrow (as in Skelton's mock elegy on 'Philip Sparrow').
232 toys abroad i.e. there is a little game afoot about my names: trifling gifts, such as a knighthood (Sir Richard) and a new surname (Plantagenet).

Madam, I was not old Sir Robert's son.
Sir Robert might have eat his part in me
Upon Good Friday and ne'er broke his fast.   235
Sir Robert could do well – marry, to confess –
Could he get me. Sir Robert could not do it.
We know his handiwork. Therefore, good mother,
To whom am I beholding for these limbs?
Sir Robert never holp to make this leg.   240
LADY FALCONBRIDGE Hast thou conspirèd with thy brother too,
That for thine own gain shouldst defend mine honour?
What means this scorn, thou most untoward knave?
BASTARD Knight, knight, good mother, Basilisco-like.
What, I am dubbed, I have it on my shoulder.   245
But mother, I am not Sir Robert's son,
I have disclaimed Sir Robert and my land;
Legitimation, name, and all is gone.
Then, good my mother, let me know my father –
Some proper man I hope. Who was it, mother?   250
LADY FALCONBRIDGE Hast thou denied thyself a Falconbridge?
BASTARD As faithfully as I deny the devil.
LADY FALCONBRIDGE King Richard Cœur-de-lion was thy father.
By long and vehement suit I was seduced
To make room for him in my husband's bed.   255
Heaven! lay not my transgression to my charge
That art the issue of my dear offence,
Which was so strongly urged past my defence.

236–7 do well – marry, to confess – / Could . . . me. Sir] *This edn;* do: well – marry, to confess – / Could . . . me? Sir;
Alexander, conj. Vaughan (subst.); do well, marrie to confesse / Could . . . me sir F; do well, marry, to confess! /
Could . . . me! Sir F4   237 he get] *Pope;* get F   256 Heaven!] *Knight;* Heauen F   256 to my] F; to thy *conj. Staunton*
257 That] F; Thou F4

234–5 Sir Robert . . . fast Compare Heywood's
Proverbs (1546), sig. D4: 'He may his part on Good
Friday eat, / And fast never the worse, for ought he
shall get' (Tilley P75).
   236 do copulate.
   238 his handiwork God's handiwork was the
creation of the world; Ps. 19 (Prayer-Book version):
'the firmament showeth his handiwork'. If the
Bastard has this verse in mind, there is an irreverent
tone, especially since in Elizabethan slang 'fair
work and good workmanship' refers to begetting
children (Honigmann).
   239 beholding beholden, indebted.
   240 holp helped.
   242 That Who.
   244 Basilisco-like In saying 'Knight, knight'

the Bastard imitates the ridiculous, boastful character named Basilisco, in *Soliman and Perseda* (c.
1589–92), 1.3.166–75.
   252 faithfully . . . devil Echoing the services of
baptism and confirmation: 'Dost thou renounce
the devil and all his works . . . ?'
   256 Heaven ! In the name of heaven; the
equivalent of 'Heavens' and 'O heaven!' See
supplementary note.
   257 dear offence grievous wrong, the offence
which has cost me dear. In the light of what the
Bastard says next, there should be a latent meaning
of an apparent offence that leads to good; compare
1H4 1.2.216: 'I'll so offend to make offence a
skill.'

BASTARD Now by this light, were I to get again,
    Madam, I would not wish a better father.   260
    Some sins do bear their privilege on earth,
    And so doth yours: your fault was not your folly,
    Needs must you lay your heart at his dispose,
    Subjected tribute to commanding love,
    Against whose fury and unmatchèd force   265
    The aweless lion could not wage the fight,
    Nor keep his princely heart from Richard's hand.
    He that perforce robs lions of their hearts
    May easily win a woman's. Ay, my mother,
    With all my heart I thank thee for my father.   270
    Who lives and dares but say thou didst not well
    When I was got, I'll send his soul to hell.
    Come, lady, I will show thee to my kin,
     And they shall say, when Richard me begot,
    If thou hadst said him nay, it had been sin.   275
    Who says it was, he lies; I say 'twas not.
                 Exeunt

2.1 *Enter, before Angiers*, PHILIP, *King of France, Lewis* [*the*] DAUPHIN,
CONSTANCE, ARTHUR, [*lords, and soldiers, at one door; at the other, Duke of*]
AUSTRIA [*with soldiers*]

KING PHILIP [*Embraces Austria*] Before Angiers well met, brave
    Austria. –

Act 2, Scene 1 2.1] *Rowe³; Scæna Secunda* F 0 SD *Enter . . . soldiers*] *Capell (subst.); Enter before Angers, Philip
King of France, Lewis, Daulphin, Austria, Constance, Arthur.* F 1, 18 SH KING PHILIP] *Dyce²*, conj. *Theobald; Lewis* F

---

259 to get to be begotten.
261 do . . . earth are venial and immune from
punishment on earth. See p. 24 above.
263–7 Needs . . . hand According to legend,
while King Richard was imprisoned by the Duke of
Austria, a hungry lion was placed in his cell, and
when the lion roared Richard thrust his hand down
its throat and ripped out its heart.
264 Subjected Compare the Book of Common
Prayer (1559), sig. 09: 'Let . . . wives . . . be in sub-
jection unto their own husbands in all things.'
268–70 See supplementary note.
270–2 With . . . hell The Bastard imitates his
new-found father. Like a king he will command
everyone's assent that her dear offence was pri-
vileged, and, as the instrument of a king's will, she
should not have to answer to others for it.
276 says it was i.e. says it was a sin to say
'yea'.
276 'twas not A final, playful flourish, if an actor

can suggest a pun on 'naught' (i.e. wicked,
naughty). Compare Middleton and Rowley, *A Fair
Quarrel* (1617), 5.1, sig. 11: 'I say she's naught
. . . Your intended bride is a whore.'

Act 2, Scene 1
0 SD.1 before Angiers In contemporary theatres
the upper stage represented the top of the city
walls, and the tent of the King of France stood to
one side. See illustration 1, p. 2 above.
0 SD.2 DAUPHIN 'Dolphin' or 'Daulphin',
typical spellings found in F, suggest how the title
was pronounced.
0 SD.3 AUSTRIA Wearing the lion skin which
figures in 141–5 and 291–4. See also 3.2.0 SD and
supplementary note.
1 *KING PHILIP For variations in speech
headings here, and at 18 and 149, see Textual
Analysis, p. 184 below.

Arthur, that great forerunner of thy blood,
Richard, that robbed the lion of his heart
And fought the holy wars in Palestine,
By this brave duke came early to his grave,   5
And for amends to his posterity,
At our importance hither is he come
To spread his colours, boy, in thy behalf,
And to rebuke the usurpation
Of thy unnatural uncle, English John.   10
Embrace him, love him, give him welcome hither.
ARTHUR God shall forgive you Cœur-de-lion's death
The rather that you give his offspring life,
Shadowing their right under your wings of war.
I give you welcome with a powerless hand   15
But with a heart full of unstainèd love.
Welcome before the gates of Angiers, duke.
KING PHILIP A noble boy! Who would not do thee right?
AUSTRIA Upon thy cheek lay I this zealous kiss
As seal to this indenture of my love: 20
That to my home I will no more return
Till Angiers and the right thou hast in France,
Together with that pale, that white-faced shore,
Whose foot spurns back the ocean's roaring tides
And coops from other lands her islanders,   25
Even till that England, hedged in with the main –

---

18 A] F; Ah, *Honigmann, conj. Fleay*

2 forerunner . . . blood i.e. his predecessor but not necessarily his direct ancestor.

5 By this brave duke Austria. Historical accounts said that Richard died of wounds after the siege of Limoges, but the popular romance of *Cuer du Lyon* (sig. Q5) conflated the Viscount Limoges and the Archduke of Austria, who earlier had imprisoned Richard. (See 1.1.263–7 n.)

7 importance importunity.

8 colours flags.

10 unnatural unloving. Natural love was between blood relations. See *FQ* IV, 9, 1–2: 'dear affection unto kindred sweet . . . natural affection'.

13 offspring On stage this word, like 'forerunner' and 'posterity' above, would suggest that Arthur is Cœur-de-lion's direct descendant, instead of his elder brother's son.

14 Shadowing . . . wings Normally a potent image of heavenly protection, but the likes of Austria are all that helpless Arthur can appeal to. Compare Ps. 63.7: 'Because thou hast been mine helper, therefore under the shadow of thy wings

will I rejoice.' Donne's *Prebend Sermon*, No. 2 (ed. J. Mueller, 1971), explores the manifold meanings of the image for young David and for all Christians in the wilderness.

23 pale . . . shore The chalk cliffs facing France were supposed to have given the island the name of Albion. The quibble on 'pale', a fence or barrier, ties in with 'water-wallèd' (27).

25 coops encloses for protection. The idea of England's isolation from other lands goes back to Virgil's first Eclogue: 'The land of the Britons divided from the rest of the world'.

26–9 England . . . west A patriotic description popular in the days of the Great Armada. Shakespeare expanded this passage in John of Gaunt's speech, *R2* 2.1.40–63. See J. W. Bennett, 'Britain among the Fortunate Isles', *SP* 53 (1956), 114–40.

26–7 hedged . . . secure Compare with Greene's *Spanish Masquerado* (1589), sig. B4: 'seeing how secure we slept . . . for that we were hedged in with the sea . . . |God| brought these Spaniards to waken us out of our dreams'.

That water-wallèd bulwark, still secure
And confident from foreign purposes –
Even till that utmost corner of the west
Salute thee for her king. Till then, fair boy,   30
Will I not think of home but follow arms.

CONSTANCE O take his mother's thanks, a widow's thanks,
Till your strong hand shall help to give him strength
To make a more requital to your love.

AUSTRIA The peace of heaven is theirs that lift their swords   35
In such a just and charitable war.

KING PHILIP Well then, to work; our cannon shall be bent
Against the brows of this resisting town.
Call for our chiefest men of discipline
To cull the plots of best advantages.   40
We'll lay before this town our royal bones,
Wade to the market-place in Frenchmen's blood,
But we will make it subject to this boy.

CONSTANCE Stay for an answer to your embassy,
Lest unadvised you stain your swords with blood;   45
My Lord Chatillon may from England bring
That right in peace which here we urge in war,
And then we shall repent each drop of blood
That hot rash haste so indirectly shed.

---

37 Well then, to work;] *Theobald;* Well, then to worke F

27 **still** always.

32 a widow's thanks The first mention of one of Constance's favourite themes, the obligation to protect widows and orphans. (See 171–2 n. below, 3.1.108–11, and Jones, *Origins*, pp. 240–2.)

34 more greater. Compare Num. 26.54: 'To many thou shalt give the more inheritance, and to few thou shalt give less.'

37 bent aimed. The metaphor is taken from archery but often applied to other weapons. See *3H6* 5.1.87.

38 brows The gates are the eyes of the city, the battlements the brows or forehead.

39 discipline military training or experience.

40 cull . . . advantages choose the best positions for attack.

43 But Even though those things happen. See *OED* sv conj. 11. Compare Henry of Navarre's decision to besiege Rouen: 'The King is resolved to die but to take it' (Sir Roger Williams, *Works*, ed.

John X. Evans, 1972, p. xlvii; in a letter to Queen Elizabeth, 4 June 1591).

43 subject to this boy Historically as son of Geoffrey, Duke of Brittany, Arthur was heir to his French lands and owed homage for some of them to the French king and some to the English king. Therefore it was appropriate for King Philip to try to enforce Arthur's right to Angiers, but Shakespeare expands Arthur's claims to include the kingdom of England and all its territories. See 1.1.7–15, 2.1.151–3, and Appendix, pp. 200–3 below.

44–9 Stay . . . shed Constance's only quiet speech in the play. Her call for patience in the negotiation without unnecessary fighting makes sense here, but soon she and her cause will be destroyed by negotiation, and she will cry for war.

45 unadvised without due consideration.

49 indirectly lawlessly, pointlessly, See *OED* Indirect *a* 2a and compare *R3* 1.4.218: 'He needs no indirect or lawless course.'

Enter CHATILLON

KING PHILIP A wonder, lady! Lo, upon thy wish   50
Our messenger Chatillon is arrived.
What England says, say briefly, gentle lord;
We coldly pause for thee. Chatillon, speak.
CHATILLON Then turn your forces from this paltry siege
And stir them up against a mightier task: 55
England, impatient of your just demands,
Hath put himself in arms. The adverse winds,
Whose leisure I have stayed, have given him time
To land his legions all as soon as I.
His marches are expedient to this town,   60
His forces strong, his soldiers confident.
With him along is come the mother-queen,
An Ate stirring him to blood and strife;
With her her niece, the Lady Blanche of Spain;
With them a bastard of the king's deceased;   65
And all th'unsettled humours of the land –
Rash, inconsiderate, fiery voluntaries,
With ladies' faces and fierce dragons' spleens –
Have sold their fortunes at their native homes,
Bearing their birthrights proudly on their backs,   70

---

62 mother-queen] F4; *no hyphen in* F   63 Ate] *Rowe;* Ace F

50 **upon thy wish** in answer to your wish.
53 **coldly** calmly, dispassionately. The word comes as a surprise after France seemed so hot and eager, as if he watches himself turn his feelings on and off (Smallwood). Compare *Ado* 3.2.129–30: 'Bear it coldly but till midnight, and let the issue show itself.'
56 **impatient of** unable to endure; angry at.
58 **Whose . . . stayed** As if the busy winds were a great man whom 'I simply had to wait upon until he was unoccupied': a pretty phrase for a diplomat.
60 **expedient** speedy. In the first three acts, Shakespeare carefully emphasises John's speed and impulsiveness, as announced at 1.1.24–6, and confirmed again at 79, 223, and 3.4.11.
63 ***Ate** Goddess of discord and strife. See *Ado* 2.1.256, *LLL* 5.2.688, and compare *JC* 3.1.271: 'With Ate by his side come hot from hell'.
64 **her niece** In the old general sense of a remote female relative. In our terms she is Eleanor's granddaughter and John's niece.
65 **of the king's deceased** of the dead king (a double genitive).
66 **unsettled humours** Used as a metonymy for persons of unruly, discontented temperament.

67 **inconsiderate** reckless, not considering themselves.
67–75 **voluntaries . . . Christendom** This could refer to any of a number of expeditions of ambitious young volunteers from England: Elizabethan gentlemen who, finding no employment at home, took to foreign religious wars, under Thomas Morgan, Sir Humphrey Gilbert, Sir John Norris, Lord Willoughby, Leicester, and Sir Roger Williams. They departed in great numbers to the wars in the Low Countries (1572–86) and to France (1589–91).
68 **ladies' faces** i.e. young and beardless.
68 **spleens** hot tempers. The spleen was the seat of passions, according to the old psychology. Compare *R3* 5.3.350: 'Inspire us with the spleen of fiery dragons!'
69–71 **sold . . . new fortunes** Like the Bastard, their leader, who forsook his legal right at home for a foot of honour and war abroad.
70 As the saying goes, 'All his wardrobe (wealth) is on his back' (Tilley and Wilson w61); also 'a whole lordship on his back' (1.452).

To make a hazard of new fortunes here.
In brief, a braver choice of dauntless spirits
Than now the English bottoms have waft o'er
Did never float upon the swelling tide
To do offence and scathe in Christendom.   75
                    Drum beats
The interruption of their churlish drums
Cuts off more circumstance: they are at hand,
To parley or to fight, therefore prepare.

KING PHILIP How much unlooked for is this expedition.

AUSTRIA By how much unexpected, by so much   80
We must awake endeavour for defence,
For courage mounteth with occasion.
Let them be welcome then; we are prepared.

Enter [JOHN,] *King of England*, BASTARD, QUEEN ELEANOR, BLANCHE,
        PEMBROKE, [SALISBURY, *soldiers*] *and others*

KING JOHN Peace be to France, if France in peace permit
Our just and lineal entrance to our own.   85
If not, bleed France, and peace ascend to heaven,
Whiles we, God's wrathful agent, do correct
Their proud contempt that beats his peace to heaven.

KING PHILIP Peace be to England, if that war return
From France to England, there to live in peace.   90
England we love, and for that England's sake
With burden of our armour here we sweat.
This toil of ours should be a work of thine;
But thou from loving England art so far
That thou hast underwrought his lawful king,   95

---

75 SD *Drum beats*] *Pope; after 77* F   77–8 hand, To . . . fight,] F; hand. To . . . fight, *Pope;* hand, To . . . fight; *Capell*
89 SD KING PHILIP] *Fran.* F *(throughout rest of scene)*

73 **bottoms** ships.

73 **waft** wafted.

75 **scathe** harm.

76 **churlish** intentionally harsh, brutal. See *OED* sv 2.

77 **circumstance** detail.

77–8 ***hand . . . fight,** The squinting construction, as punctuated in F, makes sense on stage, although editors often insert a semicolon before or after the infitives.

79 **expedition** speed; military force.

83 SD Although Pembroke and Salisbury are mutes in this scene, Salisbury should be here so that he can carry John's message to Constance after 555.

85 **lineal** due by hereditary right. See 5.7.102 n.

85 **entrance** (1) taking legal possession of property, a formal assertion of ownership (see *OED* Enter *v* 2), (2) accession, as to a throne (*OED* Entrance *sb* 2).

87 **correct** punish.

88 **beats . . . to heaven** drives peace out of the world.

91 **England's** i.e. Arthur's.

93 **This toil** The task of securing Arthur's right.

95 **underwrought his** undermined its.

Cut off the sequence of posterity,
Outfacèd infant state, and done a rape
Upon the maiden virtue of the crown.
Look here upon thy brother Geoffrey's face.
These eyes, these brows, were moulded out of his;   100
This little abstract doth contain that large
Which died in Geoffrey, and the hand of time
Shall draw this brief into as huge a volume.
That Geoffrey was thy elder brother born,
And this his son, England was Geoffrey's right,   105
And this is Geoffrey's. In the name of God
How comes it then that thou art called a king,
When living blood doth in these temples beat
Which owe the crown that thou o'ermasterest?
KING JOHN From whom hast thou this great commission, France,   110
      To draw my answer from thy articles?
KING PHILIP From that supernal judge that stirs good thoughts
      In any breast of strong authority
      To look into the blots and stains of right.
      That judge hath made me guardian to this boy,   115
      Under whose warrant I impeach thy wrong,
      And by whose help I mean to chastise it.
KING JOHN Alack, thou dost usurp authority.
KING PHILIP Excuse it is to beat usurping down.
ELEANOR Who is it thou dost call usurper, France?   120

---

106 Geoffrey's. In] *Collier; Geffreyes* in F; Geffrey's in *Rowe*   106 God] *Pope;* God: F; God, *Rowe*   113 breast]
F2; beast F   119 Excuse] F; Excuse; *Malone*   120 SH ELEANOR] *Queen* F *(throughout, except / Qu. Mo / at 166
and / Old Qu / at 468)*

96 **posterity** lineal descent.

97 **Outfacèd infant state** Defied or intimidated
the authority that belongs to a child.

99 **Geoffrey's face** Once more our attention is
called to a face as evidence of true lineage. See
1.1.85 ff.

101–3 **abstract . . . volume** A legal conceit runs
through the passage, in answer to John's request for
legal entrance to his property (85). Compare
Edward III 2.1.82–3: 'Whose body is an abstract of
a brief, / Contains each general virtue in the
world'.

104 **That** Because. See *OED* That *conj.* 2.

106 **this** An actor may resolve the ambiguity by
pointing either to Angiers, to John's crown, or to
Arthur. John began his challenge with a request to
enter 'our own' city, so it is natural that Philip
should end his denial of John's legitimacy with a
gesture toward the city for possession of which they
are prepared to fight.

109 **owe** own.

109 **o'ermasterest** hold in your power.

111 **articles** list of offences in an indictment.

115 **guardian** 'Constance . . . doubting the surety
of her son, committed him to the trust of the
French king, who . . . promised to defend him'
(Holinshed, II, 274).

117 **chastise** Accent on the first syllable.

119 My usurpation is sufficiently excused by my
fighting against usurpation.

120–94 Verbal battles like these between Eleanor
and Constance, Austria and the Bastard con-
ventionally symbolised the physical action that had
to take place mostly off-stage. The prototype was
the scolding match of the two queens in *1 Tamburlaine* 3.3, while Tamburlaine and Bajazeth
fight.

CONSTANCE Let me make answer: thy usurping son.

ELEANOR Out, insolent! Thy bastard shall be king
  That thou mayst be a queen and check the world!

CONSTANCE My bed was ever to thy son as true
  As thine was to thy husband, and this boy   125
  Liker in feature to his father Geoffrey
  Than thou and John in manners, being as like
  As rain to water or devil to his dam.
  My boy a bastard! By my soul, I think
  His father never was so true begot.   130
  It cannot be, and if thou wert his mother.

ELEANOR There's a good mother, boy, that blots thy father.

CONSTANCE There's a good grandam, boy, that would blot thee.

AUSTRIA Peace!

BASTARD   Hear the crier!

AUSTRIA   What the devil art thou?

BASTARD One that will play the devil, sir, with you,   135
  And a may catch your hide and you alone.
  You are the hare of whom the proverb goes,
  Whose valour plucks dead lions by the beard;
  I'll smoke your skin-coat and I catch you right.
  Sirrah, look to't! I'faith I will, i'faith.   140

BLANCHE O, well did he become that lion's robe
  That did disrobe the lion of that robe.

---

127 John in manners,] *Neilson, conj. Vaughan;* Iohn, in manners F; John in manners; *Capell, conj. Roderick*
133 grandam] grandame F

122–33 These accusations of infidelity and bastardy damn the accuser as much as the accused, for if Geoffrey was not 'true begot' in Eleanor's marriage to Henry II, Arthur's lineal right suffers as much as Eleanor's reputation.

123 queen . . . check A metaphor from chess (with a play on 'quean' = whore). The queen of the chess-board became the most powerful piece in the game early in the sixteenth century. See Damiano de Ode, *The Pleasant and Wittie Play of the Cheastes*, tr. Rowbottom (1569).

127 manners moral character.

128 devil . . . dam The exact meaning of 'devil and his dam' (traced by Whiting (D181) back to 1350) remains uncertain, but Shakespeare's use suggests a witch who copulates with a devil and gives birth to a monster. See *Tit.* 4.2.64–5; *1H6* 1.5.5–7; *Shr.* 3.2.156; *Temp.* 1.2.319.

132 blots slanders.

134 Hear the crier In the courts of justice criers called for silence.

135 play the devil make mischief. The Vice figure in Morality plays was a witty trouble-maker, and, like the devil, the Bastard will catch the best thing about Austria, King Richard's lion skin.

136 And a If he.

136 hide A lion's hide must have been a property of the Chamberlain's Men; in any case *MND* 5.1.139 also requires it.

137–8 hare . . . beard The hare was a type of cowardice because he ran from his enemy, and to pluck a person's beard was an insult (Tilley H165).

139 smoke your skin-coat give you a drubbing. Compare Cotgrave *contrepoincte*: 'My skin-coat hath received as many knocks as a quilt hath stitches.' In northern dialect, 'to smoke' was to beat.

BASTARD It lies as sightly on the back of him
　　　　　As great Alcides' shoes upon an ass.
　　　　　But ass, I'll take that burden from your back　　　　　145
　　　　　Or lay on that shall make your shoulders crack.
AUSTRIA What cracker is this same that deafs our ears
　　　　　With this abundance of superfluous breath?
　　　　　King Philip, determine what we shall do straight.
KING PHILIP Women and fools, break off your conference.　　150
　　　　　King John, this is the very sum of all:
　　　　　England and Ireland, Anjou, Touraine, Maine,
　　　　　In right of Arthur do I claim of thee.
　　　　　Wilt thou resign them and lay down thy arms?
KING JOHN My life as soon. I do defy thee, France.　　　　　155
　　　　　Arthur of Brittaine, yield thee to my hand,
　　　　　And out of my dear love I'll give thee more
　　　　　Than e'er the coward hand of France can win.
　　　　　Submit thee, boy.
ELEANOR　　　　　　　　　Come to thy grandam, child.
CONSTANCE Do, child, go to it grandam, child.　　　　　　160
　　　　　Give grandam kingdom, and it grandam will
　　　　　Give it a plum, a cherry, and a fig.
　　　　　There's a good grandam.
ARTHUR　　　　　　　　　　　　　Good my mother, peace.
　　　　　I would that I were low laid in my grave.
　　　　　I am not worth this coil that's made for me.　　　　　165
ELEANOR His mother shames him so, poor boy, he weeps.

---

144 Alcides' shoes] *Rowe; Alcides shooes* F; *Alcides' shews Theobald; Alcides' shows Wright*　149 King Philip]
Theobald; King *Lewis* F; K.Phi. Lewis *Capell*　150 SH KING PHILIP] *Theobald; Lew.* F　152 Anjou] *Theobald;*
Angiers F

143 **sightly** handsomely, pleasing to the sight.
144 ***great Alcides' shoes** There is a play on
'shows' and 'shoes', pronounced and often spelled
the same ('shews'). See supplementary note.
147 **cracker** boaster. Compare Udall's *Roister
Doister* (1553) 1.1.35–6: 'All the day long is he
facing and cracking / Of his great acts in fighting.'
Austria puns on the Bastard's last word.
149 ***King Philip** See Honigmann, pp. xxxiv–
xxxvi, for a defence of Capell's emendation.
149 **straight** immediately.
150 **Women and fools** Who are ever quarrel-
ling.
152 ***Anjou** F's '*Angiers*' is probably a tran-

scriptional error because Shakespeare gets it right
in the identical list at 1.1.11. Angiers was capital of
Anjou, the principal territory of the Angevin
empire.
156 **Brittaine** Brittany.
158 **coward hand** In contrast to Cœur-de-lion's
hand that thrust deep in the lion's mouth to pluck
out its 'princely heart'. See 1.1.263–7 n.
160 **it** its; baby talk, used contemptuously.
162 **Give . . . a fig** Possibly suggesting more than
a bit of fruit, in the saying 'to give someone a fig'
(*ODEP* 255b, Tilley F213), a gesture of contempt.
165 **coil** turmoil.

CONSTANCE Now shame upon you, whe'er she does or no!
His grandam's wrongs, and not his mother's shames,
Draws those heaven-moving pearls from his poor eyes,
Which heaven shall take in nature of a fee.   170
Ay, with these crystal beads heaven shall be bribed
To do him justice and revenge on you.
ELEANOR Thou monstrous slanderer of heaven and earth!
CONSTANCE Thou monstrous injurer of heaven and earth,
Call not me slanderer! Thou and thine usurp   175
The dominations, royalties, and rights
Of this oppressèd boy. This is thy eldest son's son,
Infortunate in nothing but in thee.
Thy sins are visited in this poor child,
The canon of the law is laid on him,   180
Being but the second generation
Removèd from thy sin-conceiving womb.
KING JOHN Bedlam, have done.
CONSTANCE   I have but this to say,
That he is not only plaguèd for her sin,
But God hath made her sin and her the plague   185
On this removèd issue, plagued for her
And with her plague; her sin his injury,
Her injury, the beadle to her sin,
All punished in the person of this child,
And all for her. A plague upon her!   190
ELEANOR Thou unadvisèd scold, I can produce
A will that bars the title of thy son.

187 plague; her sin | *Cam.*; plague her sinne: F

167 **shame** Constance, whose defence is so often defiance, habitually picks up a word and turns it on her opponent with 'acrid *tu quoque* invective' as she does with 'blot' (133), 'grandam' (160), 'slanderer' (175), and 'will' (193). See J. C. Bucknill, *The Mad Folk of Shakespeare*, 1867, p. 270.
170 **in nature . . . fee** as a kind of fee.
171 **beads** Suggesting prayers and the rosary.
171–2 **heaven . . . revenge on you** The biblical injunction is found in Exod. 22.22–4: 'Ye shall not trouble any widow nor fatherless child. If you vex or trouble such, and so he cry unto me, I will surely hear his cry. Then shall my wrath be kindled, and I will kill you with my sword.' See 'oppressèd' (177) and 'plaguèd' (184) and at 32 above, 'a widow's thanks'.

176 **dominations** dominions.
176 **royalties** prerogatives.
177 **eldest son's son** eldest grandson (not 'the son of your eldest son').
179 **visited** punished.
180 **canon of the law** i.e. that the iniquities of the fathers shall be visited upon the children unto the third and fourth generations of them that hate God (Exod. 20.5).
183 **Bedlam** Lunatic.
184–90 See supplementary note.
186 **removèd issue** distant descendant.
191 **unadvisèd** rash.
192–4 **will . . . grandam's will** See 1.1.9 and 1.1.109 nn.

CONSTANCE Ay, who doubts that? a will, a wicked will,
    A woman's will, a cankered grandam's will.
KING PHILIP Peace, lady; pause or be more temperate,   195
    It ill beseems this presence to cry aim
    To these ill-tunèd repetitions.
    Some trumpet summon hither to the walls
    These men of Angiers. Let us hear them speak
    Whose title they admit, Arthur's or John's.   200

Trumpet sounds

Enter a CITIZEN *[and others] upon the walls*

CITIZEN Who is it that hath warned us to the walls?
KING PHILIP 'Tis France, for England.
KING JOHN   England for itself.
    You men of Angiers, and my loving subjects –
KING PHILIP You loving men of Angiers, Arthur's subjects,
    Our trumpet called you to this gentle parle –   205
KING JOHN For our advantage; therefore hear us first.
    These flags of France, that are advancèd here
    Before the eye and prospect of your town,
    Have hither marched to your endamagement.
    The cannons have their bowels full of wrath,   210
    And ready mounted are they to spit forth
    Their iron indignation 'gainst your walls.
    All preparation for a bloody siege
    And merciless proceeding by these French

---

200 SD.2 *a* CITIZEN] F; *Hubert / Honigmann, conj. Wilson* 201 SH CITIZEN] (*Cit. / here and through scene to 281*); *Hubert / Honigmann (throughout scene), conj. Wilson* 206 our] F; *your conj. Tyrwhitt* 206 advantage;] *Rowe;* advantage, F 214 French] *Dyce;* French. F; *French, Rowe*

194 **woman's will** i.e. forced or dictated by Eleanor, because 'Women will have their wills' (Tilley w723).

195 **pause** See supplementary note.

196 **this presence** A kingly way of saying 'me'.

196 **cry aim** encourage, abet; a term of archery. Thus bystanders cry 'aim' to urge on violent brawlers.

197 **ill-tunèd repetitions** One of several passages that call attention to the play's repetitious style.

200 SD. 2 CITIZEN See 325 n.

201 **warned** summoned.

202 **England for itself** The king, who is one with his realm, needs no other spokesman. See

2.1.366–7 (supplementary note), 4.2.243–6, 4.3.142–5 for the unity of the king in his natural body and the king as coextensive with the body politic.

205 **parle** One syllable.

206 **our advantage** my timely opportunity. See *OED* Advantage *sb* 4. Tyrwhitt suggested 'your advantage', which would refer to the opportunity of the citizens but would not explain why John ought to speak first.

207 **advancèd** raised.

210 **bowels** Here associated with danger and interior horrors, as in *1H6* 1.1.129: 'rush'd into the bowels of the battle'; and *R3* 3.4.100–1: 'tumble down / Into the fatal bowels of the deep'.

Confronts your city's eyes, your winking gates;   215
And but for our approach, those sleeping stones,
That as a waist doth girdle you about,
By the compulsion of their ordinance
By this time from their fixèd beds of lime
Had been dishabited, and wide havoc made   220
For bloody power to rush upon your peace.
But on the sight of us your lawful king,
Who painfully with much expedient march
Have brought a countercheck before your gates,
To save unscratched your city's threatened cheeks,   225
Behold, the French amazed vouchsafe a parle,
And now, instead of bullets wrapped in fire
To make a shaking fever in your walls,
They shoot but calm words folded up in smoke,
To make a faithless error in your ears,   230
Which trust accordingly, kind citizens,
And let us in, your king, whose laboured spirits,
Forewearied in this action of swift speed,
Craves harbourage within your city walls.
KING PHILIP When I have said, make answer to us both.   ·   235

---

215 Confronts your] *Capell;* Comfort yours F*; comfort your* F3*; confront your* Rowe*; Comforts your* Honigmann
232 us in, your] *Capell;* us in. Your F*; in us, your* Pope

215 *Confronts** If we accept F's 'Comfort' as ironic, the word makes some sense, but it goes against the implications of the speech. The French armies stand in front of the closed gates; the city, as if asleep in its bed and unaware of the danger, has been awakened by John's approach, and the city can see that the French would breach its walls, tearing aside the clothing about its waist, and would ravish it. The fanciful conceit of 'eye', 'winking', 'waist', 'beds', and 'dishabited' suggests less irony than elaboration of the merciless proceeding threatened by the French.

215 **winking** closed as in sleep.

217 **waist** belt.

220 **dishabited** (1) removed from their place of abode, dislodged, (2) undressed.

220 **wide havoc** 'wide' at first suggests a gap in a battered wall, but 'havoc' means destruction and spoliation. This use still carried the original meaning of the cry 'havoc' to an army, i.e. let every man pillage and destroy at will.

221 **peace** (1) peaceful repose, (2) a fortified place, a stronghold (see *OED* piece *sb* 10b), (3) a single person, referring to either a man or woman.

Although the connotations of a sexually attractive woman apparently did not adhere to the word until the mid seventeenth century, 'rush upon your peace' is suggestive.

223 **painfully** laboriously.

223 **expedient** speedy.

224 **countercheck** A metaphor from chess; see 2.1.123 n. If so, the play on 'peace' /'piece' at 221 could also suggest a chess-man, presumably the king, whom John has checked. See *OED* Check *sb* 1–2.

226 **amazed** astounded with fear.

227 **bullets** cannon-balls.

227–9 **wrapped in fire . . . in smoke** Compare *The Jew of Malta* 2.2.55–6: 'instead of gold / We send the bullets wrapped in smoke and fire'.

229 **smoke** i.e. breath.

230 **faithless error** lie against your sworn vows.

232 **laboured** hard-worked.

233 **Forewearied in** Exhausted by.

234 **Craves** The subject is 'spirits', not 'king', although the verb is singular.

235 **said** spoken.

Lo, in this right hand, whose protection
Is most divinely vowed upon the right
Of him it holds, stands young Plantagenet,
Son to the elder brother of this man,
And king o'er him and all that he enjoys.   240
For this down-trodden equity we tread
In warlike march these greens before your town,
Being no further enemy to you
Than the constraint of hospitable zeal,
In the relief of this oppressèd child,   245
Religiously provokes. Be pleasèd then
To pay that duty which you truly owe
To him that owes it, namely, this young prince,
And then our arms, like to a muzzled bear,
Save in aspect, hath all offence sealed up.   250
Our cannons' malice vainly shall be spent
Against th'invulnerable clouds of heaven,
And with a blessèd and unvexed retire,
With unhacked swords and helmets all unbruised,
We will bear home that lusty blood again,   255
Which here we came to spout against your town,
And leave your children, wives, and you in peace.
But if you fondly pass our proffered offer,
'Tis not the roundure of your old-faced walls
Can hide you from our messengers of war,   260

---

252 invulnerable] F2; involuerable F   259 roundure] *Capell;* rounder F

236 in . . . hand Compare Gen. 21.18: Hagar is told by God not to despair after she and her son have been cast out of Abraham's house. God tells her to 'take up the child and hold him in thine hand: for I will make of him a great people'.

237 upon to uphold.

241 down-trodden equity oppressed right or natural justice.

248 owes has a right to.

249–50 arms . . . sealed up See supplementary note.

250 Save in aspect The phrase modifies 'all offence sealed up'. Stress on the second syllable of 'aspect'.

253 unvexed retire voluntary withdrawal. See *OED* Vexed *ppl* 3.

255 bear With a play on 'bear' as an animal.

258 fondly pass foolishly disregard.

258 proffered offer The verbosity suggests the

old alliterative drama, as in *Tom Tyler* (1661 edn, sig. C2): 'I never did proffer you such an offer' (Honigmann).

259 *roundure circle, circumference. The emendation of F's 'rounder' rests on the word in Sonnet 21.7–8: 'all things rare / That heaven's air in this huge roundure hems'. It is possible that 'roundure' means simply roundness (as glossed by Cotgrave), because a circular fortress was thought to be harder to assault than one with sharp-angled walls. See Paul Ive, *Practise of Fortification* (1589), p. 7 (Honigmann).

259 old-faced walls Of uncertain meaning, but the general sense is probably that an old wall is harder to break down than a new one (Bernardino de Mendoza, *Theoric and Practice of War* (1597), p. 87). In fortifications the face was that stretch of wall between two bastions (see *OED* Face *sb* 17).

> Though all these English and their discipline
> Were harboured in their rude circumference.
> Then tell us, shall your city call us lord
> In that behalf which we have challenged it?
> Or shall we give the signal to our rage   265
> And stalk in blood to our possession?

CITIZEN In brief, we are the King of England's subjects;
From him and in his right we hold this town.

KING JOHN Acknowledge then the king, and let me in.

CITIZEN That can we not, but he that proves the king,   270
To him will we prove loyal. Till that time
Have we rammed up our gates against the world.

KING JOHN Doth not the crown of England prove the king?
And if not that, I bring you witnesses,
Twice fifteen thousand hearts of England's breed –   275

BASTARD [*Aside*] Bastards and else.

KING JOHN To verify our title with their lives.

KING PHILIP As many and as well-born bloods as those –

BASTARD [*Aside*] Some bastards too.

KING PHILIP Stand in his face to contradict his claim.   280

CITIZEN Till you compound whose right is worthiest,
We for the worthiest hold the right from both.

KING JOHN Then God forgive the sin of all those souls
That to their everlasting residence,
Before the dew of evening fall, shall fleet   285
In dreadful trial of our kingdom's king!

KING PHILIP Amen, amen! Mount, chevaliers! To arms!

BASTARD Saint George that swinged the dragon, and e'er since

---

267 subjects;| *Theobald;* subjects F; subjects, F2   287 chevaliers! To| *Capell;* Cheualiers to F; chevaliers, to *Pope*
288–9 Saint . . . door | *Pope; divided at* Saint . . . dragon, / . . . door F

261 these . . . discipline these English, skilled though they are in war (Smallwood).

263 call us lord pay homage; or does France have a serious political interest in Angiers?

264 which in which.

265 our rage my army's fury, i.e. devastating force and martial spirit. See *OED* Rage *sb* 3. The king does not mean to imply that he can turn on or off his anger.

270 proves shows that he is genuine; with the implication that he must establish it by some test.

276 Bastards and else Bastards and otherwise; Bastards and suchlike. The imperfect lines 276 and

279 suggest that he speaks simultaneously with the kings and addresses the audience (Smallwood).

278 bloods men of spirit and good birth.

280 Stand in his face Remain obstinately opposed (*OED* Stand v^1 72b).

281 compound settle, agree. See *OED* sv v 6.

285 fleet glide away (from their bodies).

288–9 Saint George . . . door From a proverb (Tilley S42): 'Like St George, who is ever on horseback and never rides'. The 'George and Dragon' was a common inn-sign in Elizabethan England. Typically the Bastard mixes the heroic and homely. The bawdy associations of 'St George', of riding, and of 'swinged' (= (1)

Sits on his horseback at mine hostess' door,
Teach us some fence! [*To Austria*] Sirrah, were I at home   290
At your den, sirrah, with your lioness,
I would set an ox-head to your lion's hide,
To make a monster of you.

AUSTRIA   Peace, no more.

BASTARD O tremble, for you hear the lion roar.

KING JOHN Up higher to the plain, where we'll set forth   295
      In best appointment all our regiments.

BASTARD Speed then to take advantage of the field.

KING PHILIP It shall be so, and at the other hill
      Command the rest to stand. God and our right!

                              Exeunt. [*Citizens remain above*]

Here, after excursions, enter the HERALD OF FRANCE *with trumpets to the*
gates

FRENCH HERALD You men of Angiers, open wide your gates   300
      And let young Arthur Duke of Brittaine in,
      Who by the hand of France this day hath made
      Much work for tears in many an English mother,
      Whose sons lie scattered on the bleeding ground;
      Many a widow's husband grovelling lies   305
      Coldly embracing the discoloured earth,
      And victory with little loss doth play
      Upon the dancing banners of the French,
      Who are at hand, triumphantly displayed,
      To enter conquerors and to proclaim   310
      Arthur of Brittaine England's king and yours.

Enter ENGLISH HERALD *with trumpet*

---

289 on his] *Pope;* on's F   290 SD *To Austria*] Rowe³; *not in* F   299 SD *Citizens remain above*] Riverside; *not in* F

thrashed, (2) copulated with) may explain why it is 'hostess' door' rather than 'host's' (see Farmer).

289 *on his F's on's' comes in a full line; therefore it is likely that the compositor elided the two words.

290 fence swordsmanship.

291 lioness harlot.

292–3 ox-head . . . monster i.e. a lion with horns, hence a cuckold and monster.

294 lion roar Identifying himself with his lion-hearted father.

299 SD.1 At about this moment Constance and Arthur retire to the tent of the King of France at

one side of the stage, where they are discovered at the beginning of Act 3. See 2.1.472 and 544.

301 Duke of Brittaine See 2.1.551 n. for Arthur's titles.

304 bleeding ground An affecting transfer of the epithet, creating an association with mother's tears; as if mother earth weeps blood and sons who bleed.

305 grovelling prostrate.

306 embracing Compare Lam. 4.5: 'They that were brought up in scarlet, embrace the dung.'

309 displayed spread out in a column; unfurled, as a banner.

ENGLISH HERALD Rejoice, you men of Angiers, ring your bells;
    King John, your king and England's, doth approach,
    Commander of this hot malicious day.
    Their armours, that marched hence so silver-bright,   315
    Hither return all gilt with Frenchmen's blood,
    There stuck no plume in any English crest
    That is removèd by a staff of France;
    Our colours do return in those same hands
    That did display them when we first marched forth,   320
    And like a jolly troop of huntsmen come
    Our lusty English, all with purpled hands,
    Dyed in the dying slaughter of their foes.
    Open your gates and give the victors way.
CITIZEN Heralds, from off our tow'rs we might behold   325
    From first to last the onset and retire
    Of both your armies, whose equality
    By our best eyes cannot be censurèd.
    Blood hath bought blood, and blows have answered blows;
    Strength matched with strength, and power confronted
      power;   330
    Both are alike, and both alike we like.
    One must prove greatest. While they weigh so even,
    We hold our town for neither, yet for both.

Enter the two kings with their powers, [ELEANOR, BLANCHE, *the* BASTARD; *Lewis the* DAUPHIN, AUSTRIA] *at several doors*

325 SH CITIZEN] *Rowe (Citi.); Hubert F (Hub. / throughout, except 368)*

314 malicious malignant, virulent. The metaphor probably comes from medicine, having to do with an ill humour, hence 'hot'. See *OED* sv *a* 5.
315–16 silver-bright . . . gilt Compare *Mac.* 2.3.112: 'His silver skin lac'd with his golden blood'.
318 staff spear.
319 Our colours Companies of soldiers guarded their colours religiously, for they were much disgraced if their banners were thrown down. Bernardino de Mendoza recommends that a general give ten crowns to the soldier who captures the enemy's colours (*Theoretic and Practice of War* (1597), p. 115).
321–3 troop . . . foes Compare *JC* 3.1.205–6: 'here thy hunters stand, / Sign'd in thy spoil, and

crimson'd in the lethe'. For the jolly sport, compare W. Cavendish, *The Country Captain and the Varietie* (1649), sig. C12ᵛ: 'Those were the days . . . such brave jests, at the death of a stag, and buck, to throw blood up and down, upon folks' faces' (Honigmann).
325 SH *CITIZEN In the Folio this speech heading and the next four of the Citizen's are erroneously assigned to 'Hubert'. See Textual Analysis, pp. 188–92 below.
328 censurèd judged unequal (?); appraised, as by spectators of a drama. Compare *Ham.* 3.2.86–7: 'after [the play] we will both our judgments join / In censure of his seeming'.
329 Blood . . . blood See 1.1.19 n.
333 SD *powers* armies.
333 SD *several* separate.

KING JOHN France, hast thou yet more blood to cast away?
    Say, shall the current of our right roam on,   335
    Whose passage, vexed with thy impediment,
    Shall leave his native channel and o'erswell
    With course disturbed even thy confining shores,
    Unless thou let his silver water keep
    A peaceful progress to the ocean?   340
KING PHILIP England, thou hast not saved one drop of blood
    In this hot trial more than we of France,
    Rather lost more. And by this hand I swear
    That sways the earth this climate overlooks,
    Before we will lay down our just-borne arms,   345
    We'll put thee down, 'gainst whom these arms we bear,
    Or add a royal number to the dead,
    Gracing the scroll that tells of this war's loss
    With slaughter coupled to the name of kings.
BASTARD Ha, majesty! how high thy glory tow'rs,   350
    When the rich blood of king is set on fire!
    O now doth Death line his dead chaps with steel,
    The swords of soldiers are his teeth, his fangs,
    And now he feasts, mousing the flesh of men
    In undetermined differences of kings.   355
    Why stand those royal fronts amazèd thus?
    Cry 'havoc', kings! Back to the stainèd field,
    You equal potents, fiery-kindled spirits.
    Then let confusion of one part confirm

---

335 roam] F (rome), *Malone;* runne F2

335 *roam on make its way. Compare *1H6*
3.1.51: 'Rome shall remedy this . . . Roam thither
then.' See supplementary note.
338 thy confining shores This assertion
threatens King Philip's own lands within France or
his right of fealty from Angiers, because 'shores'
may refer to the country bounded by a shore.
340 ocean Three syllables.
343–9 swear . . . kings France repeats the oath he
swore at 41–3 above, but now he swears by his own
hand, not the hand of Arthur, who is off-stage.
Philip reveals his real intentions by thus failing to
distinguish what he publicly claims for Arthur and
what he regards as his own (Smallwood).
344 climate part of the sky. See Cotgave, sv
Climat.
350 glory The Bastard approves of glorious,
defiant speeches, and he delivers a number of them;
therefore, he probably does not mean to mock King

Philip's declaration. He wants the kings to translate
their words into action, hence the images associated
with the mouth and applied to acts of violence.
350 tow'rs soars; a term from hawking, describing the bird's spiral rise before it dives on its
prey.
352–4 Death . . . feasts From the proverb (Dent
D138.1) 'Death devours all things.' Cotgrave sv
Feste: 'War is the dead man's holiday.'
352 chaps jaws.
354 mousing biting and tearing, as wild animals
eat their prey.
356 fronts foreheads or faces.
357 havoc Compare *JC* 3.1.272–3: 'with a
monarch's voice / Cry "Havoc!" and let slip the
dogs of war'. See 2.1.220.
358 potents powers.
359 confusion destruction, ruin.

The other's peace. Till then, blows, blood, and death! 360
KING JOHN Whose party do the townsmen yet admit?
KING PHILIP Speak, citizens, for England; who's your king?
CITIZEN The King of England, when we know the king.
KING PHILIP Know him in us that here hold up his right.
KING JOHN In us, that are our own great deputy 365
    And bear possession of our person here,
    Lord of our presence, Angiers, and of you.
CITIZEN A greater pow'r than we denies all this,
    And till it be undoubted, we do lock
    Our former scruple in our strong-barred gates, 370
    Kinged of our fears, until our fears resolved
    Be by some certain king, purged and deposed.
BASTARD By heaven, these scroyles of Angiers flout you, kings,
    And stand securely on their battlements
    As in a theatre, whence they gape and point 375
    At your industrious scenes and acts of death.
    Your royal presences be ruled by me:
    Do like the mutines of Jerusalem,
    Be friends awhile, and both conjointly bend
    Your sharpest deeds of malice on this town. 380
    By east and west let France and England mount
    Their battering cannon chargèd to the mouths,
    Till their soul-fearing clamours have brawled down

---

362 who's] F2; whose F 368 SH CITIZEN] *Rowe (Citi.)*; *Fra.* F; *Hubert / Honigmann* 371 Kinged of our fears] *Malone, conj. Tyrwhitt;* Kings of our feare F; Kings are our fears *Warburton;* King'd of our fear *Collier*

364 hold up his right Some editors think he raises Arthur's hand here, but Arthur is not meant to be in sight. See 543, 'Where is she and her son?'

365 great deputy The pre-eminent deputy, second only to God; in effect, 'I need no spokesman.' Compare *LLL* 1.1.219–20, the high words of Armado to the King of Navarre: 'Great deputy, the welkin's vicegerent, and sole denominator of Navarre'.

366–7 bear . . . you having exclusive control over myself, and (unlike Arthur) capable of managing my own affairs, domains, and subjects. See supplementary note.

368 greater pow'r The citizens' fears which rule them more powerfully; but at first impression the audience must think of almighty God.

371 *Kinged . . . fears Ruled by our fears. See supplementary note.

372 deposed Carrying on the 'kinged' metaphor.

373 scroyles scurvy fellows.

375 As in a theatre A self-conscious reference to the playhouse and spectators, some of whom probably sat above and somewhat to the side, near where the citizens stood on the upper stage.

376 scenes and acts acting, performance, the place of action; also the segments of a play.

377 presences persons.

378 mutines of Jerusalem During the civil war in Jerusalem Titus besieged the city (AD 70), and the opposing factions temporarily united to resist the Romans, but the city fell anyway.

379 bend aim, direct.

382 battering cannon Heavy artillery that fired anything between forty- and sixty-pound shot (Bernardino de Mendoza, *Theoric and Practice of War* (1597), p. 92).

383 fearing frightening.

383 brawled driven or forced down with clamorous brawling.

The flinty ribs of this contemptuous city.
I'd play incessantly upon these jades,   385
Even till unfencèd desolation
Leave them as naked as the vulgar air.
That done, dissever your united strengths
And part your mingled colours once again,
Turn face to face and bloody point to point;   390
Then in a moment Fortune shall cull forth
Out of one side her happy minion,
To whom in favour she shall give the day,
And kiss him with a glorious victory.
How like you this wild counsel, mighty states?   395
Smacks it not something of the policy?
KING JOHN Now by the sky that hangs above our heads,
I like it well. France, shall we knit our pow'rs,
And lay this Angiers even with the ground,
Then after fight who shall be king of it?   400
BASTARD And if thou hast the mettle of a king,
Being wronged as we are by this peevish town,
Turn thou the mouth of thy artillery,
As we will ours, against these saucy walls,
And when that we have dashed them to the ground,   405
Why then defy each other and pell-mell
Make work upon ourselves, for heaven or hell.
KING PHILIP Let it be so. Say, where will you assault?
KING JOHN We from the west will send destruction
Into this city's bosom.   410
AUSTRIA I from the north.
KING PHILIP   Our thunder from the south
Shall rain their drift of bullets on this town.

---

385 play i.e. fire the guns; a glance at acting.

386 unfencèd unwalled, unprotected.

387 naked defenceless; houseless and wretched, as in *Lear* 3.4.28.

387 vulgar common; the citizens, who now place themselves above kings by virtue of their walls, will be reduced to ordinary status, like the plain, free air.

391 cull forth choose, with a possible quibble on 'cull' or 'coll' = to hug, by attraction to 'minion' and 'kiss'.

392 happy minion lucky favourite, darling.

395 states monarchs.

396 the policy the right thing to do; statecraft or cunning, which the Bastard enjoys it being new to him.

401 mettle spirit, courage; stuff or substance (see *OED* Metal *sb* 1f).

402 peevish headstrong; spiteful, harmful, as in the *Grafton Chronicle* (1568), 2.176: 'In derision of the king they made certain peevish and mocking rhymes.'

403 mouth See 414, 449, and 457 for the recurring image.

406 pell-mell headlong, hand to hand.

407 Make work Cause trouble, i.e. inflict pain.

407 for on behalf of.

412 their The plural suggests that the intended antecedent is 'our cannon', to which 'Our thunder' refers (411).

412 drift shower, driven along by wind.

BASTARD [*Aside*] O prudent discipline! From north to south,
         Austria and France shoot in each other's mouth.
         I'll stir them to it. – Come, away, away!   415
CITIZEN Hear us, great king. Vouchsafe awhile to stay,
         And I shall show you peace and fair-faced league.
         Win you this city without stroke or wound;
         Rescue those breathing lives to die in beds
         That here come sacrifices for the field.   420
         Persever not, but hear me, mighty kings.
KING JOHN Speak on with favour, we are bent to hear.
CITIZEN That daughter there of Spain, the Lady Blanche,
         Is niece to England. Look upon the years
         Of Lewis the Dauphin and that lovely maid.   425
         If lusty love should go in quest of beauty,
         Where should he find it fairer than in Blanche?
         If zealous love should go in search of virtue,
         Where should he find it purer than in Blanche?
         If love ambitious sought a match of birth,   430
         Whose veins bound richer blood than Lady Blanche?
         Such as she is, in beauty, virtue, birth,
         Is the young Dauphin every way complete.
         If not complete of, say he is not she,
         And she again wants nothing, to name want,   435
         If want it be not that she is not he.
         He is the half part of a blessèd man,

---

424 niece] *Collier²*; neere F   425 Dauphin] Dolphin F *(Dol., Dolph.*, Dolphine, Daulphin *throughout)*   434 complete of] F; completed *Sisson*   434 of,] F; oh! *Hanmer*; all, *conj. Wilson*

413 **O prudent discipline!** The Bastard proposed similar tactics, however, at 381.
421 **Persever** Accent on the second syllable.
422 **favour** permission.
422 **bent** inclined.
424 ***niece** Because the equivalent passage in *TR* (2.333) is 'Neece to K. *John*' and F spells the word 'neece' at 64, 469, and 521, the Folio's 'neere to England' is probably a misreading.
425 **Lewis** The second syllable barely pronounced.
426–41 The series of *if*-clauses followed by main clauses and climaxed by an *Oh* is a familiar pattern in Elizabethan love poems, as in Sidney's *Astrophil and Stella* (*Poems*, ed. W. A. Ringler, 1962), third song. See *FQ* III, 3, 1 on the three qualities of true love.
428 **zealous** fervent, religious; hence 'loving virtue or the soul'. Compare Sonnet 27: 'For then

my thoughts . . . / Intend a zealous pilgrimage to thee.'
430 **love ambitious** aspiring love; emulation.
430 **a match of birth** i.e. a dynastic union.
431 **bound** contain. See 442.
432–6 **Such . . . he** Both are perfect in themselves, but they will be more perfect together, like the lovers who have all of their love but can have more from each other. See Donne, 'Lovers' Infiniteness'.
434 **complete of** perfect thereof or therein. For the adverbial use of 'of' compare Marston, *Antonio and Mellida* (1602), ed. Hunter, 5.2.256–7: 'he that hath the best parts of – I'll prick him down for my husband'.
435 **wants** lacks.
436 **If . . . not** Unless it be want.
437–40 **He . . . him** That men and women are only half-complete until they unite is traceable at least to Aristophanes' myth in Plato's *Symposium*.

Left to be finishèd by such as she,
And she a fair divided excellence,
Whose fullness of perfection lies in him.   440
O, two such silver currents when they join
Do glorify the banks that bound them in;
And two such shores to two such streams made one,
Two such controlling bounds shall you be, kings,
To these two princes if you marry them.   445
This union shall do more than battery can
To our fast-closèd gates; for at this match,
With swifter spleen than powder can enforce,
The mouth of passage shall we fling wide ope
And give you entrance. But without this match,   450
The sea enragèd is not half so deaf,
Lions more confident, mountains and rocks
More free from motion – no, not Death himself
In mortal fury half so peremptory
As we to keep this city.

BASTARD   Here's a stay   455
That shakes the rotten carcass of old Death
Out of his rags. Here's a large mouth indeed,
That spits forth death and mountains, rocks and seas,
Talks as familiarly of roaring lions
As maids of thirteen do of puppy-dogs!   460
What cannoneer begot this lusty blood?

---

455 stay] F; flaw *conj. Johnson;* 'stay!' *Kittredge*

The Elizabethan proverb narrows the conception to 'Women receive perfection by men' (Tilley w718).

437 blessèd The false syllables here and in 'finishèd' (438), 'closèd' (447), and 'enragèd' (451) add to the artificial language.

441 two . . . currents The marriage of two rivers, a metaphor in vogue among Elizabethan poets. Spenser carries it farthest, *FQ* IV, II.

441–4 silver . . . controlling bounds In contrast to 335–40, where the current of John's right threatens to overflow confining shores unless the silver water is allowed to take its peaceful course. Now both kings can control the banks in peace by controlling Blanche and Lewis.

445 princes princes of the blood; a term applied to both male and female descendants of a sovereign.

446 battery heavy blows by battering cannons.

447 match With a pun on the match or wick that lights powder in a cannon. See *OED* sv *sb²* 2.

448 spleen flash of energy. See 5.7.50 and *MND* 1.1.145–6.

448 enforce i.e. strive to open a passage, make way. See *OED* sv *v* 6.

451 sea . . . deaf i.e. the angry sea which cannot hear above its own roar. Compare *R2* 1.1.18–19: 'full of ire, / In rage, deaf as the sea, hasty as fire' (Dent s169.2). See supplementary note.

452–3 mountains . . . motion A commonplace (Dent m1214.1, r151).

454 peremptory determined.

455 stay check, or hindrance. See supplementary note.

456–7 Death . . . rags Death was often depicted as an emaciated corpse in tatters, as, for example, in Dürer's woodcut of *The Four Horsemen* (E. Panofsky, *Albrecht Dürer*, 1948, no. 284). There may be a play on 'rags' as fustian rhetoric.

460–1 As . . . blood On the Bastard's style, see pp. 24–5 above.

He speaks plain cannon-fire and smoke and bounce.
He gives the bastinado with his tongue.
Our ears are cudgelled, not a word of his
But buffets better than a fist of France.   465
Zounds! I was never so bethumped with words
Since I first called my brother's father Dad.
[KING PHILIP *and* LEWIS *move aside and whisper*]
ELEANOR Son, list to this conjunction, make this match,
Give with our niece a dowry large enough,
For by this knot thou shalt so surely tie   470
Thy now unsured assurance to the crown
That yon green boy shall have no sun to ripe
The bloom that promiseth a mighty fruit.
I see a yielding in the looks of France.
Mark how they whisper. Urge them while their souls   475
Are capable of this ambition,
Lest zeal now melted by the windy breath
Of soft petitions, pity, and remorse,
Cool and congeal again to what it was.
CITIZEN Why answer not the double majesties   480
This friendly treaty of our threatened town?
KING PHILIP Speak England first, that hath been forward first
To speak unto this city: what say you?
KING JOHN If that the Dauphin there, thy princely son,
Can in this book of beauty read, 'I love',   485

468 match,| F2; match F   477 Lest| F4; Least F

462 **speaks . . . cannon** Compare *Ado* 2.1.247–8: 'She speaks poniards, and every word stabs.'
462 **bounce** bang.
463 **the bastinado** a beating, usually with a club or stick.
465 **buffets better** As in contests of buffeting, which are described in old romances, wherein each contender stood while the other took his turn with his fists. Cœur-de-lion killed Austria's son in such a duel (Honigmann).
467 **called . . . Dad** A perfect bastardly twist of an old saying. Honigmann suggests a play on the verb 'to dad' (= to beat, thump) in northern dialect.
468–79 Eleanor's whispered counsel to John recalls her similar secret advice to him at 1.1.40–3, while others whisper. See 503–20, 3.3.18–69 and 4.2.68.
471 **unsured** doubtful, not free from care. *OED* records only this passage for the participial form.
472 **yon** Implying that Arthur is nearby but not

necessarily in view. If the audience has seen him go with his mother into France's tent, the meaning of 'yon' is apparent.
472 **green** young. See 3.4.145.
476 **capable of** susceptible to. See 3.1.12.
477 **zeal now melted** eagerness for (1) this match, (2) Arthur's rights. See supplementary note.
478 **remorse** compassion.
479 **to what it was** to the calculating zeal for Arthur that France had before, in contrast to the warmer zeal he now has for the wedding.
481 **treaty** entreaty. There is probably a glance at 'treaty' as a proposal for discussion of terms.
485 **book . . . love** The book is William Lily and John Colet's *A Short Introduction to Grammar* (1549), sig. B3ᵛ, where the paradigm begins '*Amo*, I love'. The book of beauty is Blanche (T. W. Baldwin, *Shakespeare's Small Latine*, 1944, I, 569).

Her dowry shall weigh equal with a queen,
For Anjou and fair Touraine, Maine, Poitiers,
And all that we upon this side the sea
(Except this city now by us besieged)
Find liable to our crown and dignity,   490
Shall gild her bridal bed and make her rich
In titles, honours, and promotions,
As she in beauty, education, blood,
Holds hand with any princess of the world.

KING PHILIP What sayst thou, boy? Look in the lady's face.   495

LEWIS I do, my lord, and in her eye I find
A wonder or a wondrous miracle,
The shadow of myself formed in her eye,
Which being but the shadow of your son,
Becomes a sun and makes your son a shadow.   500
I do protest I never loved myself
Till now enfixèd I beheld myself
Drawn in the flattering table of her eye.

Whispers with Blanche

BASTARD [*Aside*] Drawn in the flattering table of her eye!
Hanged in the frowning wrinkle of her brow!   505
And quartered in her heart! he doth espy
Himself love's traitor. This is pity now,

---

487 Anjou] *Pope²; Angiers* F   500 sun] *Rowe³; sonne* F   507 traitor.] F4 *(subst.); traytor,* F   507 now,] F4*; now;* F

487–9 *Anjou . . . Except this city* This passage indicates that Shakespeare meant to distinguish between the city of Angiers and the territory of Anjou. The Folio names the territory as Angiers (here and at 2.1.152), although elsewhere (1.1.11 and 2.1.528) the reading is 'Aniowe' and 'Aniow', easily misread as 'Aniers' in an Elizabethan hand.

490 **Find liable** Regard as subject to, subservient.

492 **promotions** preferments. Marriage itself promoted a woman to real social status, but here the word is probably the equivalent of perquisites.

493 **education** upbringing. See supplementary note.

494 **Holds hand with** Matches, equals.

496–503 **I . . . eye** The practice of lovers known as 'looking babies' in the eyes. One sees his own reflection, which looks like a little boy (*pupulus*); see K. Garvin, *TLS*, 5 Dec. 1936, p. 1016, and Sidney, *Astrophil and Stella*, 11.

498 **shadow** picture or reflection.

500 **Becomes . . . shadow** Turns into my true being, the ideal of me in her and the object of my worship, which renders my former self as a poor reflection, an unreal appearance. 'Becomes a sun' also suggests the brightness of her eyes that befits his image. See *TGV* 4.2.118–21.

501–3 **loved . . . eye** As in courtly love the lover loves his good qualities seen in his mistress, so he loves himself but in a higher register, through her. G. Chapman, *Ovid's Banquet of Sense* (1595), stanza 51; Beauty is doomed unless it loves 'enamoured (like good self-love) with her own, / Seen in another, then tis heaven alone' (Honigmann).

503 **flattering . . . eye** The 'table' is a board or flat surface on which a picture is painted, and since the Dauphin says that the portrait is flattering, we may expect the infatuation to be short-lived. Sonnet 24 uses similar images and concludes that the eyes 'draw but what they see, know not the heart'.

506 **quartered** lodged.

That hanged and drawn and quartered there should be
In such a love so vile a lout as he.
BLANCHE My uncle's will in this respect is mine.   510
If he see aught in you that makes him like,
That anything he sees which moves his liking,
I can with ease translate it to my will;
Or if you will, to speak more properly,
I will enforce it eas'ly to my love.   515
Further I will not flatter you, my lord,
That all I see in you is worthy love,
Than this: that nothing do I see in you –
Though churlish thoughts themselves should be your
        judge –
That I can find should merit any hate.   520
KING JOHN What say these young ones? What say you, my niece?
BLANCHE That she is bound in honour still to do
What you in wisdom still vouchsafe to say.
KING JOHN Speak then, Prince Dauphin; can you love this lady?
LEWIS Nay, ask me if I can refrain from love,   525
For I do love her most unfeignedly.
KING JOHN Then do I give Volquessen, Touraine, Maine,
Poitiers and Anjou, these five provinces
With her to thee, and this addition more:
Full thirty thousand marks of English coin.   530
Philip of France, if thou be pleased withal,
Command thy son and daughter to join hands.
KING PHILIP It likes us well. Young princes, close your hands.

---

528 Anjou] F4; *Aniow* F   533 well. Young princes,] F4 *(subst.); well young Princes:* F

508 hanged . . . quartered The punishment for treason was to be hanged, cut down alive, disembowelled (i.e. drawn), and cut into four pieces.

509 In such a love (1) Professing such feelings of love, (2) Toward such a person as his beloved. See *OED* Love *sb* 1 and 9. Elizabethan poems frequently hover between these two meanings of love, as in Sonnet 105.5.

510–20 My uncle . . . hate We hear only Blanche's reply to the Dauphin's whispered entreaty.

512 That anything That thing whatever it may be. Blanche is emphatic on the point, as is Petruchio about his absolute possession of Kate in *Shr.* 3.2.230–2: 'she is my house, / . . . My horse, my ox, my ass, my anything'.

513–15 translate it . . . enforce it Blanche seems to imply a coolness and a calculated propriety, but the speech as a whole calls for a balance of encouragement and guarded restraint.

513 will desire.

514 properly precisely.

519 churlish ungenerous.

527 Volquessen The ancient country of Velocasses, in the vicinity of Rouen, now called Vexin.

528 One of two identical lines in *John* and *TR* (2.410). See 5.4.42 below.

529 addition With a possible quibble on the 'sum' of money as an addition.

530 thirty thousand marks About £20,000 because a mark amounted to 65 new pence. This cash dowry is presumably what John had promised would be 'equal with a queen' (486).

533 likes pleases.

533–4 close . . . lips The formal gestures of a legal betrothal. Some authorities thought that only the joining of hands was necessary; others included a kiss (Honigmann).

AUSTRIA And your lips too, for I am well assured,
    That I did so when I was first assured.   535
               [They join hands and kiss]
KING PHILIP Now, citizens of Angiers, ope your gates,
    Let in that amity which you have made,
    For at Saint Mary's Chapel presently
    The rites of marriage shall be solemnised. –
    Is not the Lady Constance in this troop?   540
    I know she is not, for this match made up,
    Her presence would have interrupted much.
    Where is she and her son? Tell me, who knows.
LEWIS She is sad and passionate at your highness' tent.
KING PHILIP And by my faith, this league that we have made   545
    Will give her sadness very little cure.
    Brother of England, how may we content
    This widow lady? In her right we came,
    Which we, God knows, have turned another way,
    To our own vantage.
KING JOHN   We will heal up all,   550
    For we'll create young Arthur Duke of Brittaine
    And Earl of Richmond, and this rich fair town
    We make him lord of. Call the Lady Constance.
    With speedy messenger bid her repair
    To our solemnity. I trust we shall,   555
    If not fill up the measure of her will,

---

539 rites] F4; rights F   541 not,] F3; not F   543 son? . . . knows.] *Steevens*³; sonne, . . . knowes? F

535 I . . . assured Compare Erasmus, *Enchiridion*, trans. R. Himelick, 1963, p. 115: 'fools, as the comic poet says, . . . think nothing right except what they themselves do.' The poet is Terence, *The Brothers* 1.99–100.
535 assured engaged to be married.
535 SD *They . . . kiss* The kiss completes the arch of an analogy in this scene. As the Bastard persuades France and England to join forces against Angiers, to destroy it, and then to fight each other until Fortune should 'kiss' (394) one or the other, so the Citizen persuades them to join Blanche and the Dauphin in a kissing compact.
538 presently at once.
540–4 In *TR* Constance is present 'in this troop', she does interrupt, and she is left behind with Arthur when the others leave for the wedding.
544 passionate grieved, sorrowful. Compare

TGV 1.2.121: 'Poor forlorn Proteus, passionate Proteus'. See supplementary note.
548–50 In . . . vantage King Philip has, after all, some concern for Constance, which he shows again at 3.4.22 and 106. Here he admits ruefully that he has broken his promises for his own advantage.
551 create . . . Duke of Brittaine The earlier dialogue implies that Arthur is already Duke of Brittany: John calls him Arthur of Brittaine (2.1.156), and the Herald of France styles him Duke of Brittaine (2.1.301). Historically he inherited the titles to Brittany and Richmond from his mother's father.
552–3 town . . . lord of In some early sources, Arthur's father is called 'Count of Angiers', so Shakespeare may think of Angiers as part of Arthur's patrimony (Honigmann), but see Appendix, pp. 201–2 below.
555 our solemnity i.e. the marriage ceremony.

Yet in some measure satisfy her so
That we shall stop her exclamation.
Go we as well as haste will suffer us
To this unlooked-for, unpreparèd pomp.   560
Exeunt [all but the Bastard]
BASTARD Mad world, mad kings, mad composition!
John, to stop Arthur's title in the whole,
Hath willingly departed with a part,
And France, whose armour conscience buckled on,
Whom zeal and charity brought to the field   565
As God's own soldier, rounded in the ear
With that same purpose-changer, that sly devil,
That broker that still breaks the pate of faith,
That daily break-vow, he that wins of all,
Of kings, of beggars, old men, young men, maids –   570
Who having no external thing to lose
But the word 'maid', cheats the poor maid of that –
That smooth-faced gentleman, tickling Commodity,
Commodity, the bias of the world,
The world, who of itself is peisèd well,   575

558 stop her exclamation i.e. stop her mouth with some commodity. The Bastard picks up the 'stop', in the sense of plugging a hole, again at 562, and Constance reverts to it at 3.4.32; also see 3.1.299 and 4.2.120.

561–86 See pp. 34–6 above on contemporary models for this speech.

561 composition agreement, compact.

562 stop . . . whole prevent Arthur's claim to the whole of his realm and plug a dangerous hole. Compare *2H6* 3.1.288: 'A breach that craves a quick expedient stop'.

563 departed parted.

564–8 armour . . . faith The Bastard mocks France with biblical metaphors of God's soldiers: 2 Cor. 6–7: 'The power of God . . . the *armour* of righteousness'; Eph. 6.11–17: 'Put on the whole *armour of God* . . . the breast plate of righteousness . . . the shield of *faith* . . . the sword of the spirit, which is the word of God's; also Isa. 59.17: 'For he put on righteousness, as an habergeon, and an helmet of salvation upon his head . . . and was clad with *zeal* as a cloak' (Geneva).

566 rounded whispered.

567 With By.

568 broker pander, go-between. Compare *Ham.* 1.3.127: 'Do not believe his vows, for they are brokers.' See 582.

569 wins of gets the better of.

571–2 Who . . . cheats 'Who' seems to refer to 'maids', but the subject of 'cheats' is 'Commodity'.

573 smooth-faced smiling, fair, pleasing. Compare *R3* 5.5.32–4: 'let their heirs . . . / Enrich the time to come with smooth-fac'd peace, / With smiling plenty, and fair prosperous days'. The devil's charming deceptions may be implied here; compare *Lear* 3.4.143: 'The Prince of Darkness is a gentleman.'

573 tickling exciting a craving or delicate itching to do something. See *OED* sv *ppl a.* Most editors follow Onions, saying that it implies flattering, but the local meaning suggests seduction and drawing away from a good purpose.

573 Commodity Self-interest at the expense of honour and the general welfare. What the audience has seen operating throughout this scene is finally named (Smallwood).

574 bias The off-centred weight or lop-sided form of a wooden ball used in the game of bowls. It causes the ball to run obliquely on a perfectly flat lawn (see 576). Compare Bacon, 'Of Wisdom for a Man's Self', *Essays* (1625), on self-loving officers, treasurers, generals, and other false servants who stand upon their own centre and 'crooketh' the affairs of their masters, setting a 'bias upon their bowl, or their own petty ends'. See supplementary note.

575 peisèd balanced. Compare F. Sabie, *Adam's Complaint* (1596), sig. B1ᵛ: 'For thee he fram'd earth's even-poised globe, / Hanging it in the air to human wonder' (Honigmann).

Made to run even upon even ground,
Till this advantage, this vile-drawing bias,
This sway of motion, this Commodity,
Makes it take head from all indifferency,
From all direction, purpose, course, intent;   580
And this same bias, this Commodity,
This bawd, this broker, this all-changing word,
Clapped on the outward eye of fickle France,
Hath drawn him from his own-determined aid,
From a resolved and honourable war,   585
To a most base and vile-concluded peace.
And why rail I on this Commodity?
But for because he hath not wooed me yet.
Not that I have the power to clutch my hand
When his fair angels would salute my palm,   590
But for my hand, as unattempted yet,
Like a poor beggar raileth on the rich.
Well, whiles I am a beggar I will rail,
And say there is no sin but to be rich;
And being rich, my virtue then shall be   595
To say there is no vice but beggary.
Since kings break faith upon commodity,
Gain, be my lord, for I will worship thee.   *Exit*

---

582 this all-changing word] *Pope;* this all-changing-word F; that all-changing-world F2   **584** own-determined] *Capell;* no hyphen in F

577 vile-drawing leading or enticing toward base or morally degrading actions. Compare *3H6* 3.3.74–7: 'Look therefore, Lewis, that by this league and marriage / Thou draw not on thy danger and dishonor; / For though usurpers sway the rule a while, / Yet heav'ns are just, and time suppresseth wrongs.'

578 sway of motion (1) deviation from a course of action, (2) political power that inclines or controls.

579 take head from take the power or force away from. See *OED* Head *sb* 31. The usual gloss, 'rush away', is unverified by contemporary usage, the earliest citation in *OED* 55a coming from 1674, and even that use of 'take head' means to rush forward.

579 indifferency impartiality.

582 all-changing *word (1) 'all' as the receiver of the action; hence 'Commodity' is the word that changes all people and all resolutions away from chaste or honourable vows. See *OED* All E.7 *adv*, and compare *Lear* 3.2.6: 'all-shaking thunder'. (2) 'word' as the object of change, implying that the

word 'Commodity' is ever-changing, for it has many synonyms, as the Bastard has just shown. Compare *R2* 5.5.66: 'in this all-hating world', i.e. a world full of hate. See supplementary note.

583 Clapped on Presented to, put before.

583 the outward eye As distinct from the inward spiritual eye, the eye of reason and conscience, which led France to buckle on his armour. See supplementary note.

584 his own-determined aid the support that he intended to give Arthur.

588 But for because Merely because.

589 clutch close.

590 angels Gold coins having St Michael and the dragon stamped on one side. There is probably a quibble on 'angel', 'salute', and 'rail' (= rial or royal), which were all the names of coins.

590 salute kiss.

591 unattempted untested or untempted; literally, 'against which no attempt has been made'.

597 upon on account of.

3.1 *Enter* CONSTANCE, ARTHUR, *and* SALISBURY [*from the tent*]

CONSTANCE Gone to be married? Gone to swear a peace?
    False blood to false blood joined. Gone to be friends?
    Shall Lewis have Blanche and Blanche those provinces?
    It is not so; thou hast misspoke, misheard.
    Be well advised, tell o'er thy tale again.   5
    It cannot be, thou dost but say 'tis so.
    I trust I may not trust thee, for thy word
    Is but the vain breath of a common man.
    Believe me, I do not believe thee, man;
    I have a king's oath to the contrary.   10
    Thou shalt be punished for thus frighting me,
    For I am sick and capable of fears,
    Oppressed with wrongs and therefore full of fears,
    A widow, husbandless, subject to fears;
    A woman, naturally born to fears;   15
    And though thou now confess thou didst but jest,
    With my vexed spirits I cannot take a truce,
    But they will quake and tremble all this day.
    What dost thou mean by shaking of thy head?
    Why dost thou look so sadly on my son?   20
    What means that hand upon that breast of thine?
    Why holds thine eye that lamentable rheum,
    Like a proud river peering o'er his bounds?
    Be these sad signs confirmers of thy words?
    Then speak again, not all thy former tale,   25

Act 3, Scene 1 3.1| *Theobald; Actus Secundus* F; Act II Scene II *White, Honigmann* 3 Blanche| F4; *Blaunch* F *(and at 34)* 15 born| F3; borne F 16–17 jest, . . . spirits| *Rowe;* iest . . . spirits, F

Act 3, Scene 1

3.1 The Folio unaccountably heads this scene *Actus Secundus*, but nearly all editors since Theobald begin Act 3 here rather than at 74 (as in the Folio) because the stage is not cleared before the wedding-party enters.

0 SD If, in the original staging, the French pavilion stood to one side of the 'city gates' (presumably one of the doors in the tiring-house wall), the ensuing dialogue took place just outside the tent.

8 breath . . . man As opposed to a king's oath at 10 (Smallwood).

8 common man In her anger Constance speaks to Salisbury as if he is a servant or other inferior person: 'man' (9), 'fellow' (36, 62), and her repeated use of the contemptuous 'thou', in contrast with Salisbury's deferential 'you'.

12 capable of susceptible to.

12–15 fears Repetition of the closing word of successive clauses (antistrophe or counterturn) is seldom used because it is harder than beginning the line with the same word.

16–17 *jest, . . . spirits The plain sense requires a comma after 'jest', but without the comma Constance could mean 'you play with or joust with my agitated mind'; 'truce' suggests that a 'jest' may be a 'geste' as well. See *R2* 1.3.95 and *Err.* 2.2.8.

17 take a truce make peace.

21 hand . . . breast John Bulwer, *Chironomia* (1644), p. 47, recommends this gesture for orators, 'who with a peaceable meekness bringing the quiet hand unto the breast, by the forcible achievements of that pronunciation, procure a dreadful influence to fall upon their auditory'.

22 rheum tear.

But this one word: whether thy tale be true.
SALISBURY As true as I believe you think them false
    That give you cause to prove my saying true.
CONSTANCE O, if thou teach me to believe this sorrow,
    Teach thou this sorrow how to make me die,   30
    And let belief and life encounter so
    As doth the fury of two desperate men
    Which in the very meeting fall and die.
    Lewis marry Blanche! O boy, then where art thou?
    France friend with England! What becomes of me?   35
    Fellow, be gone: I cannot brook thy sight;
    This news hath made thee a most ugly man.
SALISBURY What other harm have I, good lady, done
    But spoke the harm that is by others done?
CONSTANCE Which harm within itself so heinous is   40
    As it makes harmful all that speak of it.
ARTHUR I do beseech you, madam, be content.
CONSTANCE If thou that bid'st me be content wert grim,
    Ugly, and sland'rous to thy mother's womb,
    Full of unpleasing blots and sightless stains,   45
    Lame, foolish, crooked, swart, prodigious,
    Patched with foul moles and eye-offending marks,
    I would not care, I then would be content,
    For then I should not love thee; no, nor thou
    Become thy great birth nor deserve a crown.   50
    But thou art fair, and at thy birth, dear boy,
    Nature and Fortune joined to make thee great.
    Of Nature's gifts thou mayst with lilies boast,

---

26 one word To say one word means to make a simple statement. The one word Constance wants is 'The tale is (not) true' (Honigmann).

27 them the French and English kings.

32 fury . . . men Compare with W. Lightfoote's *Complaint of England* (1587), sig. 113: 'the picture of *Fury*, who is painted with a sword in his hand, and for the impatient desire of revenge wherewith he is inflamed, desperately rusheth upon a javelin, slaying himself' (Honigmann).

42 content calm, quiet.

44 sland'rous disgraceful.

45 blots dark patches.

45 sightless unsightly.

46 prodigious monstrous, portentous; as one deformed or with a birthmark.

50 deserve a crown Because 'A fair face must

have good conditions' (Tilley F5); and an ugly face implies an evil mind.

51–2 But . . . great Compare S. Daniel, *Complaint of Rosamond* (1592), *Poems*, ed. A. C. Sprague, 1930, 78–81: 'The blood I stained was good and of the best, / My birth had honour, and my beauty fame; / Nature and Fortune join'd to make me blest, / Had I had grace t'have known to use the same' (Honigmann).

52–5 Nature . . . corrupted Your parents, Nature and Fortune, legitimately joined to make you, but Fortune has since become a whore, having been seduced away from Nature and having abandoned her role as your parental protector.

53–4 lilies . . . rose The familiar attributes of female beauty (see 2.1.68), with a suggestion of the English rose and French lily.

And with the half-blown rose. But Fortune, O,
She is corrupted, changed, and won from thee;   55
Sh'adulterates hourly with thine uncle John,
And with her golden hand hath plucked on France
To tread down fair respect of sovereignty,
And made his majesty the bawd to theirs.
France is a bawd to Fortune and King John –   60
That strumpet Fortune, that usurping John.
Tell me, thou fellow, is not France forsworn?
Envenom him with words, to get thee gone
And leave those woes alone which I alone
Am bound to underbear.

SALISBURY   Pardon me, madam,   65
I may not go without you to the kings.

CONSTANCE Thou mayst, thou shalt, I will not go with thee;
I will instruct my sorrows to be proud,
For Grief is proud and makes his owner stoop.
To me and to the state of my great grief   70
Let kings assemble, for my grief's so great
That no supporter but the huge firm earth
Can hold it up.
                    [*Sits on the ground*]
Here I and sorrows sit,
Here is my throne, bid kings come bow to it.

                              [*Exit Salisbury*]

---

68 sorrows] F; Sorrow *Rowe²*   69 Grief] *Rowe;* greefe F   69 and] F; an't *Honigmann (after anon. conj. Cam.)*
69 stoop.] *Pope;* stoope, F; stout. *Hanmer*   73 SD *Sits . . . ground*] *Not in* F; *placed at 73, Kittredge; after 69, Smallwood;*
after 72, Capell; after 74, Theobald. Wording varies: Sits down on the floor / Theobald; throwing herself upon it / Capell;
Seats herself on the ground / Dyce; she seats herself on the knoll / Wilson   74 SD.1 *Exit Salisbury*] *not in* F; *Exeunt Salisbury*
with Arthur / Smallwood (Matchett, Oxford subst.)

---

54 **half-blown** half-blossomed.
56 **adulterates** commits adultery. Compare
Rev. 17.2, the whore of Babylon 'with whom have
committed fornication the kings of the earth'
(Honigmann), and see 2.1.97–8.
56 **hourly** With a play on 'whorely' (i.e.
whorishly). Compare *AYLI* 2.7.26–8: 'from hour
to hour, we ripe and ripe, / And then from hour to
hour, we rot and rot'.
57 **plucked on** incited.
63 **Envenom . . . words** Vituperate upon him;
poison his ears.
65 **underbear** suffer, endure. Compare *R2*
1.4.29: 'patient underbearing of his fortune'.
69 **Grief . . . stoop** A person afflicted with sorrow
must bow to it because Grief itself is proud.
Compare Ecclus. 11.27 as paraphrased by T.
White, *Sermon at Paul's Cross* (1589), sig. E4ᵛ: 'for

the affliction of an hour will make the proudest
stoop and sit upon the ground and forget all former
felicity' (Honigmann).
70–4 **To me . . . bow to it** Kings must come to pay
homage (or worship) before the majesty and throne
of my vast and exalted sorrow. See supplementary
note.
73 SD *Sits . . . ground* Possibly on a grassy bank;
Shakespeare's company used one as a property in
MND 2.2.40 and *Ham.* 3.2.39, and it would be
appropriate if her 'throne' were slightly raised. See
supplementary note.
74 *SD.1 The action continues without pause.
Nothing is said of Arthur and Salisbury in the rest
of the scene, but Arthur presumably stays with his
mother and Salisbury could re-enter among the
attendants.

Enter KING JOHN, [*hand in hand with* KING PHILIP *of*] *France,* [*Lewis the*] DAUPHIN, BLANCHE, ELEANOR, *Philip* [*the* BASTARD], AUSTRIA, [*and attendants*]

KING PHILIP 'Tis true, fair daughter, and this blessèd day   75
    Ever in France shall be kept festival.
    To solemnise this day the glorious sun
    Stays in his course and plays the alchemist,
    Turning with splendour of his precious eye
    The meagre cloddy earth to glittering gold.   80
    The yearly course that brings this day about
    Shall never see it but a holiday.
CONSTANCE A wicked day, and not a holy day. [*Rises*]
    What hath this day deserved? what hath it done
    That it in golden letters should be set   85
    Among the high tides in the calendar?
    Nay, rather turn this day out of the week,
    This day of shame, oppression, perjury.
    Or if it must stand still, let wives with child
    Pray that their burthens may not fall this day,   90
    Lest that their hopes prodigiously be crossed.
    But on this day let seamen fear no wreck,
    No bargains break that are not this day made;
    This day all things begun, come to ill end,
    Yea, faith itself to hollow falsehood change.   95
KING PHILIP By heaven, lady, you shall have no cause
    To curse the fair proceedings of this day.

---

74 SD.2–4] *Actus Tertius, Scœna prima. Enter King Iohn, France, Dolphin, Blanch, Elianor, Philip, Austria, Constance.* F; *Theobald first continued the scene unbroken and without Constance's re-entry*   82 holiday] *Cam.;* holy day F; Holy-day F4
83 SD *Rises*] *Kittredge; not in* F; *Rising / Theobald*

77–8 sun . . . course Compare Joshua 10.13–14: 'the sun abode in the middes of the heaven . . . And there was no day like that before it, nor after it.' See 5.5.1–2 below.

78–80 alchemist . . . gold Compare Sonnet 33, the 'sovereign eye' of the sun 'Kissing with golden face the meadows green / Gilding pale streams with heavenly alchemy'. As in the same sonnet, Constance's next speech calls attention to the shame that clouds this false glory, and she prays that before sunset (110) this 'painted peace' will turn to armed discord.

80 meagre poor, barren.

85 golden letters For a very special day, printed red on calendars, red being synonymous with gold (see *LLL* 5.2.44 and *OED* Red *adj* 3).

86 high tides high times, great festivals. Elizabethan calendars noted 14 July, the anni-

versary of Leicester's entertainment of the queen, in black, but 7 September, her birthday, and 17 November, her accession day, in red.

87 turn . . . week Compare Job 3.3–8: 'Let the day perish, wherein I was born . . . Let it not be joined unto the days of the year, nor let it come into the count of the months.'

89 stand still remain.

89–94 let . . . ill end Old almanacs designated for each month certain favourable and unfavourable days for planting, harvesting, taking physic, and other important business.

91 prodigiously by producing monstrous births.

92 But Except.

94 begun . . . ill end 'An ill beginning an ill ending' (Tilley B261).

Have I not pawned to you my majesty?
CONSTANCE You have beguiled me with a counterfeit
    Resembling majesty, which being touched and tried,   100
    Proves valueless. You are forsworn, forsworn.
    You came in arms to spill enemies' blood,
    But now in arms you strengthen it with yours.
    The grappling vigour and rough frown of war
    Is cold in amity and painted peace,   105
    And our oppression hath made up this league.
    Arm, arm, you heavens, against these perjured kings!
    A widow cries; be husband to me, God!
    Let not the hours of this ungodly day
    Wear out the day in peace; but ere sun set,   110
    Set armèd discord 'twixt these perjured kings!
    Hear me, O, hear me!
AUSTRIA   Lady Constance, peace.
CONSTANCE War, war, no peace! Peace is to me a war.
    O Limoges, O Austria, thou dost shame
    That bloody spoil. Thou slave, thou wretch, thou coward!   115
    Thou little valiant, great in villainy!

---

105 cold] F; cool'd *Hanmer;* clad *Capell* 108 God] *Oxford;* heauens F 110 day] *Theobald;* daies F; day's *Honigmann* 110 sun set] *Wilson, conj. Fleay;* Sun-set F

98 pawned pledged.

99 counterfeit portrait ; false coin (on which an image of a king could be stamped).

100 touched tested ; as gold was rubbed on a touchstone to determine its purity.

102–3 'You came *in war* to destroy my enemies but now you strengthen them *in embraces*' (Johnson). The pun on 'arms' is further complicated if Constance implies that the marriage alliance also enhances their blood lines, quartering the arms of England and France (Honigmann).

103 in arms arm in arm with John.

103 yours your blood relative.

105 *cold . . . painted* The contrast between rough war and smooth peace is belied by France's vows of friendship and peace with England, false as his vows to go to war for Arthur's rights. See *Ham.* 3.1.50–2 on the painted word v. the ugly thing.

106 our oppression Not necessarily implying that Arthur is still on stage, but it is natural that he should stay with his mother, as Kemble and Macready's prompt-books indicate.

106 this league In Macready's production the two kings have by this time seated themselves next to each other on a dais, so they could clasp hands at appropriate moments. See 192 ff.

107–12 Arm . . . me See supplementary note on these Medea-like curses.

108 A widow cries Compare Exod. 22.22–4: 'Ye shall trouble no widow, nor fatherless child. If ye shall evil entreat them and they cry unto me, I will surely hear their out cry. And then will my wrath ware hot, and I will kill you with the sword' (Bishops' Bible). See Jones, *Origins*, pp. 240–2.

108 husband Isa. 54.4–5 assures widows that they should not forget reproaches to their widowhood, 'For he that made thee is thine husband'.

110–11 ere . . . discord An inversion of Eph. 4.26: 'Let not the sun go down upon your wrath.'

110 *sun set* Two words, if the metre and the play on 'set' in the following line are to be emphasised (Wilson).

111 perjured kings Although John has not broken a vow to Constance, he is included in other general imprecations: 'false blood' (3.1.2) and 'you think them false' (3.1.27).

113 War . . . Peace . . . war See supplementary note.

114 Limoges See 'Austria' in the notes to the list of characters.

115 spoil The lion's skin. Ovid, *Metamorphoses*, IX, 113, calls it *spolium leonis.*

Thou ever strong upon the stronger side!
Thou Fortune's champion that dost never fight
But when her humorous ladyship is by
To teach thee safety! Thou art perjured too,   120
And sooth'st up greatness. What a fool art thou,
A ramping fool, to brag and stamp and swear
Upon my party. Thou cold-blooded slave,
Hast thou not spoke like thunder on my side,
Been sworn my soldier, bidding me depend   125
Upon thy stars, thy fortune, and thy strength,
And dost thou now fall over to my foes?
Thou wear a lion's hide! Doff it for shame,
And hang a calf's-skin on those recreant limbs.
AUSTRIA O that a man should speak those words to me!   130
BASTARD And hang a calf's-skin on those recreant limbs.
AUSTRIA Thou dar'st not say so, villain, for thy life.
BASTARD And hang a calf's-skin on those recreant limbs.
KING JOHN We like not this, thou dost forget thyself.

Enter PANDULPH

KING PHILIP Here comes the holy legate of the Pope.   135
PANDULPH Hail, you anointed deputies of God!
To thee, King John, my holy errand is.
I Pandulph, of fair Milan cardinal,
And from Pope Innocent the legate here,
Do in his name religiously demand   140
Why thou against the church, our holy mother,
So wilfully dost spurn, and force perforce

---

129 calf's-skin| *Capell;* Calues skin F *(or* Calues-skin *throughout)*   131, 133 SH BASTARD| *Rowe; Phil.* F   136 God| *Oxford;* heauen F

119 **humorous** capricious.
121 **sooth'st up greatness** flatter great ones; 'up' is emphatic as in 4.3.133. See Greene, *Friar Bacon* (1594), 3.22, for this use of 'sooth up' with 'smooth flattery'.
122 **ramping** extravagant acting or 'roaring'. J. Earle, *Micro-cosmography* (1628), ed. Arber, 1868, p. 42, describes the vociferous actor as 'tragical on the stage but rampant in tiring-house, and swears oaths there which he never conned'. Compare Jonson, *Bartholomew Fair* (1614), 4.5.72: 'Peace you foul ramping jade.'
123 **Upon my party** In my support.
127 **fall over** desert.
128–9 **lion's . . . skin** See supplementary note.

130 Compare Sidney, *Arcadia* (1590 edn), p. 456: 'O God (cried out Pyrocles) that thou wert a man that usest these words unto me.'
135 **holy** A flurry of 'holy's follows, and again at 5.2.65–71; an epithet detested by many English Protestants (Honigmann).
136 **deputies of God** After Constance's excoriating rebuke of perjured kings this salutation sounds hollow.
138 **cardinal** See supplementary note.
139 **Pope Innocent** Innocent III, the champion of papal supremacy.
142 **spurn** kick; show antipathy scornfully.
142 **force perforce** by violent means, by compulsion.

Keep Stephen Langton, chosen Archbishop
Of Canterbury, from that holy see.
This, in our foresaid Holy Father's name,   145
Pope Innocent, I do demand of thee.
KING JOHN What earthy name to interrogatories
Can task the free breath of a sacred king?
Thou canst not, cardinal, devise a name
So slight, unworthy, and ridiculous   150
To charge me to an answer, as the Pope.
Tell him this tale, and from the mouth of England
Add thus much more: that no Italian priest
Shall tithe or toll in our dominions,
But as we under God are supreme head,   155
So under Him, that great supremacy
Where we do reign, we will alone uphold
Without th'assistance of a mortal hand.
So tell the Pope, all reverence set apart
To him and his usurped authority.   160
KING PHILIP Brother of England, you blaspheme in this.
KING JOHN Though you and all the kings of Christendom
Are led so grossly by this meddling priest,
Dreading the curse that money may buy out,
And by the merit of vild gold, dross, dust,   165
Purchase corrupted pardon of a man,
Who in that sale sells pardon from himself –
Though you and all the rest so grossly led,
This juggling witchcraft with revenue cherish,

---

144 see] F4 *(subst.)*; Sea F   148 task] *Theobald;* tast F; taste F3; tax *Rowe³*   155 God] *Collier MS.;* heauen F; Heav'n *Rowe*

143 Stephen Langton The monks of Canterbury proposed one candidate, John another, and the Pope rejected both, appointing Langton, whom John refused forthwith. See Holinshed, II, 295–6.
147–8 What . . . king Who on earth can force the free breath of a king to answer any questions?
147 interrogatories In law, questions formally put to an accused person.
148 *task bring to task, challenge. See supplementary note.
151 charge command.
153 Italian priest The Pope.
154 tithe or toll impose tithes or collect taxes.
155 *under God 'under heaven' in F is apparently an alteration made to conform with the statute against oaths on the stage (1606). Compare

TR 3.80: 'I reign next under God, supreme head.'
163 grossly stupidly; with a suggestion of 'earthly', as associated with money and metal.
163 meddling priest the Pope.
165 merit According to the doctrine of merit, forgiveness of sins is impossible unless one earns it by good acts, 'which [Roman Catholics] for money sake have invented, instead of the bloodshedding of Jesus Christ' (from a Protestant pamphlet, 1588; cited by Honigmann).
167 sells . . . himself damns, puts himself beyond pardon.
169 juggling cheating.
169 revenue Stress on the second syllable.

Yet I alone, alone do me oppose   170
Against the Pope and count his friends my foes.
PANDULPH Then by the lawful power that I have
    Thou shalt stand cursed and excommunicate,
    And blessèd shall he be that doth revolt
    From his allegiance to an heretic,   175
    And meritorious shall that hand be called,
    Canonised and worshipped as a saint,
    That takes away by any secret course
    Thy hateful life.
CONSTANCE   O lawful let it be
    That I have room with Rome to curse a while!   180
    Good father cardinal, cry thou 'Amen'
    To my keen curses; for without my wrong
    There is no tongue hath power to curse him right.
PANDULPH There's law and warrant, lady, for my curse.
CONSTANCE And for mine too, when law can do no right,   185
    Let it be lawful that law bar no wrong.
    Law cannot give my child his kingdom here,
    For he that holds his kingdom holds the law.
    Therefore, since law itself is perfect wrong,
    How can the law forbid my tongue to curse?   190
PANDULPH Philip of France, on peril of a curse,
    Let go the hand of that arch-heretic,

185 too. When . . . right,| *Staunton;* too, when . . . right. F; too; when . . . right, *Rowe²*

173–5 **cursed . . . heretic** A contemporary audience would see a reference to the papal bull of 1570 by which Pius V excommunicated Queen Elizabeth, declared her a heretic, released her subjects from allegiance, and called for her deposition.

174–5 **revolt . . . heretic** The 'cursed' papist doctrine of 'no faith with heretics' (*ODEP* 241b, Tilley F33).

176–7 **meritorious . . . Canonised** See supplementary note.

180 **room with Rome** Shakespeare often rhymes 'Rome' with 'room', 'doom', and 'roam'. See Kökeritz, pp. 141, 231, 238, for the possibility that all four were pronounced the same, and compare 2.1.335, where 'roam' is spelled 'rome' in F.

181–2 **cry . . . Amen . . . curses** Referring to the 'Commination Against Sinners' in the Prayer Book, taken from Deut. 27.14–26. The priest recited the curses and the congregation answered 'Amen'; but Constance plays the priest, and she

expects a priest to say 'Amen'. She is probably thinking of one versicle: 'Cursed is he that letteth in judgement the right of the . . . fatherless and widows' (Book of Common Prayer (1559)).

182–3 **without . . . right** Unless you curse along with me and acknowledge the pre-eminence of my grievance, your tongue lacks the authority and vigour to curse John fully.

185–90 **When . . . curse** Constance shifts rapidly through three senses of 'wrong': (1) her supposed lack of warrant (185), (2) injury to Arthur (187), (3) injustice as embodied in John (189). 'My curses cannot be prohibited and declared wrong-doing because the law as it is in the hands of John will not set right the injury to Arthur. The present embodiment of law is no law at all because he is absolute injustice, a violation of law, and "where no law is, there is no transgression" (Rom. 4.15); so how can law forbid me to curse?'

187 **here** on earth.

And raise the power of France upon his head,
Unless he do submit himself to Rome.
ELEANOR Look'st thou pale, France? Do not let go thy hand.   195
CONSTANCE [*To King John*] Look to it, devil, lest that France
      repent
And by disjoining hands hell lose a soul.
AUSTRIA King Philip, listen to the cardinal.
BASTARD And hang a calf's-skin on his recreant limbs.
AUSTRIA Well ruffian, I must pocket up these wrongs,   200
      Because –
BASTARD   Your breeches best may carry them.
KING JOHN Philip, what say'st thou to the cardinal?
CONSTANCE What should he say, but as the cardinal?
LEWIS Bethink you, father, for the difference
      Is purchase of a heavy curse from Rome,   205
      Or the light loss of England for a friend:
      Forgo the easier.
BLANCHE   That's the curse of Rome.
CONSTANCE O Lewis, stand fast! The devil tempts thee here
      In likeness of a new untrimmèd bride.
BLANCHE The Lady Constance speaks not from her faith,   210
      But from her need.
CONSTANCE   O, if thou grant my need,
      Which only lives but by the death of faith,
      That need must needs infer this principle,

---

196 it,] *Smallwood, conj. Maxwell;* that F; that, *Pope* 209 untrimmèd] F; and trimmed *Theobald;* uptrimmed *Dyce*

193 upon his head falling upon his person and (possibly) on the foremost ranks of his army. See *OED* Head *sb* 35 and 18a.

196 *Look to it Take care. Compare *2H6* 1.1.156: 'Look to it, lords, let not his smoothing words / Bewitch your hearts.' Many editors since Pope have tried to clarify the passage with a comma after the Folio's 'that', but the usual expression was 'Look to it'. If the manuscript read 'yt', a compositor could have misread 'that'. See Maxwell, p. 76.

200 pocket up ... wrongs put up with or swallow affronts (Tilley 170).

201 breeches (1) the loose baggy slops often worn by men, (2) the bare buttocks (breech). The sarcasm suggests an association with the verb 'to breech' or whip a coward or schoolboy. See *OED* Breech *sb* 4 and *v* 2, and compare *Wiv.* 4.1.77–9: 'if

you forget your *qui*'s, your *quae*'s, and your *quod*'s, you must be preeches' (i.e. breeched).

203 but except.

209 *untrimmèd (1) unbedded, not yet deflowered (see Farmer and Henley, Trim *v* 3, and *Tit.* 5.1.93–6), (2) her hair hanging loose as a virgin bride's (see Webster, *The White Devil* (1612), ed. J. R. Mulryne, 1970, 4.1.2).

210–11 not ... faith ... need not as she really believes but as she must, for it suits her cause or advantage. Compare the proverbs 'Need hath not law, need maketh her hither jet' and 'Need will have his course in everything' (Tilley N76 and N81).

212 My distress is caused by France's broken promise.

213 That need That necessity.

213 infer demonstrate.

That faith would live again by death of need.
O then tread down my need, and faith mounts up;   215
Keep my need up, and faith is trodden down.
KING JOHN The king is moved and answers not to this.
CONSTANCE O, be removed from him and answer well!
AUSTRIA Do so, King Philip, hang no more in doubt.
BASTARD Hang nothing but a calf's-skin, most sweet lout.   220
KING PHILIP I am perplexed and know not what to say.
PANDULPH What canst thou say but will perplex thee more
    If thou stand excommunicate and cursed?
KING PHILIP Good reverend father, make my person yours,
    And tell me how you would bestow yourself.   225
    This royal hand and mine are newly knit,
    And the conjunction of our inward souls
    Married in league, coupled and linked together
    With all religious strength of sacred vows;
    The latest breath that gave the sound of words   230
    Was deep-sworn faith, peace, amity, true love
    Between our kingdoms and our royal selves.
    And even before this truce, but new before,
    No longer than we well could wash our hands
    To clap this royal bargain up of peace,   235
    God knows, they were besmeared and overstained
    With slaughter's pencil, where revenge did paint
    The fearful difference of incensèd kings.
    And shall these hands so lately purged of blood,
    So newly joined in love, so strong in both,   240
    Unyoke this seizure and this kind regreet?
    Play fast and loose with faith? so jest with heaven?

225 yourself.| *Theobald;* your selfe? F   236 God| *Oxford;* Heauen, F   242 heaven?| *Theobald³;* heauen, F

222 **perplex thee more** 'perplex' carried the archaic connotation of confused entanglement and distraction, pulled this way and that. See *OED* sv *v* 1 and *ppl* 1, and *Cym.* 3.4.4–7.

225 **bestow yourself** behave.

226 **This royal hand** Philip has probably been holding John's hand since 192.

227–8 **conjunction . . . linked** A mixed construction. Although 'conjunction' is the subject of (is) 'married', 'coupled', and 'linked', these participles modify 'inward souls', but the effect is to emphasise 'conjunction', the union of souls symbolised by joined hands (Smallwood).

233 **even before** just before.

233 **new** immediately.

235 **clap . . . up** (1) make or settle hastily (see *Shr.*

2.1.325), (2) seal with a handshake (see *H5* 5.2.129–30, and for other variations, Dent H109.1).

237 **pencil** A wide brush.

240 **strong in both** resolute in battle and friendship.

241 **seizure** hand clasp. See *Tro.* 1.1.55–7.

241 **kind regreet** return of my salute.

242 **Play . . . loose** Be unreliable or tricky; as in a cheating game played by gipsies and vagabonds, using a trick knot in a rope or leather belt (*ODEP* 630a, Tilley P401). The point is that the knot which seemed fast was really loose' (Wilson).

242 **jest with heaven** The phrase comes from 'Non est bonum ludere cum sanctis' (Dent J45.1).

Make such unconstant children of ourselves
As now again to snatch our palm from palm,
Unswear faith sworn, and on the marriage-bed   245
Of smiling peace to march a bloody host,
And make a riot on the gentle brow
Of true sincerity? O holy sir,
My reverend father, let it not be so.
Out of your grace devise, ordain, impose   250
Some gentle order, and then we shall be blest
To do your pleasure and continue friends.
PANDULPH All form is formless, order orderless,
Save what is opposite to England's love.
Therefore to arms! Be champion of our church,   255
Or let the church our mother breathe her curse,
A mother's curse, on her revolting son.
France, thou mayst hold a serpent by the tongue,
A chafèd lion by the mortal paw,
A fasting tiger safer by the tooth,   260
Than keep in peace that hand which thou dost hold.
KING PHILIP I may disjoin my hand, but not my faith.
PANDULPH So mak'st thou faith an enemy to faith,
And like a civil war sett'st oath to oath,
Thy tongue against thy tongue. O, let thy vow   265
First made to heaven, first be to heaven performed,
That is, to be the champion of our church.
What since thou swor'st, is sworn against thyself,
And may not be performèd by thyself,

259 chafèd] *Theobald;* cafed F; chased *Pope;* caged *Sisson*

244 snatch . . . palm renege on an agreement that was sealed by clasping hands. There may be a reference to the children's game sometimes called 'slappies'. It is a duelling game in which one player extends his hands palms up; the other player rests his hands on top of them, palms down. The player whose hands are underneath tries to slap one or both of the hands on top before the player on top snatches his hands back. See I. and P. Opie, *Children's Games in Street and Playground,* 1969, pp. 244–5.
247 brow forehead or the whole countenance. See *The Rape of Lucrece* 807.
250 devise, ordain, impose France imitates the language of legal documents or proclamations.
251 gentle order peaceful arrangement.
258 hold . . . tongue A version of the familiar

saying 'I have got a wolf by the ears, I can neither hold him nor let go' (Tilley w603, Dent s228.1). Erasmus (*Enchiridion,* trans. R. Himelick, 1963, pp. 63–4) uses the saying to illustrate the dissension of soul and body which 'cannot be separated . . . nor cannot live together without continuous warfare'.
259 *chafèd furious, enraged. See supplementary note.
267 champion . . . church The King of France was commonly called 'The Eldest Son of the Church', and Pepin the Short carried the honorific title 'Liberator and Defender of the Church'. But an English audience might think of 'Defender of the Faith' with the ironies that followed the Pope's granting of the title to Henry VIII.
268–94 This tortuous speech suggests casuistic arguments.

For that which thou hast sworn to do amiss,   270
Is not amiss when it is truly done,
And being not done, where doing tends to ill,
The truth is then most done not doing it.
The better act of purposes mistook
Is to mistake again; though indirect,   275
Yet indirection thereby grows direct,
And falsehood falsehood cures, as fire cools fire
Within the scorchèd veins of one new burned.
It is religion that doth make vows kept,
But thou hast sworn against religion   280
By what thou swear'st against the thing thou swear'st,
And mak'st an oath the surety for thy truth
Against an oath. The truth thou art unsure
To swear swears only not to be forsworn –
Else what a mockery should it be to swear!   285
But thou dost swear only to be forsworn
And most forsworn, to keep what thou dost swear;
Therefore thy later vows, against thy first,
Is in thyself rebellion to thyself,
And better conquest never canst thou make   290
Than arm thy constant and thy nobler parts
Against these giddy loose suggestions;
Upon which better part our prayers come in,

---

275 again;| *Theobald;* again, F   280 religion| *Smallwood;* religion: F; religion, *Collier*   283 oath. The truth| *Johnson, conj. Heath;* oath the truth, F; oath the truth *Pope*

270–3 For . . . it The wrong you have sworn to do is not wrong if you act rightly, that is, if you do not act at all. Compare 'An unlawful oath is better broken than kept' (Tilley O7), and *2H6* 5.1.182–3: 'It is great sin to swear unto a sin, / But greater sin to keep a sinful oath.'
274–5 The . . . again When we have turned away from the true path, it is better to veer to one side on a short cut in hope of returning to the right path. 'Purpose' means motion toward a place, and 'mistake' means to take wrongfully or to transgress.
275 indirect deceitful.
276 indirection . . . direct Compare the Polonian strategy, *Ham.* 2.1.63: 'By indirections find directions out'.
277 falsehood . . . cures i.e. 'Tell a lie and find a truth' (Tilley L237); 'One deceit drives out another' (D174).
277–8 fire . . . burned See supplementary note.

281 By swearing to be true to an enemy of the church, this religious oath in itself violates your religious faith, the thing you swear by.
282 truth faith.
283–4 The truth . . . forsworn To swear loyalty to something of which you are uncertain is only to swear that you are not committing perjury. A vow to God must be kept above all others, and other pledges of faith are of less certain obligation.
289 Is The verb is singular perhaps by attraction to 'rebellion' which follows, but the intended subject may be 'to put thy later vows in opposition to thy first'.
292 suggestions temptations, promptings of the devil.
293 come in (1) enter the field (see *AYLI* 1.2.171), (2) make a pass at fencing, thrust under the opponent's guard (see *2H4* 3.2.283), consistent with 'arm' (291).

If thou vouchsafe them. But if not, then know
The peril of our curses light on thee   295
So heavy as thou shalt not shake them off
But in despair die under their black weight.
AUSTRIA Rebellion, flat rebellion!
BASTARD   Will't not be?
Will not a calf's-skin stop that mouth of thine?
LEWIS Father, to arms!
BLANCHE   Upon thy wedding-day?   300
Against the blood that thou hast marrièd?
What, shall our feast be kept with slaughtered men?
Shall braying trumpets and loud churlish drums,
Clamours of hell, be measures of our pomp?
O husband, hear me. Aye, alack, how new   305
Is 'husband' in my mouth! Even for that name
Which till this time my tongue did ne'er pronounce,
Upon my knee I beg, go not to arms
Against mine uncle.
CONSTANCE O, upon my knee made hard with kneeling   310
I do pray to thee, thou virtuous Dauphin,
Alter not the doom forethought by heaven.
BLANCHE Now shall I see thy love. What motive may
Be stronger with thee than the name of wife?
CONSTANCE That which upholdeth him that thee upholds,   315
His honour – O thine honour, Lewis, thine honour.
LEWIS I muse your majesty doth seem so cold,
When such profound respects do pull you on.
PANDULPH I will denounce a curse upon his head.
KING PHILIP Thou shalt not need. England, I will fall from thee.   320
                    [*Drops King John's hand*]
CONSTANCE O fair return of banished majesty.

---

318 on.] *Capell; on?* F

296 **as that.**
298 **Rebellion, flat rebellion** Austria repeats the word from 289 – a considerable delay. He may have tried to interrupt sooner but was prevented by the flow of Pandulph's rhetoric (Smallwood).
298 **Will't not be?** The empty exasperated rhetorical question is like *Quid hoc?* often preceding another question in Senecan plays. See *Hercules Ortaenus* 1432 ff., *Jacob and Esau* (*c.* 1554), MSR, 1.1.13, Peele *Edward I* (*c.* 1591), MSR, 1221, *1H6* 1.5.33.

303 **churlish** intentionally harsh.
304 **measures . . . pomp** music for our wedding.
312 Do not change God's preordained decree.
313 **motive** An argument or means of persuading. See *OED* sv *sb* 3.
316 **thine honour** Mrs Siddons spoke this with heavy sarcasm.
317 **I muse** I am amazed.
318 **profound respects** weighty considerations.
319 **denounce** call down.
320 **fall from** forsake.

ELEANOR O foul revolt of French inconstancy.

KING JOHN France, thou shalt rue this hour within this hour.

BASTARD Old Time the clock-setter, that bald sexton Time,
    Is it as he will? Well then, France shall rue.   325

BLANCHE The sun's o'ercast with blood. Fair day, adieu.
    Which is the side that I must go withal?
    I am with both, each army hath a hand,
    And in their rage, I having hold of both,
    They whirl asunder and dismember me.   330
    Husband, I cannot pray that thou mayst win;
    Uncle, I needs must pray that thou mayst lose.
    Father, I may not wish the fortune thine;
    Grandam, I will not wish thy wishes thrive.
    Whoever wins, on that side shall I lose,   335
    Assurèd loss, before the match be played.

LEWIS Lady, with me, with me thy fortune lies.

BLANCHE There where my fortune lives, there my life dies.

KING JOHN Cousin, go draw our puissance together.

                                [Exit Bastard]

    France, I am burned up with inflaming wrath,   340
    A rage whose heat hath this condition
    That nothing can allay, nothing but blood,
    The blood and dearest-valued blood of France.

KING PHILIP Thy rage shall burn thee up, and thou shalt turn
    To ashes, ere our blood shall quench that fire.   345
    Look to thyself, thou art in jeopardy.

KING JOHN No more than he that threats. – To arms let's hie!

                                Exeunt [severally]

---

323 SH KING JOHN] *Eng.* F 324 clock-setter] F3; *no hyphen* F 330 whirl] *Rowe²* (*subst.*); whurle F 337 lies] F; lives *Capell* 338 lives] F; li'es *Honigmann, conj. Fleay* 339 SD] *Pope; not in* F 342 allay] F; allay't *Dyce², conj. Capell* 343 dearest-valued] *Theobald; no hyphen in* F

324–5 Old Time . . . rue If changeable Time wills it, France shall regret. The Bastard thinks the outcome is in the hands of a power less predictable than John or King Philip suppose. There may be a play on 'thyme' and 'rue', which are said to grow in the same garden (Tilley R198).

324 bald sexton Time The sexton, who sets the church clock and digs graves, is combined with the image of Time or Occasion, who is bald behind (Tilley T311). See 4.2.61–2 n., 4.2.125.

326 sun's . . . day adieu Referring to the 'blessèd day' and 'glorious sun' that France hoped for at 3.1.75–7.

333 Father King Philip, her father-in-law.

339 Cousin Kinsman.

340–3 wrath . . . France According to the theory of humours, one's own blood quenches burning choler, but John's fiery wrath is so great that it needs the best blood of France too. See *3H6* 2.1.79–88.

341 condition attribute.

346 in jeopardy in danger; connoting that the risks are evenly divided, as in the older meaning associated with games like chess. See Spenser, *FQ* III, 1, 22, 6.

3.2 *Alarums, excursions. Enter* BASTARD *with Austria's head* [*and the lion's skin*]

BASTARD Now by my life, this day grows wondrous hot;
　　　　Some airy devil hovers in the sky
　　　　And pours down mischief. Austria's head lie there,
　　　　While Philip breathes.

Enter KING JOHN, ARTHUR, HUBERT

KING JOHN Hubert, keep this boy. Philip, make up: 5
　　　　My mother is assailèd in our tent,
　　　　And ta'en I fear.
BASTARD　　　　　　　　My lord, I rescued her,
　　　　Her highness is in safety, fear you not.
　　　　But on, my liege, for very little pains
　　　　Will bring this labour to an happy end.   10

　　　　　　　　　　　　　　　　　　　　　Exeunt

3.3 *Alarums, excursions, retreat. Enter* [KING] JOHN, ELEANOR, ARTHUR, BASTARD, HUBERT, *lords*

KING JOHN [*To Eleanor*] So shall it be; your grace shall stay behind
　　　　So strongly guarded. [*To Arthur*] Cousin, look not sad,
　　　　Thy grandam loves thee, and thy uncle will
　　　　As dear be to thee as thy father was.
ARTHUR O, this will make my mother die with grief!   5
KING JOHN [*To Bastard*] Cousin, away for England, haste before,
　　　　And ere our coming see thou shake the bags
　　　　Of hoarding abbots; imprisoned angels

Act 3, Scene 2 3.2] *Scæna Secunda.* F 0 SD *and the lion's skin*] Kemble (subst.); *not in* F 10 SD *Exeunt*] Rowe; *Exit* F Act 3, Scene 3 3.3] *No scene division in* F 1 SD] Hanmer; *not in* F 2 SD] Pope; *not in* F 6 SD] Pope; *not in* F

Act 3, Scene 2
0 SD *head . . . skin* A severed head was a stock property, used again in *Mac.* 5.9 and *Cym.* 4.2. See supplementary note.

2 airy devil The daemons of the air raised storms in thunder and lightning, here a metaphor for the din of battle, especially cannon fire. See supplementary note.

4 *Philip See Textual Analysis, p. 184 below.

4 breathes rests, catches his breath.

5 make up advance, rally your men. See *OED* Make *v* 96.

6–7 My mother . . . her See supplementary note.

7–10 rescued . . . labour The Bastard thinks of the battle as birth pains, perhaps because he has now earned the right to be a Plantagenet by rescuing his grandmother and avenging his father's death. In *TR* (3.154–8) he exults in his revenge, but Shakespeare leaves it implicit.

Act 3, Scene 3
0 SD *retreat* A trumpet signal for withdrawal of pursuing forces.

1 stay behind i.e. in control of John's French possessions, although Shakespeare's exaggeration at 2.1.487–9 seems to leave him without any (Smallwood).

7 shake the bags extract money; behaving like a shakebag or scoundrel.

8 angels gold coins; with the usual pun.

Set at liberty. The fat ribs of peace
Must by the hungry now be fed upon.   10
Use our commission in his utmost force.
BASTARD Bell, book, and candle shall not drive me back,
When gold and silver becks me to come on.
I leave your highness. Grandam, I will pray,
If ever I remember to be holy,   15
For your fair safety. So I kiss your hand.
ELEANOR Farewell, gentle cousin.
KING JOHN   Coz, farewell.

                                            [*Exit Bastard*]

ELEANOR Come hither, little kinsman; hark, a word.
                     [*She takes Arthur aside*]
KING JOHN Come hither, Hubert. O, my gentle Hubert,
We owe thee much. Within this wall of flesh   20
There is a soul counts thee her creditor,
And with advantage means to pay thy love,
And, my good friend, thy voluntary oath
Lives in this bosom, dearly cherishèd.
Give me thy hand. I had a thing to say,   25
But I will fit it with some better time.
By heaven, Hubert, I am almost ashamed
To say what good respect I have of thee.
HUBERT I am much bounden to your majesty.
KING JOHN Good friend, thou hast no cause to say so yet,   30
But thou shalt have, and creep time ne'er so slow,
Yet it shall come for me to do thee good.
I had a thing to say, but let it go.

8–9 imprisoned . . . liberty] F; set at liberty / Imprison'd angels *White, conj. Walker* 17 SD] *Pope; not in* F
18 SD] *Malone (subst. Pope); not in* F   26 time] *Pope;* tune F

---

10 hungry i.e. hungry soldiers, since John said earlier (1.1.48) that 'Our abbeys and our priories shall pay / This expedition's charge.'

11 his its.

12 Bell . . . candle The symbols used in the ritual of excommunication (Tilley B276).

13 becks beckons. The passage recalls the Bastard's speech on Commodity, 2.1.598: 'Gain, be my lord, for I will worship thee.'

17 Coz Cousin, kinsman.

18 Implying that Eleanor is privy to the king's plot (for other whispering, see 1.1.40–3, 2.1.468–79 and 4.2.68).

20 We owe thee much The script lacks any

specific sign of what John means here; it may be taken as another random statement like the unspecified 'voluntary oath' (23), while John gropes for a show of favour.

22 advantage gain, profit in the form of money. See 2.1.577.

23 voluntary oath Wilson thought part of a scene containing this oath might have been deleted by Shakespeare. If so, it was a wise choice, for the imprecise reference adds to the king's smarmy tone.

26 *time See supplementary note.

28 respect esteem.

29 bounden obliged.

The sun is in the heaven, and the proud day,
Attended with the pleasures of the world,   35
Is all too wanton, and too full of gauds
To give me audience. If the midnight bell
Did with his iron tongue and brazen mouth
Sound on into the drowsy ear of night,
If this same were a churchyard where we stand,   40
And thou possessèd with a thousand wrongs;
Or if that surly spirit, melancholy,
Had baked thy blood and make it heavy-thick,
Which else runs tickling up and down the veins,
Making that idiot, laughter, keep men's eyes   45
And strain their cheeks to idle merriment –
A passion hateful to my purposes –
Or if that thou couldst see me without eyes,
Hear me without thine ears, and make reply
Without a tongue, using conceit alone,   50
Without eyes, ears, and harmful sounds of words;
Then, in despite of broad-eyed watchful day,
I would into thy bosom pour my thoughts.
But, ah, I will not! Yet I love thee well,
And by my troth, I think thou lov'st me well.   55
HUBERT So well that what you bid me undertake,

39 ear] *Dyce, conj. Collier;* race F; face *Sisson* 43 heavy-thick] *Pope;* heauy, thicke F 52 broad-eyed] *Pope;* brooded F

36 gauds trifling ornaments, showy toys.
37 give me audience John, normally the one to give an audience, displaces the metaphor, as if he stands in attendance before the sovereign eye of heaven.
38 brazen With a connotation of 'shameless'.
39 Sound on Continue striking.
39 *ear See supplementary note.
41 thou . . . wrongs i.e. if you were a villain I could speak my mind to you. 'Possessed with' means obsessed with or dominated by, but the image of a midnight churchyard also suggests 'possessed by devils' (Smallwood).
43 baked . . . thick Fear, among other causes of melancholy, burns blood to ashes, hence, congeals or thickens it and makes one sullen. Compare Nashe, *Terrors of the Night* (1594), in *Works*, ed. R. B. McKerrow, 1904, rev. edn 1958, 1, 354: 'the grossest part of our blood is the melancholy humour, which . . . still thickening as it stands still, engendreth many misshapen objects in our imaginations'.

43 heavy-thick The Folio's punctuation 'heavy, thick' is not to be trusted in this case. Compare *R2* 2.2.30: 'I cannot be sad, so heavy sad.'
44 tickling tingling, provoking laughter.
45 idiot A natural fool or professional jester.
45 keep lodge in.
47 passion emotion.
50 using conceit alone by thought, mental images or speculation. Compare Donne, 'The Ecstasy' (23), where a sympathetic observer refined by love can grow 'all mind' and might understand the soul's language directly, without eyes or ears.
51 harmful i.e. harmful to the speaker.
52 *broad-eyed watchful day vigilant day with its eyes wide open like divine providence. See supplementary note.
53 Compare Guevara, *Golden Epistles*, trans. Fenton (1582), sig. T1ᵛ: 'So simple ought we to be towards our friend, as in his bosom to pour our secrets'; see Dent (B546.2).

Though that my death were adjunct to my act,
By heaven, I would do it.

KING JOHN   Do not I know thou wouldst?
Good Hubert, Hubert, Hubert, throw thine eye
On yon young boy. I'll tell thee what, my friend,   60
He is a very serpent in my way,
And wheresoe'er this foot of mine doth tread,
He lies before me. Dost thou understand me?
Thou art his keeper.

HUBERT   And I'll keep him so
That he shall not offend your majesty.   65

KING JOHN Death.

HUBERT   My lord.

KING JOHN   A grave.

HUBERT   He shall not live.

KING JOHN   Enough.
I could be merry now. Hubert, I love thee.
Well, I'll not say what I intend for thee.
Remember. – Madam, fare you well;
I'll send those powers o'er to your majesty.   70

ELEANOR My blessing go with thee.

KING JOHN [*To Arthur*]   For England, cousin, go.
Hubert shall be your man, attend on you
With all true duty. – On toward Calais, ho!

                                            Exeunt

66 My lord.] F; My lord? *Rowe*   67 now.] *Rowe;* now, F   73 Calais] *Rowe³; Callice* F

57 **adjunct to** connected with, consequent
upon.

58 **Do not . . . wouldst** The instant reply suggests
that, although John may be agitated with fear, he
has by calculation waited for an unqualified promise
from Hubert before he shows his purpose.

61 **serpent in my way** A variation on the saying
about a lion in the path (Tilley L312), but compare
Gen. 49.16–17: 'Dan shall judge his people . . . shall
be a serpent by the way, an adder by the path,
biting the horse heels, so that his rider shall fall
backward.'

64–5 **I'll keep . . . majesty** Hubert's guarded
tone implies that 'I'll keep him so' masks a nearly
full understanding of the king's meaning (Smallwood).

65 **offend** harm, strike so as to hurt.

66 **My lord.** I retain the Folio's period, whereas
most editors since Rowe have replaced it with a
question mark. Surely Hubert understands John's
trend of thought by now (Sisson), and 'My lord' is
a grim sign of attention implying tacit agreement. If
an actor wishes to turn the phrase to a question, he
should probably suggest feigned incomprehension,
another small delay of a definite commitment.

68 **I'll . . . thee** John yet again is wary of too
explicit a promise; the politician leaves room for
further manoeuvre (Smallwood).

70 **powers** forces.

71 **My . . . thee** With grisly connotations in any
case, but especially ironic if spoken to Arthur.

3.4 *Enter* [KING PHILIP *of*] *France*, [*Lewis the*] DAUPHIN, PANDULPH, *attendants*

KING PHILIP   So, by a roaring tempest on the flood,
        A whole armado of consorted sail
        Is scattered and disjoined from fellowship.
PANDULPH   Courage and comfort. All shall yet go well.
KING PHILIP   What can go well when we have run so ill?   5
        Are we not beaten? Is not Angiers lost?
        Arthur ta'en prisoner? Divers dear friends slain?
        And bloody England into England gone,
        O'erbearing interruption spite of France?
LEWIS   What he hath won, that hath he fortified.   10
        So hot a speed with such advice disposed,
        Such temperate order in so fierce a cause,
        Doth want example. Who hath read or heard
        Of any kindred action like to this?
KING PHILIP   Well could I bear that England had this praise,   15
        So we could find some pattern of our shame.
                Enter CONSTANCE [*with her hair down*]
        Look who comes here! A grave unto a soul,
        Holding th'eternal spirit against her will,
        In the vile prison of afflicted breath.
        I prithee, lady, go away with me.   20

Act 3, Scene 4   3.4] *Scæna Tertia.* F   0 SD PANDULPH] *Pandulpho* F   2 consorted] *This edn, conj. Keightley;* conuicted F; collected *Pope;* conjuncted *conj. Maxwell*   16 SD *with her hair down*] *This edn; her Hair dischevel'd / Capell*   19 vile] vilde F

Act 3, Scene 4

1–3 So...scattered If King Philip begins in mid
speech, comparing the attack of John's army to a
devastating storm at sea, 'So' should be taken as
'Even so' or 'Just so'. The image alludes to the
providential storm that scattered the Spanish
Armada.
   1 flood ocean.
   2 armado The common form of 'armada'.
   2 *consorted sail ships joined together in a
group. Compare R. Hakluyt, *Principal Navigations,*
I, ii, 222 (1598–1600): 'all these consorted to go to
Goa together'; and W. Dampier, *New Voyage
Round the World* (1967), I, 39: 'We sailed from
hence . . . we consorted because Captain Yanky . . .
was afraid the French would take away his bark.'
See supplementary note.
   3 fellowship With a pun on 'fellow ships'.
   5 run run our course; run away (punning on
Pandulph's 'go' meaning 'walk').

11 advice prudence, forethought.
13 Doth want example Is without precedent.
15 bear With a play on 'o'erbearing'.
16 pattern example to look to; i.e. our shame is
as unprecedented as his invincible speed and
efficiency.
16 SD *Enter* CONSTANCE That she should enter
right after 'pattern of our shame' is a silent
comment on France's perfidy. See A. Harbage,
'Choral juxtaposition in Shakespeare', in S.
Homan (ed.), *Shakespeare's 'More than Words Can
Witness'*, 1980, pp. 108–14.
17–19 grave . . . breath See supplementary
note.
19 vile prison . . . breath (1) the same vile prison
in which the breath is confined; that is, the body
(Mason), (2) the body of which the breath is an
attribute. Compare 'gap of breath' (32) and 'having
breath to cry' (37), implying that breath is a sign of
life.

CONSTANCE Lo, now! now see the issue of your peace!
KING PHILIP Patience, good lady, comfort, gentle Constance.
CONSTANCE No, I defy all counsel, all redress,
       But that which ends all counsel, true redress:
       Death! Death, O amiable, lovely Death,   25
       Thou odoriferous stench, sound rottenness,
       Arise forth from the couch of lasting night,
       Thou hate and terror to prosperity,
       And I will kiss thy detestable bones,
       And put my eyeballs in thy vaulty brows,   30
       And ring these fingers with thy household worms,
       And stop this gap of breath with fulsome dust,
       And be a carrion monster like thyself.
       Come, grin on me, and I will think thou smil'st,
       And buss thee as thy wife. Misery's love,   35
       O come to me!
KING PHILIP   O fair affliction, peace.
CONSTANCE No, no, I will not, having breath to cry.
       O that my tongue were in the thunder's mouth;
       Then with a passion would I shake the world,
       And rouse from sleep that fell anatomy   40

---

21 Lo, now!] *Capell;* Lo; now: F; Lo! now – *Honigmann*   25 Death! Death,] *Honigmann;* Death, death, F; Death; death, *Pope;* Death, death; *Theobald*

23 **defy** despise, reject (*OED* sv 5).

23 **redress** relief, assistance.

25–35 **Death . . . wife** This invocation of Death as a repulsive but seductive bridegroom has been compared to the violent rhetoric in *Rom.* 3.2.73–85, 4.3.30–57, and 4.5.35–40. Constance's vision is distinct because in her despair she loves the very gruesomeness of the figure she conjures.

25 **amiable, lovely** desirable and loving (see *Oth.* 3.4.59 and *Shr.* 3.2.123).

27 **couch . . . night** Compare Job 17.13: 'Though I hope, yet the grave shall be mine house, and I shall make my bed in the dark.'

27 **lasting** everlasting.

28 Whom prosperous men fear and hate; recalling Ecclus. 41.1: 'O Death, how bitter is the remembrance of thee to man . . . that hath prosperity.'

29 **detestable** Accented on the first and third syllables, as in *Rom.* 4.5.56, 5.3.45.

30 **vaulty** arched, cavernous.

31 **household** familiar, like regular inmates.

32 **gap of breath** mouth.

32 **fulsome** loathsome.

33 **carrion monster** One who feeds on rotting corpses, the 'dust' (32).

34 **grin** The fixed, empty grin on a skull or corpse. The pangs of death are said to make one grin in black despair (*2H6* 3.3.24).

35 **buss** kiss sensually. Coarse, wanton kissing 'is in keeping with the rest of Constance's exaggerated and hysterical language' (Wright). See Hibbard, pp. 140–1.

36 **affliction** afflicted one; the abstract for the concrete, as 'prosperity' (28).

37 **to cry** i.e. to cry 'war!' as she did in response to 'Lady Constance, peace!' (3.1.113–29).

38–9 **tongue . . . world** Seneca's Medea (423–5) cries out that 'This day shall do, shall do that whereof no day shall e'er be dumb. I will storm |*invadam*| the gods and shake |*quatiam*| the world |*cuncta*|.'

39 **passion** burst of anger.

40 **fell** fierce, cruel.

40 **anatomy** Death in the form of a skeleton or emaciated corpse. The figure is no longer the ghastly bridegroom but the fourth horseman of the Apocalypse, who arises at the thunderous call of the cherubim near Christ's throne (Rev. 6.1–8).

Which cannot hear a lady's feeble voice,
Which scorns a modern invocation.
PANDULPH Lady, you utter madness, and not sorrow.
CONSTANCE Thou art too holy to belie me so.
    I am not mad: this hair I tear is mine, 45
    My name is Constance, I was Geoffrey's wife,
    Young Arthur is my son, and he is lost.
    I am not mad. I would to God I were,
    For then 'tis like I should forget myself.
    O, if I could, what grief should I forget! 50
    Preach some philosophy to make me mad,
    And thou shalt be canonised, cardinal,
    For, being not mad, but sensible of grief,
    My reasonable part produces reason
    How I may be delivered of these woes, 55
    And teaches me to kill or hang myself.
    If I were mad, I should forget my son,
    Or madly think a babe of clouts were he.
    I am not mad; too well, too well I feel
    The different plague of each calamity. 60
KING PHILIP Bind up those tresses. O what love I note
    In the fair multitude of those her hairs,
    Where but by chance a silver drop hath fall'n.
    Even to that drop ten thousand wiry friends
    Do glue themselves in sociable grief, 65

42 modern] F; mother's *Heath* 44 too holy] *This edn, conj. Maxwell;* holy F; not holy F4; unholy *Steevens* 48 God] *Oxford;* heauen F 64 friends] *Rowe*[3]; fiends F

41 **lady's feeble voice** i.e. any human voice. Only the Lord through the voice of thunder can call the ultimate avengers forth at doomsday.
42 **modern** ordinary.
44 ***too holy** Since the line in F lacks a syllable, something may have been left out. I follow Maxwell's 'too holy', which keeps the scornful tone that 'not holy' or 'unholy' lose (p. 473).
48–50 **I would . . . forget** Compare *Lear* 4.6.281–2: 'Better I were distract, / So should my thoughts be sever'd from my griefs.'
49 **like** likely.
51 An inversion of the usual remedies for melancholy or despair: good counsel, comfort, and persuasion that cure heart-eating passions (Burton, *Anatomy of Melancholy* (ed. Holbrook Jackson, 1932), 2.2.6.2 and 3.4.2.6.
53 **sensible of** aware of or capable of feeling.

55 **be delivered of** (1) be delivered from, (2) give birth to; the second meaning is suggested by the sequence of images: bussing her husband Death (35), the babe of clouts as substitute for her son (58), and her fondness for grief as for her lost child (90 ff.) (Honigmann).
58 **babe of clouts** rag doll.
60 **different plague** distinct and increasingly painful affliction.
63 **silver drop** tear.
64 **wiry *friends** hairs, probably silver hairs by attraction to 'silver drop'. The associations of this conceit in the sonnet tradition are with fine golden threads and with the strings of a musical instrument, not with modern steel wires. See Sonnet 130.4.
65 **sociable** sympathetic.

Like true, inseparable, faithful loves,
Sticking together in calamity.
CONSTANCE To England, if you will.
KING PHILIP   Bind up your hairs.
CONSTANCE Yes, that I will; and wherefore will I do it?
I tore them from their bonds and cried aloud,   70
'O that these hands could so redeem my son,
As they have given these hairs their liberty!'
But now I envy at their liberty,
And will again commit them to their bonds,
Because my poor child is a prisoner.   75
And father cardinal, I have heard you say
That we shall see and know our friends in heaven.
If that be true, I shall see my boy again;
For since the birth of Cain, the first male child,
To him that did but yesterday suspire,   80
There was not such a gracious creature born,
But now will canker-sorrow eat my bud
And chase the native beauty from his cheek,
And he will look as hollow as a ghost,
As dim and meagre as an ague's fit,   85
And so he'll die; and rising so again,
When I shall meet him in the court of heaven
I shall not know him. Therefore never, never
Must I behold my pretty Arthur more.
PANDULPH You hold too heinous a respect of grief.   90
CONSTANCE He talks to me that never had a son.
KING PHILIP You are as fond of grief as of your child.
CONSTANCE Grief fills the room up of my absent child,

68 To ... will Constance responds to the implications of France's last speech – in effect, 'If you
truly sympathise with my plight, attack England.'
It is unnecessary to assume (with Wilson) that she
replies to France's invitation to 'go away with me'
(20) and that the intervening dialogue was added
later.

73 envy at begrudge.

79 Cain The birth of Cain is as far back as any
birth. But there must be more to the name here, as
in Northumberland's grief for Hotspur, *2H4*
1.1.157 ff.: 'let one spirit of the first-born Cain /
Reign in all bosoms', i.e. let universal fratricide
prevail. If so, Constance implies that Arthur will
die at the hand of kinsmen, re-enacting the first
murder on earth.

80 suspire draw his (first) breath.
81 gracious full of graces.
82–3 canker-sorrow ... beauty 'The canker
soonest eats the fairest rose' (Dent c56).
84 hollow emaciated.
88 know recognise. See supplementary note.
90 heinous grave, severe; sinful, because in its
excess it cuts a person off from Christian comfort.
90 respect regard.
91 A scornful assertion of a parent's privilege to
grieve excessively, for a celibate priest cannot
imagine Constance's feelings. This form of the
familiar saying probably originated with Shakespeare; compare *3H6* 5.5.63 and *Mac.* 4.3.216,
and see Tilley C341, *ODEP* 120b.
93 room vacant spot.

Lies in his bed, walks up and down with me,
Puts on his pretty looks, repeats his words,   95
Remembers me of all his gracious parts,
Stuffs out his vacant garments with his form.
Then have I reason to be fond of grief?
Fare you well; had you such a loss as I,
I could give better comfort than you do.   100
I will not keep this form upon my head, [*Tears her hair*]
When there is such disorder in my wit.
O Lord! my boy, my Arthur, my fair son!
My life, my joy, my food, my all the world!
My widow-comfort, and my sorrows' cure!   *Exit*   105
KING PHILIP   I fear some outrage, and I'll follow her.   *Exit*
LEWIS   There's nothing in this world can make me joy,
Life is as tedious as a twice-told tale,
Vexing the dull ear of a drowsy man;
And bitter shame hath spoiled the sweet world's taste,   110
That it yields nought but shame and bitterness.
PANDULPH   Before the curing of a strong disease,
Even in the instant of repair and health,
The fit is strongest. Evils that take leave,
On their departure most of all show evil.   115
What have you lost by losing of this day?
LEWIS   All days of glory, joy, and happiness.
PANDULPH   If you had won it, certainly you had.
No, no; when Fortune means to men most good,
She looks upon them with a threat'ning eye.   120
'Tis strange to think how much King John hath lost

---

101 SD *Tears her hair*] Kittredge; *Tearing off her head-cloaths* / Pope; *Throwing away her head-dress* / Capell
110 world's] Pope; *words* F; *word's* Malone   114–15 leave, . . . departure] Capell; *leaue . . . departure,* F; *leave, . . .*
departure, F4

96 **Remembers** Reminds.
97 **Stuffs out** Fills out as with padding.
101 **this form** the orderly arrangement of my
hair.
101 SD *Tears her hair* As Constance entered
with her hair down, so she must leave the stage with
that emblem of inner disorder.
106 **some outrage** violence, fury, implying
suicide. See 56.
108 Compare 'Tales twice told [are] ungrateful'
(Dent T53.1).
110 **bitter shame** shame for the loss of glory
(117), not for what has happened to Constance.

110 ***world's** See supplementary note.
111 **That** In that.
113 **in the instant** at the very moment.
113 **repair** recovery, restoration.
114 **fit** crisis of an illness.
114–15 **Evils . . . evil** Pandulph seems to refer to
exorcism of evil, but the passage may derive from
a saying, perhaps related to 'When bale [= need] is
highest boot [= help] is nighest' (Tilley B59,
ODEP 28a).
119–20 **when . . . eye** Reversing the proverb
'When Fortune most doth smile, then will she
frown' (Dent F598.1).

In this which he accounts so clearly won.
Are not you grieved that Arthur is his prisoner?
LEWIS   As heartily as he is glad he hath him.
PANDULPH Your mind is all as youthful as your blood.   125
    Now hear me speak with a prophetic spirit,
    For even the breath of what I mean to speak
    Shall blow each dust, each straw, each little rub
    Out of the path which shall directly lead
    Thy foot to England's throne. And therefore mark: 130
    John hath seized Arthur, and it cannot be
    That whiles warm life plays in that infant's veins,
    The misplaced John should entertain an hour,
    One minute, nay, one quiet breath of rest.
    A sceptre snatched with an unruly hand,   135
    Must be as boist'rously maintained as gained,
    And he that stands upon a slipp'ry place,
    Makes nice of no vile hold to stay him up.
    That John may stand, then Arthur needs must fall;
    So be it, for it cannot be but so.   140
LEWIS   But what shall I gain by young Arthur's fall?
PANDULPH You, in the right of Lady Blanche your wife,
    May then make all the claim that Arthur did.
LEWIS   And lose it, life and all, as Arthur did.
PANDULPH How green you are and fresh in this old world!   145
    John lays you plots; the times conspire with you,
    For he that steeps his safety in true blood,
    Shall find but bloody safety, and untrue.
    This act so evilly borne shall cool the hearts
    Of all his people and freeze up their zeal   150
    That none so small advantage shall step forth

---

138 vile] vilde F   146 you plots] F; your plots *conj. Malone*   149 borne] F; born F3

127 **breath** whisper, utterance.

128 **dust** speck of dust.

128 **rub** obstacle or irregularity in the ground (from the game of bowls). Compare Holinshed, VI, 303: 'Whereby appeareth how dangerous it is to be a rub, when a king is disposed to sweep an alley'.

133 **misplaced** in the wrong place, i.e. usurping.

135–6 **sceptre . . . gained** See supplementary note.

136 **boist'rously** violently.

137 **slipp'ry place** Recalling Ps. 73.18: 'Surely thou hast set [the wicked] in slippery places, and castest them down into desolation.'

138 **Makes nice of** Is fastidious about.

140 **So be it** Amen. Pandulph pretends not to be responsible. He merely prophesies.

142 **right of Lady Blanche** Arthur's claim passed to his sister Eleanor, but neither *John* nor *TR* mentions her.

146 **lays you plots** devises plans for you.

149 **borne** carried out; punning on 'born', i.e. so evilly conceived.

151 **advantage** favourable opportunity.

To check his reign but they will cherish it;
No natural exhalation in the sky,
No scope of nature, no distempered day,
No common wind, no customèd event,   155
But they will pluck away his natural cause
And call them meteors, prodigies, and signs,
Abortives, presages, and tongues of heaven,
Plainly denouncing vengeance upon John.
LEWIS May be he will not touch young Arthur's life,   160
But hold himself safe in his prisonment.
PANDULPH O sir, when he shall hear of your approach,
If that young Arthur be not gone already,
Even at that news he dies, and then the hearts
Of all his people shall revolt from him,   165
And kiss the lips of unacquainted change,
And pick strong matter of revolt and wrath
Out of the bloody fingers' ends of John.
Methinks I see this hurly all on foot;
And O, what better matter breeds for you   170
Than I have named. The bastard Falconbridge
Is now in England ransacking the church,
Offending charity. If but a dozen French
Were there in arms, they would be as a call
To train ten thousand English to their side,   175
Or as a little snow, tumbled about,
Anon becomes a mountain. O noble Dauphin,

---

154 scope] F; scape *Pope*

---

152 check restrain (see 2.1.123).
152 reign sovereignty; with a pun on 'rein'.
152 it Referring to 'advantage'.
153 exhalation fiery vapour or meteor.
154 *scope of nature liberty or licence within natural causes, a natural irregularity (Wilson). Compare *MM* 1.2.127–8: 'So every scope by the immoderate use / Turns to restraint' (*OED* Scope *sb* 7a and 7b). Pope emended to 'scape', meaning a mistake (*OED* Scape *sb*¹ 3), the approximate meaning whether spelled 'scape' or 'scope'.
154 distempered stormy.
156 his its.
157 meteors Any luminous appearances in the heavens.
158 Abortives Abnormalities, monstrous births.
161 hold consider.
167–8 pick . . . John John's crimes will be as

evident as if on his bloody fingers' ends (Tilley F244).
167 strong matter (1) powerful evidence (*OED* Strong *adj* 16b), (2) evil-smelling with pus or other corrupt matter in a wound.
168 bloody fingers' ends Compare *Mac.* 5.2.16–17: 'Now does he feel / His secret murders sticking on his hands.'
169 hurly tumult.
173 Offending charity Sinning against the law of love.
174 call decoy or call-bird; call-to-arms.
175 train entice. The implications of deception here and in Pandulph's previous speech prepare for the Dauphin's bad faith and the Melun episode (5.4).
176–7 little . . . mountain The earliest example of 'Like a snowball, that rolling becomes bigger' (Tilley s595).

Go with me to the king. 'Tis wonderful
What may be wrought out of their discontent
Now that their souls are topful of offence.   180
For England go; I will whet on the king.
LEWIS Strong reasons makes strange actions. Let us go;
If you say ay, the king will not say no.

Exeunt

4.1 [*A Prison.*] *Enter* HUBERT *and* EXECUTIONERS [*with irons and rope*]

HUBERT Heat me these irons hot, and look thou stand
Within the arras. When I strike my foot
Upon the bosom of the ground, rush forth
And bind the boy which you shall find with me
Fast to the chair. Be heedful; hence, and watch.   5
EXECUTIONER I hope your warrant will bear out the deed.
HUBERT Uncleanly scruples! Fear not you; look to't.
                              [*Executioners withdraw*]
Young lad, come forth; I have to say with you.

Enter ARTHUR

ARTHUR Good morrow, Hubert.
HUBERT   Good morrow, little prince.
ARTHUR As little prince, having so great a title   10
To be more prince, as may be. You are sad.
HUBERT Indeed I have been merrier.
ARTHUR   Mercy on me!
Methinks nobody should be sad but I:
Yet I remember, when I was in France,

180 offence.] *Knight;* offence, F 182 makes] F; make *Capell* 182 strange] F; strong F2 **Act 4, Scene 1**
4.1] *Actus Quartus, Scæna prima.* F 7 scruples!] *Rowe³;* scruples, F4; scruples F 7 SD *Executioners withdraw*]
Honigmann; not in F; *Exeunt Officers / Capell*

180 offence the people's displeasure at John's
crimes; John's crimes themselves.
182 *strange unusual. Editors often emend after
F2's 'strong', but if the compositor of F read the
first 'strong' in the line correctly, he is not likely to
have mistaken the second (Sisson).

Act 4, Scene 1
0 SD *A Prison* The Tower of London, presumably. Although Holinshed placed the prison in
Falaise, a seat of the dukes of Normandy, Shakespeare implies that Arthur is no longer in France
(see **14** below). His disguise as a ship-boy (4.3.4)

suggests the vicinity of the docks, where he can pass
unnoticed, and the prison is apparently on the main
road to Bury St Edmunds (4.3.11 and 20).
0 SD *Executioners* 'tormentors' in Holinshed
(II, 286), called 'attendants' in *TR*.
0 SD *irons* Probably instruments used for
cauterising or branding. See Stage History, pp.
17–19 above.
7 Uncleanly Morally impure, improper.
9 Good morrow Good morning.
10–11 As . . . be Considering my right to be a
greater prince, I am as little a one as possible.

Young gentlemen would be as sad as night,   15
Only for wantonness. By my christendom,
So I were out of prison and kept sheep,
I should be as merry as the day is long,
And so I would be here but that I doubt
My uncle practises more harm to me.   20
He is afraid of me, and I of him.
Is it my fault that I was Geoffrey's son?
No, indeed, is't not, and I would to God
I were your son, so you would love me, Hubert.

HUBERT [*Aside*] If I talk to him with his innocent prate   25
He will awake my mercy, which lies dead;
Therefore I will be sudden, and dispatch.

ARTHUR Are you sick, Hubert? You look pale today.
In sooth, I would you were a little sick,
That I might sit all night and watch with you.   30
I warrant I love you more than you do me.

HUBERT [*Aside*] His words do take possession of my bosom. –
Read here, young Arthur. [*Shows the warrant*]
          [*Aside*]   How now, foolish rheum?
Turning dispiteous torture out of door?
I must be brief, lest resolution drop   35
Out of mine eyes in tender womanish tears. –
Can you not read it? Is it not fair writ?

ARTHUR Too fairly, Hubert, for so foul effect:
Must you with hot irons burn out both mine eyes?

HUBERT Young boy, I must.

ARTHUR   And will you?

---

18 be as] F; be *Pope*   23 indeed] F2; in deede F   23 is't] F; it's F2   23 God] *Oxford;* heauen F   25 SD]
Rowe; not in F   29 In sooth] *Rowe;* Insooth F   32 SD *aside*] *Capell; not in* F   33 SD.1 *Shows the warrant*]
Not in F; *showing a paper* / *Rowe³*   33 SD.2 *Aside*] *Rowe³; not in* F   35 lest] F4; least F   38 effect:] *Capell;*
effect, F; effect. *Rowe*

15–16 Young . . . wantonness i.e. they affected
the melancholy humour; wantonness means
'whim'.
16 By my christendom By my christening;
hence, 'by my faith as a Christian'.
17 So If.
19 doubt fear.
20 practises plots.
27 sudden swift and ruthless. Compare *R3*
1.3.345–8: 'be sudden in the execution . . . [lest
Clarence] move your hearts to pity'.

27 dispatch do away with him, kill.
29 sooth truth.
31–2 warrant . . . bosom See p. 51 above.
33 rheum tears. Probably a pun on 'room':
Arthur's words take possession of all the room in
Hubert's bosom, so torture is turned out of door
(Smallwood).
35 brief quick.
37 fair clearly.
38 effect purpose.
39 See supplementary note.

HUBERT	And I will.	40

ARTHUR Have you the heart? When your head did but ache,
       I knit my handkercher about your brows
       (The best I had, a princess wrought it me)
       And I did never ask it you again;
       And with my hand at midnight held your head;   45
       And like the watchful minutes to the hour,
       Still and anon cheered up the heavy time,
       Saying, 'What lack you?' and 'Where lies your grief?'
       Or 'What good love may I perform for you?'
       Many a poor man's son would have lien still,   50
       And ne'er have spoke a loving word to you;
       But you at your sick-service had a prince.
       Nay, you may think my love was crafty love,
       And call it cunning. Do, and if you will.
       If heaven be pleased that you must use me ill,   55
       Why then you must. Will you put out mine eyes?
       These eyes that never did nor never shall
       So much as frown on you?
HUBERT   I have sworn to do it,
       And with hot irons must I burn them out.
ARTHUR Ah, none but in this iron age would do it.   60
       The iron of itself, though heat red-hot,
       Approaching near these eyes, would drink my tears

---

46 minutes] *Pope;* minutes, F   **58** you] *Rowe³;* you. F

40 will you? (1) are you going to? (2) do you wish to?

42 handkercher The common pronunciation of 'handkerchief'.

43 wrought worked, embroidered.

46 like . . . hour vigilant like the minutes that number the hour. The epithet 'watchful' is transferred from Arthur to the 'minutes' that his dear questions seemed to tick off, to pass the otherwise slow time. Compare *R2* 5.5.50–2: 'For now hath time made me his numb'ring clock. / My thoughts are minutes, and with sighs they jar / Their watches on unto mine eyes.'

47 Still and anon Ever and anon, constantly.

48 grief pain.

49 good love act of kindness.

50 lien lain (two syllables). See *Ham.* Q2 5.1.173.

52 your sick-service your service in sickness; as at 4.2.191 where 'fearful action' means the gesture or action of fear (Wright).

53 crafty feigned. Compare *2H4* Induction 37: 'crafty-sick'.

54 and if if.

55–6 If . . . must Proverbial (Tilley M1331).

60 iron age The cruel age of treachery and greed, when all proper affection or compassion (*pietas*) lay vanquished. Desire for gold and other wealth made friend unsafe from friend (Ovid, *Metamorphoses*, 1, 127–50).

61–6 The iron . . . eye 'The personification of iron and fire, here and in lines 103–20, brings together the imagery of fire and heat with constant personifications of the play. Arthur's elaborate conceit, becoming more elaborate with every blunt response from Hubert (71, 74, 90, 104, 111), shows words for once succeeding against brutality and power' (Smallwood).

61 of itself according to its own nature.

61 heat heated.

And quench his fiery indignation
Even in the matter of mine innocence;
Nay, after that, consume away in rust   65
But for containing fire to harm mine eye.
Are you more stubborn-hard than hammered iron?
And if an angel should have come to me
And told me Hubert should put out mine eyes,
I would not have believed him – no tongue but Hubert's.   70

HUBERT   [*Stamps*] Come forth.

    [*Executioners come forward with rope, irons, etc.*]
             Do as I bid you do.

ARTHUR   O save me, Hubert, save me! My eyes are out
Even with the fierce looks of these bloody men.

HUBERT   Give me the iron, I say, and bind him here.

ARTHUR   Alas, what need you be so boist'rous-rough?   75
I will not struggle, I will stand stone-still.
For God's sake, Hubert, let me not be bound!
Nay hear me, Hubert; drive these men away,
And I will sit as quiet as a lamb.
I will not stir nor wince nor speak a word   80
Nor look upon the iron angerly.
Thrust but these men away, and I'll forgive you,
Whatever torment you do put me to.

HUBERT   Go stand within; let me alone with him.

---

63 his] *Capell;* this F; their *Rowe;* its *Rowe*3   64 matter] F; water *Dyce*2, *conj. Williams*   66 eye] F; eyes *Dyce*2
67 stubborn-hard] *Theobald*2; *no hyphen in* F   70 him – no tongue but Hubert's] *Dyce;* him: no tongue but
Huberts F; a tongue but Hubert's *Pope*   71 SD.1 *stamps*] *Pope (subst.); not in* F   71 SD.2 *Executioners . . . etc.*]
Capell; not in F   75 boist'rous-rough] *Theobald; no hyphen in* F   76 stone-still] *Rowe; no hyphen in* F   77 God's]
Oxford; heauen F   80 wince] F2; winch F

63 his its. The Folio's reading 'this' has been
defended as meaning 'the indignation *thus* produced by the iron being made red-hot for such an
inhuman purpose' (Malone), but Arthur would
scarcely stipulate 'this' before he sees the hot irons.
The error may have occurred by attraction to 'this
iron age' and 'these eyes'.

63 fiery indignation Compare 2.1.212 'iron
indignation', 3.1.340 'inflaming wrath', and
4.2.103 'burn in indignation'. Hot irons symbolise
John's violent emotions.

64 matter . . . innocence tears. 'Matter' denotes
the fluid substances of the body. Compare H.
Constable, *Diana, Poems,* ed. Grundy, 1960, 1.3.11:
'O that the matter of mine eye had might / To
quench the flames that from thine eye do come'

('matter' is the reading in the Todd MS.; the 1592
edn has 'water').

66 But for containing Only because it contains.

67 hammered iron wrought iron.

70 no . . . Hubert's I would have believed no
tongue but Hubert's.

72 See illustration 6, p. 19 above, for Fuseli's
depiction of this moment.

75 boist'rous violently, fiercely. Pandulph's
prophecy of Arthur's death includes the word
(3.4.136).

76–9 stone-still . . . lamb The two proverbial
phrases strike a simple note in Arthur's eloquence
(Whiting s772a, Tilley l.34).

81 angerly angrily; another childish touch.

84 Go stand within i.e. 'go into the next room',
not behind the arras as in 2 above.

EXECUTIONER I am best pleased to be from such a deed.   85

[Exeunt Executioners]

ARTHUR Alas, I then have chid away my friend!
He hath a stern look but a gentle heart.
Let him come back, that his compassion may
Give life to yours.

HUBERT   Come, boy, prepare yourself.

ARTHUR Is there no remedy?

HUBERT   None but to lose your eyes.   90

ARTHUR O God, that there were but a mote in yours,
A grain, a dust, a gnat, a wandering hair,
Any annoyance in that precious sense;
Then feeling what small things are boist'rous there,
Your vile intent must needs seem horrible.   95

HUBERT Is this your promise? Go to, hold your tongue.

ARTHUR Hubert, the utterance of a brace of tongues
Must needs want pleading for a pair of eyes.
Let me not hold my tongue, let me not, Hubert,
Or Hubert, if you will, cut out my tongue,   100
So I may keep mine eyes. O spare mine eyes,
Though to no use but still to look on you.
Lo, by my troth, the instrument is cold
And would not harm me.

HUBERT   I can heat it, boy.

ARTHUR No, in good sooth. The fire is dead with grief,   105
Being create for comfort, to be used

---

85 SD *Exeunt Executioners*] Pope (*subst.*); not in F 91 God] *Oxford;* heauen F 91 mote] *Steevens³, conj. Upton;*
moth F 95 vile] vilde F 100 will,] *Rowe;* will F

85 Shakespeare may recall Holinshed's account, that some of those appointed to carry out the blinding 'rather forsook their prince and country than they would consent to obey the King's authority' (Smallwood).

91–5 Arthur inverts the figure of the mote and the beam (Luke 6.41–2, Matt. 7.3–5): would that Hubert had a mote in his eye so he could imagine the pain of the iron in Arthur's eyes. Christ's lesson about hypocrisy was often turned to a lesson in charity. Compare Hugh Latimer (*Works*, ed. G. E. Corrie, 1844–5, 11, 314): 'Learn from your own beams to make allowance for your neighbour's motes.'

91 mote 'moth' (F) and 'mote' were interchangeable.

98 want pleading not plead enough.

99 'May I never [or do not cause me to] hold my tongue', and as repeated 'Do not hinder me from pleading my case, Hubert.' For the different meanings see *OED* Let v¹ 13, 14, v² 2, and Sonnet 116.1.

102 still always.

102 to look on you Possibly alluding to Hubert's ugliness. See 4.2.221.

104 would not would not be able to; does not wish to.

106 create created.

106–7 create . . . extremes made for pleasure but used instead to inflict extreme pain on an innocent person (with a play on *in extremis*).

In undeserved extremes. See else yourself,
There is no malice in this burning coal;
The breath of heaven hath blown his spirit out
And strewed repentant ashes on his head.   110
HUBERT But with my breath I can revive it, boy.
ARTHUR And if you do, you will but make it blush
And glow with shame of your proceedings, Hubert.
Nay, it perchance will sparkle in your eyes,
And like a dog that is compelled to fight,   115
Snatch at his master that doth tarre him on.
All things that you should use to do me wrong
Deny their office. Only you do lack
That mercy which fierce fire and iron extends,
Creatures of note for mercy-lacking uses.   120
HUBERT Well see to live; I will not touch thine eye,
For all the treasure that thine uncle owes.
Yet am I sworn, and I did purpose, boy,
With this same very iron to burn them out.
ARTHUR O now you look like Hubert. All this while   125
You were disguisèd.
HUBERT   Peace, no more. Adieu.
Your uncle must not know but you are dead.
I'll fill these dogged spies with false reports,
And, pretty child, sleep doubtless and secure
That Hubert, for the wealth of all the world,   130
Will not offend thee.
ARTHUR   O God! I thank you, Hubert.

---

120 mercy-lacking] *Pope; mercy, lacking* F; *mercy lacking Honigmann* 131 God] *Oxford; heaven* F

107 See else yourself If you do not believe me see for yourself.

114 sparkle throw out sparks; implying the sparkle of eyes flashing with anger (*OED* sv *v* 2c, 7).

115–16 And . . . on A proverb: 'A man may cause his own dog to bite him' (Tilley M258).

116 tarre urge.

118 Deny their office Renounce their natural function; see *OED* Office *sb* 3. Compare *Cor.* 5.3.31–3: 'my young boy / Hath an aspect of intercession, which / Great Nature cries, "Deny not"'.

119–20 fire . . . uses fire and iron created notably for uses other than mercy. Two proverbs mingled: 'Fire and water have no mercy' (Tilley F254) and 'A heart of iron would melt' (Whiting H277).

121 see to live take care how to live; an inversion of Shakespeare's usual phrase – 'that ever I should live to see . . .' (*Rom.* 3.2.63). Also 'Live and look', i.e. live and have the use of your faculties, as in *Piers Plowman*, ed. Skeat, A.ix.49.

122 owes possesses, owns.

127 you are dead See supplementary note to 4.1.39.

128 dogged malicious. The word is an index of Hubert's change of mind: earlier one executioner seemed overscrupulous; now both men are dangerous spies.

129 doubtless and secure free from fear and worry.

131 offend harm.

HUBERT Silence, no more. Go closely in with me.
        Much danger do I undergo for thee.

                                                    Exeunt

4.2 *Enter* [KING] JOHN [*in pomp, crowned*], PEMBROKE, SALISBURY,
[BIGOT,] *and other lords.* [KING *sits on the throne*]

KING JOHN Here once again we sit, once again crowned
        And looked upon, I hope, with cheerful eyes.
PEMBROKE This 'once again', but that your highness pleased,
        Was once superfluous: you were crowned before,
        And that high royalty was ne'er plucked off,   5
        The faiths of men ne'er stainèd with revolt;
        Fresh expectation troubled not the land
        With any longed-for change or better state.
SALISBURY Therefore, to be possessed with double pomp,
        To guard a title that was rich before,   10
        To gild refinèd gold, to paint the lily,
        To throw a perfume on the violet,
        To smooth the ice or add another hue
        Unto the rainbow, or with taper-light
        To seek the beauteous eye of heaven to garnish,   15
        Is wasteful and ridiculous excess.
PEMBROKE But that your royal pleasure must be done,
        This act is an an ancient tale new told,
        And, in the last repeating, troublesome,
        Being urgèd at a time unseasonable.   20

Act 4, Scene 2   4.2] *Scena Secunda.* F   1 once again crowned] F3; once against crown'd F; crown'd once again *Pope*   8 longed-for change] F4; long'd-for-change F

132 **closely** secretly.

Act 4, Scene 2
1 again crowned The direction in *TR* (8.84 SD) may reflect the business here: '*Enter the Nobles [and Bishops] and crown King* John, *and then cry* "God save the King."' See supplementary note.

4 once on one occasion, i.e. once too often; the first of many insinuations in the lords' sugared language.

7 Fresh expectation Active anticipation; 'expectations' = 'demands' is a nuance not recorded until the mid seventeenth century (*OED* Expectation 3b).

10 To guard (1) To trim (a garment) with braid, lace, velvet, etc., (2) To protect.

10–16 guard . . . excess Salisbury parodies John's 'double pomp'.

14–15 taper-light . . . garnish From the saying 'To set forth the sun with a candle' or 'To light a candle at noonday' (Tilley s988).

15 the . . . eye of heaven The watchful eye which John fears, 3.3.52.

18–20 tale . . . unseasonable Compare Ecclus. 22.6: 'A tale out of time is as music in mourning: but wisdom knoweth the seasons of correction and doctrine.'

19 troublesome vexatious; inclined to cause a disturbance in the realm.

20 unseasonable Five syllables with increased stress on the fourth, as in *R2* 3.2.106 and *The Rape of Lucrece* 581.

SALISBURY In this the antique and well-noted face
   Of plain old form is much disfigurèd,
   And like a shifted wind unto a sail,
   It makes the course of thoughts to fetch about,
   Startles and frights consideration,   25
   Makes sound opinion sick and truth suspected
   For putting on so new a fashioned robe.
PEMBROKE When workmen strive to do better than well,
   They do confound their skill in covetousness,
   And oftentimes excusing of a fault   30
   Doth make the fault the worser by th'excuse.
   As patches set upon a little breach
   Discredit more in hiding of the fault
   Than did the fault before it was so patched.
SALISBURY To this effect, before you were new crowned   35
   We breathed our counsel; but it pleased your highness
   To overbear it, and we are all well pleased,
   Since all and every part of what we would
   Doth make a stand at what your highness will.
KING JOHN Some reasons of this double coronation   40
   I have possessed you with, and think them strong.
   And more, more strong, when lesser is my fear,
   I shall indue you with. Meantime, but ask
   What you would have reformed that is not well,

---

21 antique] *Pope;* Anticke F 21 well-noted] *Pope; no hyphen in* F 26 suspected] F; suspect *conj. anon in Cam.*
29 covetousness] F; covetize *conj. Capell* 31 worser] *Smallwood, conj. Maxwell;* worse F 42 when lesser] *Tyrwhitt in Steevens²;* then lesser F; then less F2; the less that *Rowe³;* the lesser *Pope;* than lesser *Collier*

21 **antique** Accent on the first syllable, and a play on the meaning 'antic', anticipating 'dis-figurèd' in the next line.
 21 **well-noted** familiar.
 22 **old form** customary behaviour.
 24 **to fetch about** to veer round or tack.
 25 **consideration** reflection (upon the motive for this coronation or upon the legitimacy of your title).
 27 **so new . . . robe** a robe of so new a fashion, i.e. against custom.
 28–31 **strive . . . excuse** i.e. leave well enough alone.
 29 **covetousness** excessive eagerness, desire.
 30–1 **excusing . . . excuse** The earliest recorded use in English of the saying 'to excuse is to accuse', from Jerome, 'Dum excusare credis, accusas' (*ODEP* 234a).

30, 31, 33, 34 **fault** The repetition implies John's defective right to the crown.
 31 *****worser** See supplementary note.
 32–4 **patches . . . patched** Compare Matt. 9.16: 'no man pieceth an old garment with a piece of new cloth: for that should fill it up, taketh away from the garment, and the breach is worse'.
 36 **breathed** spoke.
 37 **overbear** overrule.
 38–9 **all . . . will** 'all our hopes and wishes go no further than your royal will allows' (Smallwood).
 39 **make a stand** (1) stop short, pause, as after speaking or fighting, (2) hold our ground, as against an opponent.
 41 **possessed you with** informed you of.
 42 *****when lesser** See supplementary note.
 43 **indue** furnish. The context of the clothes metaphors (27, 32–4) suggests the root meaning – to put on clothing, cover.

And well shall you perceive how willingly   45
I will both hear and grant you your requests.
PEMBROKE Then I – as one that am the tongue of these
To sound the purposes of all their hearts,
Both for myself and them, but chief of all,
Your safety, for the which myself and them   50
Bend their best studies – heartily request
Th'enfranchisement of Arthur, whose restraint
Doth move the murmuring lips of discontent
To break into this dangerous argument:
If what in rest you have in right you hold,   55
Why then your fears – which, as they say, attend
The steps of wrong – should move you to mew up
Your tender kinsman and to choke his days
With barbarous ignorance and deny his youth
The rich advantage of good exercise?   60
That the time's enemies may not have this
To grace occasions, let it be our suit
That you have bid us ask, his liberty,
Which for our goods we do no further ask
Than whereupon our weal, on you depending,   65
Counts it your weal he have his liberty.

Enter HUBERT

50 safety,| *Johnson;* safety: F 50 them| F; they *Pope* 60 exercise?| *Pope;* exercise, F 63 ask,| *Rowe³;* aske F
64–5 ask / Than| *Collier;* aske, / Then, F; aske, / Than, F2 66 weal| *Rowe;* weale: F 66 SD| *Collier; not in* F;
Taking him apart / Capell

46 **requests** See supplementary note.

48 **sound** proclaim; with a suggestion of ringing a bell or sounding a trumpet.

48 **purposes** intentions; proposals for discussion.

50 **Your safety** i.e. For your safety.

50 **them** they; 'myself and them' repeats that phrase from 49 and uses the accusative by attraction to 'for'.

51 **Bend . . . studies** Direct their (or our) best efforts.

52 **enfranchisement** release from prison.

55 **rest** quiet possession. See supplementary note.

56–60 **Why . . . exercise** The argument or enquiry takes the form of an indirect question. The people ask, says Pembroke, why your fears should

move you to mew up your tender kinsman, etc. (Wright).

56–7 **fears . . . wrong** 'A guilty conscience is never without fear' (Tilley c606).

57 **mew up** confine; as in a mew or coop for hawks.

60 **exercise** training fit for a prince.

61–2 **time's . . . occasions** discontented people who are opposed to the present state of affairs may not seize this as a pretext for attack.

62–3 *let . . . ask, his liberty** let the concession, which you have bid us ask for, be Arthur's liberty (Smallwood).

64 **goods** things advantageous to us.

65–6 **our weal . . . your weal . . . his liberty** the true reciprocity of king and subject, whereby our welfare depends on yours and yours on Arthur's freedom, which makes you and us secure.

KING JOHN Let it be so. I do commit his youth
 To your direction. – Hubert, what news with you?
 [*Hubert whispers to the King*]
PEMBROKE This is the man should do the bloody deed.
 He showed his warrant to a friend of mine.   70
 The image of a wicked heinous fault
 Lives in his eye; that close aspect of his
 Doth show the mood of a much troubled breast,
 And I do fearfully believe 'tis done
 What we so feared he had a charge to do.   75
SALISBURY The colour of the king doth come and go
 Between his purpose and his conscience,
 Like heralds 'twixt two dreadful battles set.
 His passion is so ripe it needs must break.
PEMBROKE And when it breaks, I fear will issue thence   80
 The foul corruption of a sweet child's death.
KING JOHN [*Coming forward*] We cannot hold mortality's strong hand.
 Good lords, although my will to give is living,
 The suit which you demand is gone and dead.
 He tells us Arthur is deceased tonight.   85
SALISBURY Indeed we feared his sickness was past cure.
PEMBROKE Indeed we heard how near his death he was,
 Before the child himself felt he was sick.
 This must be answered either here or hence.
KING JOHN Why do you bend such solemn brows on me?   90
 Think you I bear the shears of destiny?

73 Doth] *Dyce;* Do F; Does F4   78 set] F; sent *Theobald*

69 should . . . deed i.e. because Hubert is ugly.
See 221–5, 257, 263–6, and 4.3.123. In John
Barton's production, Hubert had a hideous birthmark on his face.
71–3 See 3.3.48–53 and compare Sallust, *War
with Jugurtha* (Loeb), 113.3: 'the conflict in his
mind was reflected in his expression and eyes,
which though he was silent, revealed the secrets of
his heart' (*occulta pectoris patefecisse*).
72 close aspect furtive look. Stress on the
second syllable of 'aspect'.
73 *Doth I follow Dyce's emendation because
the assonance of 'Do show the mood' is un-
euphonious. However, in the fifteenth and sixteenth
centuries 'Do' was sometimes used with the third-
person singular indicative, as in *MND* 3.2.99 Q2:
'I'll charm his eyes against she do appear.'
77 his purpose . . . conscience his evil design

and his conscience that reproaches him for it
(Wright).
78 'twixt . . . set appointed to confer between two
armies readied for battle.
79–81 The metaphor of a bursting abscess often
suggested hatred and civil disorder. See supplementary note.
81 corruption pus.
84 demand urge.
84 gone and dead hopeless and of no effect, as
in a 'gone case'; 'dead and gone' was already a
cliché.
85 tonight last night (*OED* sv 3).
89 answered . . . hence Compare 'die here and
live hence', 5.4.29.
90 bend . . . brows scowl.
91 shears of destiny With which Atropos, one
of the three Fates, cuts the thread of life.

Have I commandment on the pulse of life?
SALISBURY It is apparent foul-play, and 'tis shame
That greatness should so grossly offer it.
    So thrive it in your game! and so farewell.   95
PEMBROKE Stay yet, Lord Salisbury. I'll go with thee
And find th'inheritance of this poor child,
His little kingdom of a forcèd grave.
That blood which owed the breadth of all this isle,
Three foot of it doth hold; bad world the while!   100
This must not be thus borne, this will break out
To all our sorrows, and ere long, I doubt.
                             Exeunt [lords]

KING JOHN They burn in indignation. I repent.
There is no sure foundation set on blood,
No certain life achieved by others' death.   105

               Enter MESSENGER

A fearful eye thou hast. Where is that blood
That I have seen inhabit in those cheeks?
So foul a sky clears not without a storm,
Pour down thy weather: how goes all in France?
MESSENGER From France to England. Never such a power   110
For any foreign preparation
Was levied in the body of a land.
The copy of your speed is learned by them,

---

95 game!] *Capell;* game, F   105 SD] *Johnson; following 103* F   110 England. Never] *Johnson, conj. Roderick;* England, neuer F

92 **commandment on** command over.
93 **apparent** evident, manifest.
94 **grossly offer** plainly or clumsily attempt.
95 **So . . . game** May you suffer accordingly; i.e. as you played foul, so may you fare the worse in your other intrigues.
97–8 **inheritance . . . little kingdom** Imlying that, despite Arthur's right to a great inheritance, by murder he rules only a little grave.
98 **forcèd** violently brought about; involuntary.
99–100 **That . . . hold** See supplementary note.
99 **owed** possessed.
100 **the while** these times. Compare *1H4* 2.4.132: 'God help the while! a bad world, I say.'
101 **break out** See 79–81 n.
102 **doubt** fear.

104–5 **no . . . death** Fulfilling Pandulph's prediction, 3.4.147–8.
106 **fearful** expressing fear; causing fear in others.
107 **inhabit** abide.
109 **weather** tempest.
110 **From . . . England** i.e. All in France goes from France to England.
110 **power** army.
111 **preparation** Five syllables; 'foreign preparation' suggests an expeditionary force which will invade a foreign land (*OED* sv *sb* 3).
112 **the body of a land** a nation, the body politic.
113 They have learned to imitate the speed that you showed in France. See 2.1.60 n.
113 **copy** model or pattern (for emulation).

For when you should be told they do prepare,
The tidings comes that they are all arrived.   115
KING JOHN O, where hath our intelligence been drunk?
Where hath it slept? Where is my mother's care?
That such an army could be drawn in France,
And she not hear of it?
MESSENGER   My liege, her ear
Is stopped with dust: the first of April died   120
Your noble mother; and as I hear, my lord,
The Lady Constance in a frenzy died
Three days before; but this from rumour's tongue
I idly heard – if true or false I know not.
KING JOHN Withhold thy speed, dreadful Occasion!   125
O, make a league with me till I have pleased
My discontented peers. What? Mother dead?
How wildly then walks my estate in France!
Under whose conduct came those powers of France
That thou for truth giv'st out are landed here?   130
MESSENGER Under the Dauphin.

Enter BASTARD *and* PETER OF POMFRET

KING JOHN   Thou hast made me giddy
With these ill tidings. – Now, what says the world
To your proceedings? Do not seek to stuff
My head with more ill news, for it is full.
BASTARD But if you be afeared to hear the worst,   135
Then let the worst, unheard, fall on your head.

---

117 care] F; ear *Dyce²*, *conj. Walker*

115 comes A singular verb often follows 'news'
or 'tidings', even though 'tidings' takes a plural
demonstrative pronoun at 132.
117 care See supplementary note.
118 drawn levied.
121–4 and . . . not The historical Constance is
said to have died in 1201, Eleanor in 1204; the
messenger's disclaimer is Shakespeare's usual way
of indicating uncertainty (Honigmann).
124 idly heard i.e. heard an idle rumour.
125 Withhold thy speed Alerting the audience
again to John's sudden inability to control the
speed of events.
125 Occasion Opportunity, crisis. See supplementary note.
126 make a league agree to a peaceful alliance.
126 pleased appeased.

128 wildly in confusion.
128 estate fortunes, affairs.
129 conduct command.
131 SD POMFRET i.e. Pontefract in Yorkshire.
Holinshed identifies Peter as a hermit 'about
York', but Shakespeare adds the place name
probably because of fearful associations with the
castle, reputed site of the murders of Richard II
and of the barons opposed to Richard III.
133 your proceedings If the emphasis is on
'your', John implies that he hopes for a shred of
good news.
135–6 'To know the worst is good' (*ODEP* 435a)
and the variation 'It is good to fear the worst'
(Tilley W912). The Bastard now speaks sharply to
the king, with good effect; and his stern tone
continues at 165–6 and at 5.1.65–73 (Smallwood).

KING JOHN Bear with me, cousin, for I was amazed
Under the tide, but now I breathe again
Aloft the flood and can give audience
To any tongue, speak it of what it will.   140
BASTARD How I have sped among the clergymen
The sums I have collected shall express,
But as I travelled hither through the land,
I find the people strangely fantasied,
Possessed with rumours, full of idle dreams,   145
Not knowing what they fear, but full of fear.
And here's a prophet that I brought with me
From forth the streets of Pomfret, whom I found
With many hundreds treading on his heels,
To whom he sung in rude harsh-sounding rhymes,   150
That ere the next Ascension Day at noon,
Your highness should deliver up your crown.
KING JOHN Thou idle dreamer, wherefore didst thou so?
PETER Foreknowing that the truth will fall out so.
KING JOHN Hubert, away with him; imprison him,   155
And on that day at noon, whereon he says
I shall yield up my crown, let him be hanged.
Deliver him to safety and return,
For I must use thee.
                    [*Exit Hubert with Peter*]
                         O my gentle cousin,
Hear'st thou the news abroad, who are arrived?   160
BASTARD The French, my lord; men's mouths are full of it.
Besides, I met Lord Bigot and Lord Salisbury
With eyes as red as new-enkindled fire,
And others more, going to seek the grave

143 travelled] F4 (travel'd); trauail'd F   150 harsh-sounding] *Pope; no hyphen in* F

137 amazed (1) struck with terror (compare 'fearful eye', 106 n.), (2) confused.
138–9 Under . . . flood Implying divine retribution; compare Ps. 88.15–17 (Prayer-Book version): 'thy terrors have I suffered . . . Thy wrathful displeasure goeth over me: and the fear of thee hath undone me. They came round about me daily like water.'
139 Aloft the flood Above the waves.
141 sped succeeded or failed.
143 travelled The Folio's spelling 'travail'd' implies the sub-meaning here.

144 strangely fantasied full of uncommon fancies. See supplementary note 4.2.144–8.
145–6 rumours . . . they fear Compare *Mac.* 4.2.19–20: 'when we hold rumor / From what we fear, yet know not what we fear'.
151 Ascension Day See supplementary note.
153 idle foolish.
153 dreamer John is contemptuous, like Caesar rejecting the soothsayer (*JC* 1.2.24): 'He is a dreamer, let us leave him.'
158 safety confinement.
163 as red . . . fire i.e. enraged (Tilley F247).

Of Arthur, whom they say is killed tonight   165
On your suggestion.
KING JOHN   Gentle kinsman, go
And thrust thyself into their companies;
I have a way to win their loves again.
Bring them before me.
BASTARD   I will seek them out.
KING JOHN Nay, but make haste; the better foot before.   170
O, let me have no subject enemies
When adverse foreigners affright my towns
With dreadful pomp of stout invasion.
Be Mercury, set feathers to thy heels,
And fly like thought from them to me again.   175
BASTARD The spirit of the time shall teach me speed.   *Exit*
KING JOHN Spoke like a sprightful noble gentleman.
Go after him, for he perhaps shall need
Some messenger betwixt me and the peers,
And be thou he.
MESSENGER   With all my heart, my liege.   [*Exit*] 180
KING JOHN My mother dead!

Enter HUBERT

HUBERT My lord, they say five moons were seen tonight:
Four fixèd, and the fift did whirl about
The other four in wondrous motion.
KING JOHN Five moons?
HUBERT   Old men and beldams in the streets   185

165–6 Of . . . suggestion] *Rowe³; one line in* F   180 SD] *Rowe; not in* F

165 tonight last night.
166 suggestion evil incitement.
167 companies i.e. company; as in *Ham.* 2.2.14.
168 a way . . . again John's plan to win back the nobles is never revealed. The striking feature of this speech is that John conspicuously ignores the implied accusation 'On your suggestion' (Smallwood).
170 the better foot before Proverbial (Tilley F570, *ODEP* 47b).
171 subject enemies i.e. enemies among my subjects.
173 dreadful full of fear and awe (as of a great military display – hence 'pomp'). John's dread builds during the scene: 'dreadful battles' with

conscience (78), the fury of 'dreadful Occasion' (125), and 'dreadful motion of a murderous thought' (255).
173 stout bold.
176 The spirit of the time Occasion, who like Mercury has wings on her feet. See supplementary note to 4.2.125.
177 sprightful spirited; with a play on 'spirit' in the previous line.
182–4 five . . . motion One of the natural irregularities of the heavens that, according to Pandulph, the common folk would interpret as a sign of God's vengeance (3.4.153–9).
183 fift A common form of 'fifth'.
185 beldams hags.

Do prophesy upon it dangerously.
Young Arthur's death is common in their mouths,
And when they talk of him, they shake their heads,
And whisper one another in the ear.
And he that speaks doth gripe the hearer's wrist,   190
Whilst he that hears makes fearful action
With wrinkled brows, with nods, with rolling eyes.
I saw a smith stand with his hammer, thus,
The whilst his iron did on the anvil cool,
With open mouth swallowing a tailor's news,   195
Who, with his shears and measure in his hand,
Standing on slippers, which his nimble haste
Had falsely thrust upon contrary feet,
Told of a many thousand warlike French
That were embattailèd and ranked in Kent.   200
Another lean, unwashed artificer
Cuts off his tale and talks of Arthur's death.
KING JOHN Why seek'st thou to possess me with these fears?
Why urgest thou so oft young Arthur's death?
Thy hand hath murdered him. I had a mighty cause   205
To wish him dead, but thou hadst none to kill him.
HUBERT No had, my lord? Why, did you not provoke me?
KING JOHN It is the curse of kings to be attended
By slaves that take their humours for a warrant
To break within the bloody house of life,   210

---

207 No had] F; Had none *Rowe*³

186 **prophesy upon** make it the text of a
disruptive speech against the government; a habit
associated with Puritan preachers who took occasion to call for reform.

187 **Arthur's . . . mouths** Hubert carries out his
intention to spread rumours of the boy's death
(4.1.128). Shakespeare follows Holinshed (II, 286):
'For the space of fifteen days this rumour
incessantly ran through both the realms of England
and France, and there was ringing for him through
towns and villages, as it had been for his funerals.'

191 **fearful action** gestures of fear.

191 **action** Three syllables.

197 **slippers** 'tailors generally work barefooted'
(Malone).

198 **contrary** wrong; accent on the second
syllable, as in *Ham.* 3.2.211.

199 **a many thousand** Before numeral adjectives 'a' expresses an approximate estimate
(*OED* A *Adj*² 2).

200 **embattailèd** marshalled to fight, set in
order of battle.

203 **possess . . . fears** infuse me with these fears;
furnish me with this frightening news.

206 **wish him dead** Compare *R2* 5.6.39–40:
'Though I did wish him dead, / I hate the
murderer, love him murdered. 'King Henry's terse
frankness and John's fearful complaint mark the
distance between their characters. The phrase can
imply a command; compare *R3* 4.2.18: 'I wish the
bastards dead, / And I would have it suddenly
perform'd.'

207 **No had** Had I not. A reply to a negative
frequently took the form 'No did?' 'No is?' 'No
have?'

209 **humours** moodiness (as also at 214).

210 **bloody house of life** The adjective is
proleptic; breaking into the house (the human
body) thereby bloodies it. See supplementary
note.

And on the winking of authority
To understand a law, to know the meaning
Of dangerous majesty, when perchance it frowns
More upon humour than advised respect.

HUBERT Here is your hand and seal for what I did.   215

                [Shows the warrant]

KING JOHN O, when the last account 'twixt heaven and earth
Is to be made, then shall this hand and seal
Witness against us to damnation!
How oft the sight of means to do ill deeds
Make deeds ill done! Hadst not thou been by,   220
A fellow by the hand of nature marked,
Quoted, and signed to do a deed of shame,
This murder had not come into my mind.
But taking note of thy abhorred aspect,
Finding thee fit for bloody villainy,   225
Apt, liable to be employed in danger,
I faintly broke with thee of Arthur's death,
And thou, to be endearèd to a king,
Made it no conscience to destroy a prince.

HUBERT My lord –   230

KING JOHN Hadst thou but shook thy head or made a pause

---

215 SD] *This edn; not in* F   220 Make] F; Makes *Theobald*   230 lord –] *Rowe³;* lord. F

211 **winking** looking or nodding as a command. Compare Thomas Elyot, *Dictionary* (1538), *Nictus*, 'a winking, as when one doth signify his mind to an other by looking'.

214 More out of caprice than deliberate consideration.

215 **hand and seal** A detail not in the sources; probably a reference to the blame that Secretary Davison took for the execution of Mary Queen of Scots.

216–23 i.e. Your disfigured face gave me a natural warrant just as I gave you a legal warrant to do the deed. Hence we both must answer for it.

218 **us** Ambiguous, but John probably refers to himself alone (the royal 'we') rather than to Hubert. John is nothing if not self-centred in this scene (Smallwood).

220 **Make** The plural suggested by 'means' and 'deeds' (Abbott 412).

221 **marked** stamped with a sign; destined, as with the mark of Cain (224).

222 **Quoted** Annotated or inscribed; known. Compare *AWW* 5.3.205: 'He's quoted for a most perfidious slave'. Davies, I, 112, says 'quoted' is a 'playhouse word. The characters who are to be called by the prompter's boy to be ready for the scene are quoted by him in the margin of the play.'

222 **signed** sealed (*OED* sv v 3); suggesting that Hubert is branded with an evil sign on his face. See 71–2, 257, 264.

224 **aspect** Stress on the second syllable.

226 **danger** mischief.

227 **faintly . . . thee** hinted to you what was on my mind.

231–41 'These reproaches, vented against Hubert, are not the words of art or policy, but the eruptions of a mind swelling with consciousness of crime, and desirous of discharging its misery on another' (Johnson).

231 **made a pause** hesitated.

When I spake darkly what I purposèd,
Or turned an eye of doubt upon my face,
As bid me tell my tale in express words,
Deep shame had struck me dumb, made me break off,   235
And those thy fears might have wrought fears in me.
But thou didst understand me by my signs
And didst in signs again parley with sin,
Yea, without stop, didst let thy heart consent,
And consequently thy rude hand to act   240
The deed which both our tongues held vile to name.
Out of my sight, and never see me more!
My nobles leave me, and my state is braved,
Even at my gates, with ranks of foreign powers.
Nay, in the body of this fleshly land,   245
This kingdom, this confine of blood and breath,
Hostility and civil tumult reigns
Between my conscience and my cousin's death.
HUBERT Arm you against your other enemies;
I'll make a peace between your soul and you.   250
Young Arthur is alive. This hand of mine
Is yet a maiden and an innocent hand,
Not painted with the crimson spots of blood.
Within this bosom never entered yet
The dreadful motion of a murderous thought   255
And you have slandered nature in my form,
Which howsoever rude exteriorly,
Is yet the cover of a fairer mind
Than to be butcher of an innocent child.
KING JOHN Doth Arthur live? O, haste thee to the peers,   260
Throw this report on their incensèd rage,
And make them tame to their obedience!

---

241 vile| vilde F   246 breath,| F4; breath F3; breathe F

234 **As bid** As if to bid.
234 **express** unmistakable.
237–8 **signs . . . sin** In fact Hubert was perfectly explicit at 3.3.66, 'He shall not live' (Smallwood). See supplementary note.
238 **parley** speak. Compare Sylvester, *Du Bartas* (1605), 1.3.951: 'As bashful suitors, seeing strangers by, / Parley in silence with their hand or eye.'
239 **stop** hesitation.
239–40 **let . . . to act** For 'to' after 'let', see *OED* Let v¹ and Abbott 349–50.

243 **my state** the realm.
245 **this fleshly land** the domain of my flesh; John's private person as distinct from his realm.
246 **confine** territory: prison.
248 **my cousin's death** i.e. my crime.
254–5 **never . . . thought** Not exactly true if we take 3.3.66 and much of 4.1 seriously. See 3.3.66 n.
255 **motion** impulse.
256 **nature** natural feeling, affection. See *Ham.* 1.5.81.

Forgive the comment that my passion made
Upon thy feature, for my rage was blind,
And foul imaginary eyes of blood   265
Presented thee more hideous than thou art.
O, answer not! but to my closet bring
The angry lords with all expedient haste.
I conjure thee but slowly; run more fast.

                          Exeunt [severally]

4.3 *Enter* ARTHUR *on the walls [disguised as a ship-boy]*

ARTHUR The wall is high, and yet will I leap down.
  Good ground, be pitiful and hurt me not.
  There's few or none do know me; if they did,
  This ship-boy's semblance hath disguised me quite.
  I am afraid, and yet I'll venture it.   5
  If I get down and do not break my limbs,
  I'll find a thousand shifts to get away.
  As good to die and go, as die and stay.
            [Leaps down]
  O me, my uncle's spirit is in these stones.
  Heaven take my soul, and England keep my bones.   *Dies* 10

        Enter PEMBROKE, SALISBURY, *and* BIGOT

SALISBURY Lords, I will meet him at Saint Edmundsbury;
  It is our safety, and we must embrace
  This gentle offer of the perilous time.
PEMBROKE Who brought that letter from the cardinal?
SALISBURY The Count Melun, a noble lord of France,   15
  Whose privity with me o'th'Dauphin's love
  Is much more general than these lines import.

Act 4, Scene 3   4.3] *Scæna Tertia.* F   0 SD *disguised as a ship-boy*] Dyce; not in F; *disguis'd* / Theobald   8 SD]
Rowe; not in F   15 Melun] Rowe; Melloone F *(or* Melloone, Meloon *throughout)*   16 privity with me] *This edn;*
priuate with me F; *private warrant conj.* Wilson   16 o'th'] *This edn;* of the F   16 love] Theobald; loue, F

267 closet private apartment.
268 expedient speedy.
269 conjure charge solemnly, adjure.
269 but slowly John has, of course, been speaking quickly and excitedly (Smallwood).

Act 4, Scene 3
7 shifts stratagems; changes of clothing.
10 The form at the beginning of a will, as in

Shakespeare's: 'First I commend my soul into the hands of God . . . and my body to the earth.'
11 him Lewis the Dauphin. The pronoun without reference implies that they enter in mid dialogue. Comprare 3.1.1.
16 privity private counsel or secret thoughts. See supplementary note.
17 general unrestricted, liberal. Compare *Edward III* 2.1.163: 'Bid her be free and general as the sun.'

BIGOT Tomorrow morning let us meet him then.
SALISBURY Or rather then set forward, for 'twill be
　　Two long days' journey, lords, or ere we meet.　　　　20

Enter BASTARD

BASTARD Once more today well met, distempered lords!
　　The king by me requests your presence straight.
SALISBURY The king hath dispossessed himself of us,
　　We will not line his thin bestainèd cloak
　　With our pure honours, nor attend the foot　　　　25
　　That leaves the print of blood where'er it walks.
　　Return, and tell him so. We know the worst.
BASTARD Whate'er you think, good words I think were best.
SALISBURY Our griefs and not our manners reason now.
BASTARD But there is little reason in your grief.　　　　30
　　Therefore 'twere reason you had manners now.
PEMBROKE Sir, sir, impatience hath his privilege.
BASTARD 'Tis true – to hurt his master, no man else.
SALISBURY This is the prison. [*Sees Arthur*] What is he lies here?
PEMBROKE O death made proud with pure and princely beauty!　　35
　　The earth had not a hole to hide this deed.
SALISBURY Murder, as hating what himself hath done,
　　Doth lay it open to urge on revenge.
BIGOT Or when he doomed this beauty to a grave,
　　Found it too precious-princely for a grave.　　　　40
SALISBURY Sir Richard, what think you? Have you beheld,

---

24 thin bestainèd] *Rowe;* thin-bestained F; sin-bestained *Collier MS.*　33 man] F2; mans F; manners *Honigmann*　34 SD] *Pope (subst.); not in* F　40 precious-princely] *Capell;* precious Princely F　41 Have you beheld,] F3 *(subst.);* you have beheld, F

21 **Once more today** He first met the barons seeking Arthur's grave.
21 **distempered** disordered by passion.
24 **line** furnish a lining to; repair or strengthen from within, hence, to fortify.
25 **attend** wait upon; implying homage.
25–6 **foot . . . walks** Recalling 3.3.62, 4.1.2, and 4.2.57. Compare E. Daunce, *Brief Discourse of the Spanish State* (1590), sig. D2ᵛ: 'Machiavel . . . maintaineth that where the Pope and Cardinals set footing, they leave most fearful prints of confusion' (Honigmann).
28 **good words** fair speech. Compare Marlowe, *The Jew of Malta* 5.2.61: 'good words; be not so furious'.
29 **griefs** grievances, injuries.
29 **reason** speak, control our conduct.

32 **impatience . . . privilege** i.e. anger is a law unto itself.
33 'Anger punishes itself' (Tilley A247).
40 **too . . . grave** 'The bodies of princes were not buried in the ground, but embalmed and placed in a sepulchre or vault' (Wilson).
41 **Sir Richard** Apart from the Bastard's own comic use of it at 1.1.185, this is the only time his knightly title is used, suggesting Salisbury's anxiety to enlist support (Smallwood).
41 *Have you beheld A happy emendation. The series of rhetorical questions begins with 'what think you?', and 'beheld . . . read or heard' imply 'the likes of this outrage'. F's 'you have beheld' has been defended on the ground that Salisbury means 'you have had a good look'.

Or have you read or heard? or could you think,
Or do you almost think, although you see,
That you do see? Could thought, without this object,
Form such another? This is the very top,   45
The height, the crest, or crest unto the crest
Of murder's arms. This is the bloodiest shame,
The wildest savagery, the vildest stroke
That ever wall-eyed wrath or staring rage
Presented to the tears of soft remorse.   50
PEMBROKE All murders past do stand excused in this,
And this, so sole and so unmatchable,
Shall give a holiness, a purity,
To the yet-unbegotten sin of times,
And prove a deadly bloodshed but a jest,   55
Exampled by this heinous spectacle.
BASTARD It is a damnèd and a bloody work,
The graceless action of a heavy hand –
It that it be the work of any hand.
SALISBURY If that it be the work of any hand?   60
We had a kind of light what would ensue.
It is the shameful work of Hubert's hand,
The practice and the purpose of the king,
From whose obedience I forbid my soul,
Kneeling before this ruin of sweet life,   65
And breathing to his breathless excellence
The incense of a vow, a holy vow,

---

42 heard?] *Capell;* heard, F   42 think,] *Pope;* thinke? F   48 vilest] vildest F   54 yet-unbegotten] *Pope;* yet vnbegotten F   54 sin of times] F; sins of Time *Pope*

42–4 could . . . see? Although you see it, could you either conceive or even begin to conceive what you see?

44–5 Could . . . another? Without this spectacle, could you imagine its equal? An 'object' may be the sight of a thing that excites pity or horror, as in *Tim.* 4.3.123–4.

46–7 the crest . . . arms A coat-of-arms may be surmounted by a helmet, with a plume or badge on top of that.

49 wall-eyed having fierce, glaring eyes; associated with anger.

49 staring wild.

50 remorse pity.

51 do . . . this are judged innocent in comparison to this.

51–4 All . . . times Compare A. Colynet, *True History* (1591), p. 402: 'ye that are famous for any notorious wickedness, rejoice, for your infamy is justified by the raging cruelty of . . . Dominican Fryers' (Honigmann).

52 sole unique.

54 times times to come.

56 Exampled by Furnished with the precedent of.

58 graceless beyond forgiveness.

58 heavy oppressive (*OED* sv *adj* 23). The gloss 'wicked' is not supported by historical evidence.

61 light foresight.

63 practice and . . . purpose contrivance and evil design.

64–5 Salisbury unswears his oath of fealty to John in ritual terms, emphasising its solemnity. Pandulph incited such disobedience, 3.1.174–5.

66 breathing uttering with passion.

Never to taste the pleasures of the world,
Never to be infected with delight
Nor conversant with ease and idleness,   70
Till I have set a glory to this hand,
By giving it the worship of revenge.

PEMBROKE ⎱ Our souls religiously confirm thy words.
BIGOT   ⎰

Enter HUBERT

HUBERT Lords, I am hot with haste in seeking you.
                Arthur doth live, the king hath sent for you.   75
SALISBURY O, he is bold, and blushes not at death! –
                Avaunt, thou hateful villain, get thee gone!
HUBERT I am no villain.
SALISBURY   Must I rob the law? [*Draws*]
BASTARD Your sword is bright, sir; put it up again.
SALISBURY Not till I sheathe it in a murderer's skin.   80
HUBERT Stand back, Lord Salisbury, stand back I say!
                By heaven, I think my sword's as sharp as yours.
                I would not have you, lord, forget yourself,
                Nor tempt the danger of my true defence,
                Lest I, by marking of your rage, forget   85
                Your worth, your greatness, and nobility.
BIGOT Out, dunghill! Dar'st thou brave a nobleman?
HUBERT Not for my life, but yet I dare defend
                My innocent life against an emperor.
SALISBURY Thou art a murderer.
HUBERT   Do not prove me so;   90
                Yet I am none. Whose tongue soe'er speaks false,
                Not truly speaks; who speaks not truly, lies.
PEMBROKE Cut him to pieces.
BASTARD [*Drawing*]   Keep the peace, I say.

---

78 SD *Draws*] *Kittredge; not in* F; *Drawing his sword* / *Pope*

69 **infected with** affected by, so as to corrupt.

71–2 **set . . . revenge** (1) added glory to my hand by dedicating it to an honourable revenge, (2) affixed an aura of holiness to Arthur's hand, by avenging.

77 **Avaunt** Contemptuous, as if Salisbury is driving away a dog. See Cotgrave, sv *Devant*.

79 **put it up** put it away (lest it lose its brightness). Compare Othello's assured warning (*Oth.* 1.2.59): 'Keep up your bright swords, for the dew will rust them.'

84 **tempt** risk.

84 **my true defence** the defence of my honesty and innocence.

90–1 **Do . . . none** Do not make me a murderer; I am not one yet.

91–2 **Whose . . . lies** After being forced to challenge a man above his rank and being scorned for it, Hubert gives Salisbury the lie and thus steps up the pressure for a proper duel.

SALISBURY Stand by, or I shall gall you, Falconbridge.
BASTARD Thou wert better gall the devil, Salisbury.   95
          If thou but frown on me, or stir thy foot,
          Or teach thy hasty spleen to do me shame,
          I'll strike thee dead. Put up thy sword betime,
          Or I'll so maul you and your toasting-iron,
          That you shall think the devil is come from hell.   100
BIGOT What wilt thou do, renownèd Falconbridge,
          Second a villain and a murderer?
HUBERT Lord Bigot, I am none.
BIGOT   Who killed this prince?
HUBERT 'Tis not an hour since I left him well.
          I honoured him, I loved him and will weep   105
          My date of life out for his sweet life's loss.
SALISBURY Trust not those cunning waters of his eyes,
          For villainy is not without such rheum;
          And he, long traded in it, makes it seem
          Like rivers of remorse and innocency.   110
          Away with me, all you whose souls abhor
          Th'uncleanly savours of a slaughter-house,
          For I am stifled with this smell of sin.
BIGOT Away toward Bury, to the Dauphin there!
PEMBROKE There, tell the king, he may enquire us out.   115
                                        Exeunt lords
BASTARD Here's a good world. Knew you of this fair work?
          Beyond the infinite and boundless reach
          Of mercy, if thou didst this deed of death,
          Art thou damned, Hubert.
HUBERT Do but hear me, sir —
BASTARD   Ha! I'll tell thee what.   120

---

106 life's] *Rowe;* liues F 115 There,] *Theobald;* There F 117–19 Beyond . . . Hubert] *As relined by Pope;* Beyond
. . . mercy, / . . . Hubert F

94–102 The lords refuse to consider Hubert's claim to defend his honour like a gentleman and are about to hack him to pieces, but the Bastard 'seconds' Hubert, and when Bigot acknowledges that action, the lords must fight fairly or withdraw.
94 by aside.
94 gall wound.
97 hasty spleen sudden and fiery temper.
99 toasting-iron A contemptuous name for a sword; the first recorded use. Nym would use his sword only to toast cheese, *H5* 2.1.9.
106 date term.
109 traded skilled.
110 remorse See 50 n.
112 uncleanly dirty; morally or spiritually impure.
112 savours odours.
115 enquire us out seek out by asking.

Thou'rt damned as black – nay nothing is so black –
Thou art more deep damned than Prince Lucifer.
There is not yet so ugly a fiend of hell
As thou shalt be, if thou didst kill this child.

HUBERT Upon my soul –

BASTARD   If thou didst but consent   125
To this most cruel act, do but despair,
And if thou want'st a cord, the smallest thread
That ever spider twisted from her womb
Will serve to strangle thee; a rush will be a beam
To hang thee on. Or wouldst thou drown thyself,   130
Put but a little water in a spoon,
And it shall be as all the ocean,
Enough to stifle such a villain up.
I do suspect thee very grievously.

HUBERT If I in act, consent, or sin of thought,   135
Be guilty of the stealing that sweet breath
Which was embounded in this beauteous clay,
Let hell want pains enough to torture me!
I left him well.

BASTARD   Go, bear him in thine arms.
I am amazed, methinks, and lose my way   140
Among the thorns and dangers of this world.
How easy dost thou take all England up!
From forth this morsel of dead royalty,
The life, the right, and truth of all this realm
Is fled to heaven; and England now is left   145
To tug and scamble and to part by th'teeth
The unowed interest of proud-swelling state.
Now for the bare-picked bone of majesty,

---

121 black –... black – | *Riverside;* blacke,... blacke, F; black –...black; *Rowe³*   124–6 child. Upon... act, do| *Rowe;* childe. Upon... Act: do F; child – Upon... act. Do *conj. Maxwell*   125 soul – | *Pope;* soule. F   142–3 up!... royalty,| *Theobald;* up,... Royaltie? F   147 proud-swelling| *Pope; no hyphen in* F

121–2 as black... Prince Lucifer Lucifer, the 'son of morning' or the morning star, fell down from heaven into the pit (Isa. 14.12, Geneva gloss).

126–33 It was thought that guilty people were prone to ill fortune.

135 Echoing the general confession for Holy Communion: 'our manifold sins . . . which we . . . most grievously have committed, by thought, word, and deed'. Compare Hubert's equally dubious denial, 4.2.254–5.

142 England The unity of king and country. See 2.1.91, 202, where Arthur is also thus designated.

143–5 From... heaven Now that Arthur's soul has gone to heaven, the essential spirit of legitimate order and loyalty has left the body politic. The Bastard assesses the entire situation: the death of the rightful heir, the French invasion, and the baronial revolt.

146 scamble struggle for.

147 unowed of uncertain ownership, not owed to anyone (since there is no rightful king).

Doth dogged war bristle his angry crest
And snarleth in the gentle eyes of peace.   150
Now powers from home and discontents at home
Meet in one line, and vast confusion waits
As doth a raven on a sick-fall'n beast,
The imminent decay of wrested pomp.
Now happy he, whose cloak and centure can   155
Hold out this tempest. Bear away that child,
And follow me with speed. I'll to the king.
A thousand businesses are brief in hand,
And heaven itself doth frown upon the land.

                                                    Exeunt

5.1 *Enter* KING JOHN *and* PANDULPH, *attendants*

KING JOHN [*Giving the crown*] Thus have I yielded up into your hand
    The circle of my glory. [*Kneels*]
PANDULPH [*Places crown upon John's head*] Take again
    From this my hand, as holding of the Pope,
    Your sovereign greatness and authority.
KING JOHN Now keep your holy word: go meet the French,   5
    And from his holiness use all your power
    To stop their marches 'fore we are inflamed.
    Our discontented counties do revolt;
    Our people quarrel with obedience,
    Swearing allegiance and the love of soul   10

---

155 centure] *Moore Smith;* center F; cincture *Pope;* ceinture *Maxwell in Honigmann* 158 in] F; at *Rowe* 159 SD *Exeunt*] *Rowe; Exit* F **Act 5, Scene 1** 5.1] *Actus Quartus, Scæna prima.* F 0 SD PANDULPH] F; PANDULPH *with the Crown / Capell* 1 SD *giving the crown*] *Pope (at 2 after* glory; *not in* F 2 SD.1 *Kneels*] *This edn; not in* F 2 SD.2 *places . . . head*] *Wilson; not in* F; *giving back the Crown / Capell; giving John the Crown / Malone* 3 Pope,] F3; Pope F

149 dogged currish, cruel.
151 powers from home i.e. the invading French troops.
152 Meet in one line i.e. join forces on a single path or file. Compare *The Proceedings of the Earl of Leicester for the Relief of Sluce* (1590), sig. B2; 'Leicester tried to reconcile all his allies "to recure all seditious wounds, and to draw all in one line to the relief of this besieged town' (Honigmann). See *Ham.* 3.4.210.
154 imminent . . . pomp This and 142–5 show what the Bastard thinks of John's claims to the throne and of his prospects. Pandulph predicted as much for 'misplaced John', his 'sceptre snatched', and his 'slipp'ry place' (3.4.133–7).
154 wrested pomp usurped authority.

155 centure cincture, girdle, or belt.
158 are brief in hand i.e. are now in hand and must be dispatched quickly (Capell).
159 See supplementary note.

Act 5, Scene 1
1–2 See supplementary note.
1 I John uses the singular here and at 2 ('my') but returns to the royal plural when he receives the crown again. He normally reserves the singular for passionate outbursts (1.1.25, 2.1.155, etc.) or private discourse (3.3.25–70, 4.2 *passim*).
8 counties nobles, earls; or shires (?). See supplementary note.
10 love of soul deep loyalty, since the soul is the seat of real, not professed, sentiments (Schmidt).

To stranger blood, to foreign royalty.
This inundation of mistempered humour
Rests by you only to be qualified.
Then pause not, for the present time's so sick
That present med'cine must be ministered,   15
Or overthrow incurable ensues.
PANDULPH It was my breath that blew this tempest up,
Upon your stubborn usage of the Pope,
But since you are a gentle convertite,
My tongue shall hush again this storm of war   20
And make fair weather in your blust'ring land.
On this Ascension Day, remember well,
Upon your oath of service to the Pope,
Go I to make the French lay down their arms.   *Exit*
KING JOHN Is this Ascension Day? Did not the prophet   25
Say that before Ascension Day at noon
My crown I should give off? Even so I have.
I did suppose it should be on constraint.
But, heav'n be thanked, it is but voluntary.

Enter BASTARD

BASTARD All Kent hath yielded; nothing there holds out   30
But Dover Castle. London hath received,
Like a kind host, the Dauphin and his powers.
Your nobles will not hear you, but are gone
To offer service to your enemy,
And wild amazement hurries up and down   35
The little number of your doubtful friends.
KING JOHN Would not my lords return to me again
After they heard young Arthur was alive?
BASTARD They found him dead and cast into the streets,
An empty casket, where the jewel of life   40
By some damned hand was robbed and ta'en away.

---

11 stranger blood] *Theobald;* stranger-bloud F

11 **stranger** alien.
12–13 You alone can cure the ills of England, controlling this tumult of humours.
13 **qualified** abated, restored to balance.
14 **present** current.
15 **present** immediate.
18 **stubborn** wilful.
19 **gentle convertite** pliant man, newly converted.

21 **make fair weather** pacify.
25–9 See supplementary note.
35 **wild amazement** panic.
35 **hurries up and down** drives confusedly about.
36 **doubtful** fearful; of questionable loyalty.
40 **empty . . . life** Recalling 4.2.210.
41 **some damned hand** Compare 4.3.58–9, and see supplementary note.

KING JOHN That villain Hubert told me he did live.

BASTARD So, on my soul, he did, for aught he knew.
But wherefore do you droop? Why look you sad?
Be great in act, as you have been in thought. 45
Let not the world see fear and sad distrust
Govern the motion of a kingly eye.
Be stirring as the time, be fire with fire,
Threaten the threat'ner, and outface the brow
Of bragging horror. So shall inferior eyes, 50
That borrow their behaviours from the great,
Grow great by your example and put on
The dauntless spirit of resolution.
Away, and glister like the god of war
When he intendeth to become the field. 55
Show boldness and aspiring confidence.
What, shall they seek the lion in his den,
And fright him there? and make him tremble there?
O, let it not be said! Forage, and run
To meet displeasure farther from the doors, 60
And grapple with him ere he come so nigh.

KING JOHN The legate of the Pope hath been with me,
And I have made a happy peace with him,
And he hath promised to dismiss the powers
Led by the Dauphin.

BASTARD   O inglorious league! 65
Shall we, upon the footing of our land,
Send fair-play orders and make compromise,
Insinuation, parley, and base truce
To arms invasive? Shall a beardless boy,
A cockered silken wanton brave our fields, 70

---

43 aught] *Theobald²*; ought F 67 fair-play orders] *Capell*; fayre-play-orders F 70 cockered silken] *Theobald²*; cockred-silken, F; cockered, silken, *Pope*

43 for aught he knew If the pronoun is emphasised, the Bastard suggests that others (perhaps John himself) may know more (Small-wood).

44 droop become dispirited.

46 distrust lack of confidence.

48 stirring energetic.

50 bragging bullying. Compare N. Ridley, *Certain Godly . . . Conferences* (1556), sig. B5: 'they will outface, brace [brazen], and brag all men'.

55 become honour with his presence.

59 Forage Ravage, prey.

60 displeasure trouble (*OED* sv *sb* 2).

66 upon . . . of standing upon (or possibly 'When someone lands upon').

67 fair-play orders stipulations or rules for courteous dealings, chivalrous conduct.

68 Insinuation 'a privy twining or close creeping in to win favours' (T. Wilson, *Art of Rhetoric* (1553), fol. 55).

70 cockered pampered.

70 brave threaten; suggesting a splendid show.

And flesh his spirit in a warlike soil
Mocking the air with colours idly spread,
And find no check? Let us, my liege, to arms.
Perchance the cardinal cannot make your peace,
Or if he do, let it at least be said   75
They saw we had a purpose of defence.
KING JOHN Have thou the ordering of this present time.
BASTARD Away then with good courage! – [*Aside*] Yet I know
Our party may well meet a prouder foe.

Exeunt

5.2 *Enter, in arms,* [*Lewis the*] DAUPHIN, SALISBURY, MELUN, PEMBROKE,
BIGOT, *soldiers*

LEWIS My Lord Melun, let this be copied out
And keep it safe for our remembrance;
Return the precedent to these lords again,
That having our fair order written down,
Both they and we, perusing o'er these notes,   5
May know wherefore we took the sacrament,
And keep our faiths firm and inviolable.
SALISBURY Upon our sides it never shall be broken.
And, noble Dauphin, albeit we swear
A voluntary zeal and an unurgèd faith   10
To your proceedings, yet believe me, prince,
I am not glad that such a sore of time

---

78 courage! – | *This edn;* courage: F; courage! *Dyce*   78 SD] *Oxford; not in* F   Act 5, Scene 2   5.2] *Scœne Secunda.* F   0 SD SALISBURY, MELUN, PEMBROKE, BIGOT] F *(subst.);* MELUN, PEMBROKE, BIGOT, SALISBURY *Capell*   10 and an | F; and *Pope; and Capell*   10 unurgèd] *This edn;* unurg'd F

---

71 **flesh his spirit** initiate himself and his courage (as one would thrust his maiden sword into a victim; see *1H4* 5.4.130). The metaphor comes from hunting, as the young dogs are fleshed or encouraged by tasting the first kill.

72 **idly** (1) pointlessly, if they provoke no resistance, (2) carelessly, untroubled by English defenders.

77 **ordering . . . time** disposition of this pressing business.

78–9 **Yet . . . foe** Yet, considering the faintness of our side, we may very well encounter an enemy with more spirit. See supplementary note.

Act 5, Scene 2

2 **remembrance** Four syllables, as in *TN* 1.1.31.

3 **precedent** original draft.

4 **fair order** suitable agreement, the promising conditions of their treaty.

10 ***unurgèd** The addition of an artificial syllable makes the line an alexandrine, appropriate to Salisbury's weighty meditation; but if, instead, the last syllable of 'voluntary' is slurred, the line could be an irregular pentameter (Smallwood).

12–13 The 'Homily against . . . Wilful Rebellion', *Certain Sermons* (1582), sig. 2Z1, declared 'rebellion

Should seek a plaster by contemned revolt
And heal the inveterate canker of one wound
By making many. O, it grieves my soul 15
That I must draw this metal from my side
To be a widow-maker! O, and there
Where honourable rescue and defence
Cries out upon the name of Salisbury!
But such is the infection of the time 20
That for the health and physic of our right,
We cannot deal but with the very hand
Of stern injustice and confusèd wrong,
And is't not pity, O my grievèd friends,
That we, the sons and children of this isle, 25
Was born to see so sad an hour as this,
Wherein we step after a stranger, march
Upon her gentle bosom, and fill up
Her enemies' ranks – I must withdraw and weep
Upon the spot of this enforcèd cause – 30
To grace the gentry of a land remote
And follow unacquainted colours here?
What, here? O nation, that thou couldst remove,
That Neptune's arms, who clippeth thee about,
Would bear thee from the knowledge of thyself, 35

16 metal] *Rowe³;* mettle F 26 Was] F; 27 stranger, march] F; stranger march *Theobald;* stranger-march *Hanmer* 29–32 ranks –...cause –...here?] *Cam.;* rankes?...cause,...heere: F; ranks? (...cause;)...here? *Theobald;* ranks, (...cause)...Here? *Capell*

an unfit and unwholesome medicine . . . far worse than any other maladies and disorders that can be in the body of the commonwealth'. The usual saying was 'Patience is a plaster for all sores' (Tilley P107).
13 contemned revolt despicable rebellion. See *R2* 3.2.100.
14 canker gangrene.
17 there i.e. in such a situation.
18–19 i.e. where my duty to deliver and defend England from her enemies rises up and cries shame upon my good name.
19 Cries out upon Exclaims against.
21–3 right . . . wrong The opposition of legal right and moral wrong defines the dilemma of the English nobles.
22 deal act.
23 confusèd indistinguishably mingled.

26 Was A singular verb with a plural subject, influenced by the proximity of 'isle'.
27–8 step . . . bosom An image of desecration. See 3.1.246–8, 4.1.3; and *R2* 2.3.92–3.
30 Upon the spot Here in this place; because of the disgrace or stain; i.e. 'as if my tears could wash out the stain by dropping upon it'. Compare *The Rape of Lucrece* 684–5: 'that . . . lust should stain so pure a bed! / The spots whereof could weeping purify'.
30 this enforcèd cause the necessity of this undertaking.
32 unacquainted foreign.
33 remove go elsewhere.
34 clippeth embraces.
35 bear . . . thyself lift or carry you from yourself (like a stolen child), i.e. into forgetfulness. See *Ant.* 2.2.90–1.

And grapple thee unto a pagan shore,
Where these two Christian armies might combine
The blood of malice in a vein of league
And not to spend it so unneighbourly.
LEWIS A noble temper dost thou show in this,   40
And great affections wrestling in thy bosom
Doth make an earthquake of nobility.
O, what a noble combat hast thou fought
Between compulsion and a brave respect!
Let me wipe off this honourable dew,   45
That silverly doth progress on thy cheeks.
My heart hath melted at a lady's tears,
Being an ordinary inundation,
But this effusion of such manly drops,
This shower, blown up by tempest of the soul,   50
Startles mine eyes and makes me more amazed
Than had I seen the vaulty top of heaven
Figured quite o'er with burning meteors.
Lift up thy brow, renownèd Salisbury,
And with a great heart heave away this storm.   55
Commend these waters to those baby eyes
That never saw the giant world enraged,
Nor met with Fortune other than at feasts,
Full warm of blood, of mirth, of gossiping.
Come, come; for thou shalt thrust thy hand as deep   60
Into the purse of rich prosperity
As Lewis himself. So, nobles, shall you all,

---

36 grapple] *Pope;* cripple F; gripple *conj. Steevens³*   39 to spend | F; mis-spend *Hanmer;* to-spend *Steevens³*   43 thou |
F4; *not in* F   56 baby eyes] *Capell;* baby-eyes F   57 giant world] *Theobald;* giant-world F   59 warm of] F;
of warm *Dyce²*, *conj. Heath*

36 *grapple See supplementary note.
37–9 The fond hope for a crusade, whereby
Christians may forget their quarrels and unite
against a pagan enemy.
38 vein blood-vessel; temper, mood. See *1H6*
4.7.95.
44 Between what you must do and your fine
inclination not to do it. 'Respect' implies the
higher considerations of conscience or loyalty.
50 tempest of the soul spiritual combat. See
R3 1.4.44; *1 Tamburlaine* 3.2.86–7.

55 heave away remove, as if one could clear the
breast by sighs.
56 Commend Leave, bequeath.
57 giant world grown-up world, beyond a
child's experience.
58 Fortune . . . feasts See supplementary note.
59 Full warm of Very richly or generously
endowed with.
59 gossiping merriment; especially associated
with a christening or the birth of a child.
62 nobles With a pun on the gold coins, after
'purse' (61) and before 'angel' (64).

That knit your sinews to the strength of mine.
[*Trumpet sounds*]
And even there, methinks an angel spake!

Enter PANDULPH [*attended*]

Look where the holy legate comes apace,   65
To give us warrant from the hand of heaven,
And on our actions set the name of right
With holy breath.
PANDULPH   Hail, noble Prince of France.
The next is this: King John hath reconciled
Himself to Rome; his spirit is come in,   70
That so stood out against the holy church,
The great metropolis and see of Rome.
Therefore thy threat'ning colours now wind up
And tame the savage spirit of wild war,
That like a lion fostered up at hand,   75
It may lie gently at the foot of peace
And be no further harmful than in show.
LEWIS Your grace shall pardon me, I will not back.
I am too high-born to be propertied,
To be a secondary at control,   80
Or useful servingman and instrument
To any sovereign state throughout the world.
Your breath first kindled the dead coal of wars
Between this chastised kingdom and myself
And brought in matter that should feed this fire,   85
And now 'tis far too huge to be blown out

---

63 SD] *Wilson, conj. Cowden Clarke; not in* F   64 SD *Enter* PANDULPH *attended*] *Capell (after 63), Halliwell (subst., after 64); Enter Pandulpho* F *(after 63)*   72 see] F4 *(subst.); Sea* F   79 propertied,] F4; *propertied* F; propertied F2

63 knit . . . mine unite your strength with mine (Smallwood).

63 SD Trumpet sounds The stage direction fits the following line because angels are traditionally 'trumpet-tongued' (*Mac.* 1.7.19) and trumpets 'speak' (*Lear* 5.3.151).

64 angel spake The usual pun on the coin (Tilley A242, *ODEP* 767).

66 warrant A word now tainted in perfidious mouths, but used innocently by Arthur and the Bastard. See 2.1.116, 3.1.184, 4.2.209; 4.1.31, 5.2.123.

67 set seal; as on a warrant.

67–72 The language has a whiff of formal declarations of repentant heretics or phrases in papal bulls.

70 is come in has submitted, repented.

75 fostered . . . hand hand-reared.

78 shall must.

78 back withdraw.

79 propertied made a cat's paw.

80 secondary subordinate.

83–7 'A little wind kindles, much puts out the fire' (Tilley W424).

84 chastised See supplementary note to 4.3.159.

With that same weak wind which enkindled it.
You taught me how to know the face of right,
Acquainted me with interest to this land,
Yea, thrust this enterprise into my heart;   90
And come ye now to tell me John hath made
His peace with Rome? What is that peace to me?
I, by the honour of my marriage-bed,
After young Arthur, claim this land for mine;
And now it is half-conquered, must I back   95
Because that John hath made his peace with Rome?
Am I Rome's slave? What penny hath Rome borne?
What men provided? What munition sent
To underprop this action? Is't not I
That undergo this charge? Who else but I,   100
And such as to my claim are liable,
Sweat in this business and maintain this war?
Have I not heard these islanders shout out
Vive le roi! as I have banked their towns?
Have I not here the best cards for the game   105
To win this easy match played for a crown?
And shall I now give o'er the yielded set?
No, no, on my soul, it never shall be said.
PANDULPH You look but on the outside of this work.
LEWIS Outside or inside, I will not return   110
      Till my attempt so much be glorified
      As to my ample hope was promisèd
      Before I drew this gallant head of war
      And culled these fiery spirits from the world
      To outlook conquest and to win renown   115
      Even in the jaws of danger and of death.
                  [*Trumpet sounds*]

116 SD] *Rowe; not in* F

88 **know . . . right** recognise my just claim.

101 **to . . . liable** are subject to my demands for service (Smallwood).

104 *Vive le roi!* The final *e* is sounded in *Vive*. The phrase probably alludes to the name of a playing card (like king or queen in modern decks).

104 **banked their towns** As a part of the card-playing conceit (105–7), this phrase means 'won their towns', i.e. put them in the bank or in a pile of money held by one who plays against others. See supplementary note.

106 **crown** the crown of England; five shillings staked on a hand of cards.

107 **yielded set** game already won. Compare *Tit.* 5.1.100: 'As sure a card as ever won the set'.

113 **drew** levied, assembled; glancing at 'pulled these cards from the deck'.

113 **head of war** armed force, possibly the 'flower' or nucleus of an army, after *caput belli* (Honigmann).

115 **outlook** defy, outface.

What lusty trumpet thus doth summon us?

Enter BASTARD

BASTARD According to the fair play of the world,
　　　　 Let me have audience; I am sent to speak,
　　　　 My holy lord of Milan, from the king: 120
　　　　 I come to learn how you have dealt for him,
　　　　 And, as you answer, I do know the scope
　　　　 And warrant limited unto my tongue.
PANDULPH The Dauphin is too wilful-opposite
　　　　 And will not temporise with my entreaties.   125
　　　　 He flatly says, he'll not lay down his arms.
BASTARD By all the blood that ever fury breathed,
　　　　 The youth says well! Now hear our English king,
　　　　 For thus his royalty doth speak in me:
　　　　 He is prepared, and reason too he should.   130
　　　　 This apish and unmannerly approach,
　　　　 This harnessed masque and unadvisèd revel,
　　　　 This unhaired sauciness and boyish troops,
　　　　 The king doth smile at, and is well prepared
　　　　 To whip this dwarfish war, this pygmy arms   135
　　　　 From out the circle of his territories.
　　　　 That hand which had the strength, even at your door,
　　　　 To cudgel you and make you take the hatch,
　　　　 To dive like buckets in concealèd wells,

119–20 speak, . . . king:] *Theobald;* speake: . . . King F   124 wilful-opposite] *Theobald; no hyphen in* F; wilful, opposite F4
133 unhaired] *Theobald;* vn-heard F   135 this pygmy] F; these pygmy *Rowe*

118 **fair play** courtesy; continuing the card-game conceit, along with 'dealt' (121).
119–20 *****speak, . . . king:** See supplementary note.
123 **limited** appointed, specified.
124 **wilful-opposite** stubbornly opposed.
125 **temporise** make terms.
127–8 **By . . . well**! The Bastard's familiar taste for military confrontation rather than negotiation (see 2.1.350–60, 582–6; 5.1.66–76).
130 **reason** there is good reason.
131 **apish** fantastic; a sneer at artificial French manners.
132 **harnessed masque** masque in armour. See supplementary note.
132 **unadvisèd** ill-considered, foolish.
133 *****unhaired** beardless (see 5.1.69). The Folio's

'un-heared' is probably not an error since 'hair' was often spelled 'hear'.
135 **this pygmy arms** Since 'arms' was often singular, as in 2.1.249–50, 'this' need not be emended.
136 **circle** confines, compass; continuing the conceit of a masque: the playing area in a hall or theatre. Compare *H5* Prologue 13–20: 'Within this wooden O the very casques . . . within the girdle of these walls / Are now confined two mighty monarchies'.
138 **take the hatch** make a hasty exit; as dogs who are beaten leap over the lower half of the door to take cover.
139 **like buckets . . . wells** See supplementary note.

To crouch in litter of your stable planks,   140
To lie like pawns locked up in chests and trunks,
To hug with swine, to seek sweet safety out
In vaults and prisons, and to thrill and shake
Even at the crying of your nation's crow,
Thinking this voice an armèd Englishman –   145
Shall that victorious hand be feebled here,
That in your chambers gave you chastisement?
No! Know the gallant monarch is in arms
And like an eagle o'er his eyrie tow'rs
To souse annoyance that comes near his nest.   150
And you degenerate, you ingrate revolts,
You bloody Neroes, ripping up the womb
Of your dear mother England, blush for shame!
For your own ladies and pale-visaged maids,
Like Amazons, come tripping after drums,   155
Their thimbles into armèd gauntlets change,
Their needles to lances and their gentle hearts
To fierce and bloody inclination.
LEWIS   There end thy brave, and turn thy face in peace;
        We grant thou canst outscold us. Fare thee well;   160
        We hold our time too precious to be spent
        With such a brabbler.
PANDULPH   Give me leave to speak.
BASTARD No, I will speak.
LEWIS   We will attend to neither.
        Strike up the drums, and let the tongue of war

---

153 mother England] *Theobald;* Mother-England F   156 change] F; chang'd *Dyce (Collier MS.)*

141 An ignominious hiding-place, because we blemish a valuable object by placing it with a pawnbroker.

142 **hug** cuddle.

143 **thrill** shiver, tremble.

144 **your nation's crow** Possibly the crowing of a cock (*gallus*), a traditional symbol of France. See supplementary note.

147 **chambers** provinces or cities directly subject to the king (*OED* Chamber *sb* 6); as London was known as the king's chamber (*camera regis*).

149 **eagle** Symbol of sovereign power.

149 **eyrie** nest and brood high in the air.

149 **tow'rs** mounts up, soars.

150 **souse** swoop down upon; smite.

151 **ingrate revolts** ungrateful rebels.

152–3 Nero was the type of unnatural feeling. See supplementary note.

154 **maids** i.e. daughters.

157 **needles** One syllable. The frequent spelling in the Folio 'needl's' probably represents the pronunciation 'neels' or 'neelds'.

158 **inclination** propensity; possibly a quibble on leaning or bending forward, as a knight charges with a lance (Honigmann).

159 **brave** defiance; boast.

159 **turn thy** face depart.

162 **brabbler** brawler or loud talker.

Plead for our interest and our being here.   165
BASTARD Indeed, your drums being beaten, will cry out;
            And so shall you, being beaten. Do but start
            An echo with the clamour of thy drum,
            And even at hand a drum is ready braced,
            That shall reverberate all as loud as thine.   170
            Sound but another, and another shall,
            As loud as thine, rattle the welkin's ear
            And mock the deep-mouthed thunder; for at hand
            (Not trusting to this halting legate here,
            Whom he hath used rather for sport than need)   175
            Is warlike John; and in his forehead sits
            A bare-ribbed Death, whose office is this day
            To feast upon whole thousands of the French.
LEWIS Strike up our drums to find this danger out.
BASTARD And thou shalt find it, Dauphin, do not doubt.   180

                                                    Exeunt

5.3 *Alarums. Enter* [KING] JOHN *and* HUBERT

KING JOHN How goes the day with us? O, tell me, Hubert.
HUBERT Badly, I fear. How fares your majesty?
KING JOHN This fever that hath troubled me so long
            Lies heavy on me. O, my heart is sick.

                    Enter a MESSENGER

MESSENGER My lord, your valiant kinsman, Falconbridge,   5
            Desires your majesty to leave the field,
            And send him word by me which way you go.
KING JOHN Tell him toward Swinstead, to the abbey there.

Act 5, Scene 3   5.3] *Scæna Tertia.* F

167–8 Do . . . echo Just rouse an echo, like the cry
of a hound starting a hare from its hiding-place.
   169 ready braced tight, giving the best pitch.
   172 welkin's sky's. A word often used by
Shakespeare in self-consciously lofty passages. See
LLL 1.1.219, 4.2.5.
   173 deep-mouthed thunder See supplementary note.
   174 halting (1) wavering, evasive, (2) lame, like
an unsound animal.
   176–7 in . . . Death i.e. John is audaciously
hostile, ready to kill, unlike the wavering Pandulph.
See Ezek. 3.8.

177 bare-ribbed Death The skeleton or emaciated figure of Death on a horse. See 3.4.40.
   180 doubt fear.

Act 5, Scene 3
   3 This fever See supplementary note to
5.6.23.
   8 Swinstead A confusion of Swinstead, which
had no abbey, with Swineshead Abbey, near
Boston, Lincolnshire. The same error is in Foxe,
TR, and other accounts but not in Holinshed.

MESSENGER Be of good comfort, for the great supply
            That was expected by the Dauphin here   10
            Are wrecked three nights ago on Goodwin Sands.
            This news was brought to Richard but even now.
            The French fight coldly and retire themselves.
KING JOHN Ay me, this tyrant fever burns me up,
            And will not let me welcome this good news.   15
            Set on toward Swinstead. To my litter straight,
            Weakness possesseth me, and I am faint.

                                        Exeunt

5.4 *Enter* SALISBURY, PEMBROKE, *and* BIGOT

SALISBURY I did not think the king so stored with friends.
PEMBROKE Up once again! Put spirit in the French;
            If they miscarry, we miscarry too.
SALISBURY That misbegotten devil Falconbridge,
            In spite of spite, alone upholds the day.   5
PEMBROKE They say King John, sore sick, hath left the field.

        Enter MELUN *wounded [and led by soldiers]*

MELUN Lead me to the revolts of England here.
SALISBURY When we were happy, we had other names.
PEMBROKE It is the Count Melun.
SALISBURY   Wounded to death.
MELUN Fly, noble English, you are bought and sold;   10
            Unthread the rude eye of rebellion,

---

10 was] F; were *Wilson* 11 Are] F; Was *Capell* 12 now.] *Johnson*; now, F; now; *Theobald*; now: *Capell*
14 Ay] F (Aye); Ah *Pope* **Act 5, Scene 4** 5.4] *Scena Quarta.* F 2–3 French; . . . they miscarry,] *Capell*;
French, . . . they miscarry: F; French, . . . they miscarry, F3; French: . . . they miscarry, *Rowe* 6 SD *and . . . soldiers*]
Steevens; led / Capell; not in F

11 **Are** The subject 'supply' was a collective noun; also at 5.5.12–13.
11 **Goodwin Sands** Dangerous shoals four miles off the coast of Kent, near the Downs.
16 **litter** According to Holinshed (II, 335) John 'was not able to ride, but was fain to be carried in a litter presently made of twigs'.

Act 5, Scene 4
1 **stored** abundantly provided.
4 **devil** suggesting Falconbridge's uncanny powers of survival.
5 **In . . . spite** Against all odds (Ivor John);

probably a variation on 'In spite of one's teeth [beard, etc.]' (Tilley s764).
7 **revolts** Stress on the first syllable. See 5.2.151 and *OED* Revolt *sb²*, where this use of the noun comes from a different root from the usual meaning of the noun 'revolt'.
10 **bought and sold** betrayed (Tilley B787). Compare *R3* 5.3.305.
11–12 i.e. Retrace your steps that took you through the difficult passage to rebellion, as thread is drawn through a small needle's eye. See supplementary note.

And welcome home again discarded faith.
Seek out King John and fall before his feet,
For if the French be lords of this loud day,
He means to recompense the pains you take   15
By cutting off your heads. Thus hath he sworn,
And I with him, and many more with me,
Upon the altar at Saint Edmundsbury,
Even on that altar, where we swore to you
Dear amity and everlasting love.   20
SALISBURY May this be possible? May this be true?
MELUN Have I not hideous death within my view,
Retaining but a quantity of life,
Which bleeds away even as a form of wax
Resolveth from his figure 'gainst the fire?   25
What in the world should make me now deceive,
Since I must lose the use of all deceit?
Why should I then be false, since it is true
That I must die here and live hence by truth?
I say again, if Lewis do win the day,   30
He is forsworn if e'er those eyes of yours
Behold another day break in the east.
But even this night, whose black contagious breath
Already smokes about the burning crest
Of the old, feeble, and day-wearied sun –   35
Even this ill night your breathing shall expire,
Paying the fine of rated treachery,
Even with a treacherous fine of all your lives,
If Lewis by your assistance win the day.

---

14 French be lords] F; Prince be lord *Keightley;* French be lord *conj. Cam.* 15 He] F; Lewis *Honigmann*
17 more] F4; moe F 33–5 night, . . . sun –] *Kittredge;* night, . . . Sunne, F; night – . . . sun – *Capell*

12 **discarded** Coming after 'unthread', this is perhaps a pun on 'uncarded' = snarled, tangled. To 'card' is to prepare wool for spinning by combing out the impurities and snarls.

15 **He** Lewis. The lack of concord between 'the French', 'lords', and 'He' need not be a sign of corruption if Melun first thinks of 'the French' as collectively the soldiers; then 'He' refers to their leader Lewis.

23 **quantity** small piece.

24–5 **as . . . fire** as a wax shape or image melts before the fire (Tilley W137). See supplementary note.

26–9 'Dying men speak true' (Tilley M514).

27 **use** benefit, profit.

29 **hence** in the next world.

37–8 **fine . . . fine** penalty . . . end. Compare *Ham.* 5.1.106: 'Is this the fine of his fines'.

37 **rated** justly valued; perhaps implying a severe rebuke. Compare *2H6* 3.1.173–5: 'If those that care to keep your royal person / From treason's secret knife and traitor's rage / Be thus upbraided, chid, and rated at'.

Commend me to one Hubert with your king;   40
The love of him, and this respect besides,
For that my grandsire was an Englishman,
Awakes my conscience to confess all this.
In lieu whereof, I pray you bear me hence
From forth the noise and rumour of the field,   45
Where I may think the remnant of my thoughts
In peace, and part this body and my soul
With contemplation and devout desires.

SALISBURY We do believe thee, and beshrew my soul,
But I do love the favour and the form   50
Of this most fair occasion, by the which
We will untread the steps of damnèd flight,
And like a bated and retirèd flood,
Leaving our rankness and irregular course,
Stoop low within those bounds we have o'erlooked,   55
And calmly run on in obedience
Even to our ocean, to our great King John.
My arm shall give thee help to bear thee hence,
For I do see the cruel pangs of death
Right in thine eye. Away, my friends! New flight   60
And happy newness that intends old right.
                        Exeunt [leading off Melun]

---

40 Hubert] *Cam.;* Hubert, F   60 Right] F; Fight *Capell;* Bright *Collier MS.*   61 SD *leading off Melun*] *Theobald (subst.); not in* F

40–3 See p. 43 above for the importance of Melun's friendship with Hubert.

42 One of the two lines identical with *TR* (12.117). See also 2.1.528.

45 **noise and rumour** confused din, outcry.

49–50 **beshrew . . . love** may my soul be cursed if I do not love. After 'beshrew me' 'but' is not adversative, but means 'if not' (Abbott 126). See *Oth.* 4.3.78.

50–1 **favour . . . occasion** As she approaches, Occasion is charming or appealing, and she offers her forelock to be seized; but after she has passed she looks ugly.

52 **untread** retrace.

53 **bated** abated, lowered; but shading off into 'humbled' as, in 'stoop low'.

54 **rankness** overflowing, swollen as with pride.

55 **o'erlooked** risen above; connoting pride. See 3.1.23.

57 **our ocean** the great sea of authority and majesty. See supplementary note.

60 **Right** Exactly, right there.

61 **intends** proceeds toward.

61 **old right** i.e. our loyalty to the *de facto* king.

5.5 [*Lewis the*] DAUPHIN *and his train*

LEWIS   The sun of heaven, methought, was loath to set,
        But stayed and made the western welkin blush,
        When English measure backward their own ground
        In faint retire. O, bravely came we off,
        When with a volley of our needless shot,   5
        After such bloody toil, we bid good night,
        And wound our tott'ring colours clearly up,
        Last in the field and almost lords of it!

                    Enter a MESSENGER

MESSENGER   Where is my prince, the Dauphin?
LEWIS   Here: what news?
MESSENGER   The Count Melun is slain, the English lords   10
        By his persuasion are again fall'n off,
        And your supply, which you have wished so long,
        Are cast away and sunk on Goodwin Sands.
LEWIS   Ah, foul shrewd news! Beshrew thy very heart!
        I did not think to be so sad tonight   15
        As this hath made me. Who was he that said
        King John did fly an hour or two before
        The stumbling night did part our weary pow'rs?
MESSENGER   Whoever spoke it, it is true, my lord.
LEWIS   Well, keep good quarter and good care tonight;   20
        The day shall not be up so soon as I
        To try the fair adventure of tomorrow.

                                                    Exeunt

Act 5, Scene 5   **5.5**] *Scena Quinta*. F   **3** English] F; th' English *Rowe*³; the English *Capell*   **3** measure] F; measure'd
Pope   **7** wound] *Rowe*³; woon'd F   **7** tott'ring] F; tatter'd *Pope;* tattering *Malone*

Act 5, Scene 5
  3 measure tread, traverse.
  4 faint exhausted; but implying a cowardly
retreat.
  4 bravely . . . off we retired from the field in fine
style.
  5 needless i.e. as an exuberant gesture.
  7 tott'ring tattering, hanging in rags; not in
disgrace but honour. Compare *Edward II* 2.3.21:
'tottered ensign of my ancestors'.

  7 clearly freely, without embarrassment.
  11 fall'n off defected.
  14 shrewd . . . Beshrew bitter . . . Be damned.
Both words come from the noun 'shrew', a wicked
person, often called a 'cursed shrew'.
  18 stumbling night night so dark that one
stumbles.
  20 keep . . . quarter keep a good watch.
  22 To try the chances of success tomorrow (that
eluded him today).

5.6 *Enter* BASTARD *and* HUBERT, *severally* [*as in the dark*]

HUBERT Who's there? Speak ho! Speak quickly or I shoot.
BASTARD A friend. What art thou?
HUBERT   Of the part of England.
BASTARD Whither dost thou go?
HUBERT   What's that to thee?
BASTARD Why may not I demand of thine affairs,
      As well as thou of mine? –   5
      Hubert, I think.
HUBERT   Thou hast a perfect thought.
      I will upon all hazards well believe
      Thou art my friend that know'st my tongue so well.
      Who art thou?
BASTARD   Who thou wilt; and if thou please
      Thou mayst befriend me so much as to think   10
      I come one way of the Plantagenets.
HUBERT Unkind remembrance, thou and eyeless night
      Have done me shame. Brave soldier, pardon me
      That any accent breaking from thy tongue
      Should 'scape the true acquaintance of mine ear.   15
BASTARD Come, come; sans compliment, what news abroad?
HUBERT Why here walk I in the black brow of night
      To find you out.
BASTARD   Brief then; and what's the news?
HUBERT O my sweet sir, news fitting to the night,
      Black, fearful, comfortless, and horrible.   20
BASTARD Show me the very wound of this ill news.
      I am no woman, I'll not swound at it.

Act 5, Scene 6   **5.6**| *Scena Sexta.* F   **1** Who's| F4; Whose F   **3–5** What's . . . mine?| F; What's . . . demand / . . . mine?
Capell   **4–6** BASTARD Why . . . Hubert| *Dyce²*, *conj. Lloyd subst.;* Why . . . *Bast. Hubert* F   **12** eyeless| *Theobald*;
endles F

Act 5, Scene 6
0 SD *severally* by different entrances; the actors
moving as if in the dark.
  1–6 See Textual Analysis, pp. 186–8 below, on
the reassignment of these speeches.
  6 Thou . . . thought You think correctly (Wilson).
  7 upon all hazards against all odds (Smallwood).
  9 Who thou wilt Take a guess.
  11 one way Not 'got i'th'way of honesty'

(1.1.170, 181) but *got*, at any rate – in one way or
another.
  12 Unkind remembrance i.e. 'What a bad
memory I have' (Baker).
  12 *eyeless night dark, moonless. See supplementary note.
  14 accent word, utterance.
  16 sans compliment without formalities (Smallwood).
  22 swound 'swoon' plus '-d', by analogy with
'drowned' and 'bound' (adj.); internal rime with
'wound' (21) as in *The Rape of Lucrece* 1486.

HUBERT The king, I fear, is poisoned by a monk.
        I left him almost speechless and broke out
        To acquaint you with this evil, that you might   25
        The better arm you to the sudden time
        Than if you had at leisure known of this.
BASTARD How did he take it? Who did taste to him?
HUBERT A monk, I tell you, a resolvèd villain,
        Whose bowels suddenly burst out. The king   30
        Yet speaks and peradventure may recover.
BASTARD Who didst thou leave to tend his majesty?
HUBERT Why, know you not? The lords are all come back,
        And brought Prince Henry in their company,
        At whose request the king hath pardoned them,   35
        And they are all about his majesty.
BASTARD Withhold thine indignation, mighty heaven,
        And tempt us not to bear above our power!
        I'll tell thee, Hubert, half my power this night,
        Passing these flats, are taken by the tide.   40
        These Lincoln Washes have devourèd them,
        Myself, well mounted, hardly have escaped.
        Away before; conduct me to the king.
        I doubt he will be dead or ere I come.

                                                    Exeunt

33–4 not? . . . company,] F; not? . . . company; *Theobald;* not, . . . company? *conj.* Malone   41 Lincoln Washes] *Pope;* Lincolne-Washes F

---

23 **The king . . . poisoned** See supplementary note.

24 **broke out** rushed away; perhaps an association with 'speechless', implying that pent-up feelings had to break out as well.

26 i.e. I warn you so that you can prepare yourself in the emergency, lest the time's enemies take advantage of it.

27 **at leisure** after some delay (Moore Smith).

28 **Who . . . him?** Who acted as taster for him?

29 **I tell you** I assure you (*OED* Tell *v* 9).

30 **Whose . . . out** A detail from Foxe's *Acts and Monuments* or Grafton's *Chronicle*, not in Holinshed or *TR*.

38 **tempt us not** don't put us to the test. The meaning is close to the Latin root *temptare*, to try the strength of. See Gen. 22.1, 1 Cor. 10.13, and supplementary note.

39 **power** men; hence the plural 'are'.

42 **hardly** with difficulty, barely.

44 **doubt** fear.

44 **or ere** before ever; hence 'before I even come' (Abbott 131).

5.7 *Enter* PRINCE HENRY, SALISBURY, *and* BIGOT

PRINCE HENRY It is too late. The life of all his blood
Is touched corruptibly, and his pure brain
(Which some suppose the soul's frail dwelling-house)
Doth by the idle comments that it makes
Foretell the ending of mortality.   5

Enter PEMBROKE

PEMBROKE His highness yet doth speak, and holds belief
That being brought into the open air,
It would allay the burning quality
Of that fell poison which assaileth him.
PRINCE HENRY Let him be brought into the orchard here.   10
                                        [*Exit Bigot*]
Doth he still rage?
PEMBROKE   He is more patient
Than when you left him; even now he sung.
PRINCE HENRY O vanity of sickness! Fierce extremes
In their continuance will not feel themselves.
Death, having preyed upon the outward parts,   15
Leaves them insensible, and his siege is now
Against the mind, the which he pricks and wounds
With many legions of strange fantasies,
Which in their throng and press to that last hold,
Confound themselves. 'Tis strange that Death should sing.   20
I am the cygnet to this pale faint swan,

Act 5, Scene 7 5.7] *Scena Septima.* F 2 corruptibly] F; corruptedly *Capell* 11 SD] *Capell; not in* F 16 insensible,] *Hanmer, Capell (subst.);* inuisible, F; invasible, *conj. Wilson;* enfeebl'd, *conj. Maxwell;* invincible, *Smallwood* 17 mind] *Rowe³;* winde F 21 cygnet] *Rowe³;* Symet F

Act 5, Scene 7
1 **life . . . blood** vital spirits, made in the heart and transported in the veins. See Burton, *Anatomy of Melancholy* (ed. Holbrook Jackson, 1932), 1.1.2.2.
2 **touched** infected.
2 **pure** clear, normally uncorrupted. See *Ado* 5.4.87.
4 **idle comments** incoherent remarks.
5 **mortality** mortal life.
13 **vanity** delusion.
13–14 **Fierce . . . themselves** Compare Montaigne, 'Of sadness', 1, 2 (Frame trans.): the 'bleak and deaf stupor that benumbs us when accidents

surpassing our endurance overwhelm us . . . the impact of grief, to be extreme, must stun [estone] the whole soul'.
13 **extremes** intense agonies.
16 ***insensible** See supplementary note.
16–18 **his siege . . . fantasies** Compare Holinshed (II, 336), 'through anguish of mind, rather than through force of sickness, he departed this life'.
19 **hold** stronghold.
20 **Confound** Destroy.
21 **swan** Alluding to the old idea that the swan, though not a singing bird, sings once, beautifully, just before it dies (*ODEP* 791b and Tilley s1028.)

Who chants a doleful hymn to his own death,
And from the organ-pipe of frailty sings
His soul and body to their lasting rest.
SALISBURY Be of good comfort, prince, for you are born   25
To set a form upon that indigest
Which he hath left so shapeless and so rude.

JOHN *brought in* [*on a litter by* BIGOT *and attendants*]

KING JOHN Ay, marry, now my soul hath elbow-room,
It would not out at windows nor at doors.
There is so hot a summer in my bosom   30
That all my bowels crumble up to dust.
I am a scribbled form, drawn with a pen
Upon a parchment, and against this fire
So I shrink up.
PRINCE HENRY   How fares your majesty?
KING JOHN Poisoned – ill fare – dead, forsook, cast off,   35
And none of you will bid the winter come
To thrust his icy fingers in my maw,
Nor let my kingdom's rivers take their course
Through my burned bosom, nor entreat the north
To make his bleak winds kiss my parchèd lips   40
And comfort me with cold. I do not ask you much,
I beg cold comfort; and you are so strait
And so ungrateful, you deny me that.
PRINCE HENRY O that there were some virtue in my tears,
That might relieve you!

27 SD *on . . . attendants*] Capell *(subst.):* not *in* F 28 elbow-room,] F *(no hyphen);* elbow-room; Pope; elbow-room Honigmann 29 doors.] Pope; doores, F 35 Poisoned – ill fare –] Cam. *(subst.);* Poyson'd, ill fare: F, Poison'd, ill fate! Pope; Poison'd, – ill fare; – Capell

23 organ-pipe of frailty Compare W. Vallans, *A Tale of Two Swans* (1590), sig. A2ᵛ: 'The philosophers say [the swan sings] because of the spirit [which,] labouring to pass through the long and small passage of her neck, makes a noise as if she did sing' (Honigmann). For a Platonic interpretation see T. R. Waldo, 'Beyond words: Shakespeare's tongue-tied muse', in S. Homan (ed.), *Shakespeare's 'More Than Words Can Witness'*, 1980, pp. 160–76.
26–7 To create order out of the chaos of the kingdom. See supplementary note for Ovidian echoes.
28 elbow-room Proverbially, room to turn in and so live comfortably (Tilley E104), but John

means that it is easier to die out of doors. According to a Devonshire superstition, when a dying person is at the last extremity every door in the house should be opened so that the soul can go forth freely (John Brand, *Popular Antiquities*, ed. Henry Ellis, 1849, II, 231.).
32 scribbled form Like the rude, shapeless, indigest kingdom he leaves behind and the disfiguring 'form of wax' (5.4.24 and see n.).
35 ill fare With a pun on 'bad food'.
37 maw stomach.
42 cold comfort Punning on the ironic phrase for inadequate, empty consolation (Smallwood).
42 strait niggardly.
44 virtue healing power.

KING JOHN   The salt in them is hot.   45
         Within me is a hell, and there the poison
         Is, as a fiend, confined to tyrannise
         On unreprievable, condemnèd blood.

                   Enter BASTARD [*and* HUBERT]

BASTARD O, I am scalded with my violent motion
         And spleen of speed to see your majesty.   50
KING JOHN O cousin, thou art come to set mine eye.
         The tackle of my heart is cracked and burnt,
         And all the shrouds wherewith my life should sail
         Are turnèd to one thread, one little hair.
         My heart hath one poor string to stay it by,   55
         Which holds but till thy news be utterèd,
         And then all this thou seest is but a clod
         And module of confounded royalty.
BASTARD The Dauphin is preparing hitherward,
         Where God He knows how we shall answer him,   60
         For in a night the best part of my power,
         As I upon advantage did remove,
         Were in the Washes all unwarily
         Devourèd by the unexpected flood.
                              [*The King dies*]

---

48 SD *and* HUBERT | *Kemble; not in* F   60 God| *Kittredge, conj. Walker;* heauen F   60 He| *Cam.;* he F   64 SD| *Rowe;*
not in F

45 **salt . . . hot** Because tears of grief burn (see *Ham.* 4.5.155–6), as the tears of the damned are scalding (*Lear* 4.7.46–7).

46 **Within . . . hell** The common idea that sinners carry hell within them raises a question about John's salvation or damnation (Smallwood).

48 **unreprievable, condemnèd blood** blood condemned to die, without hope of reprieve from the poison.

49 **scalded . . . motion** fired with my intense desire.

50 **spleen** eagerness.

51 **set** close.

52 **tackle** rigging; if the ship's ropes are cracked and burnt through, shipwreck is imminent. Compare *3H6* 5.4.3–23.

53 **shrouds** The ropes in a ship's rigging running from the deck to the top of the masts and bracing

them against being strained sideways. A winding-sheet may be implied.

54 **thread** The notion here and in the next two lines is of weak heart-strings, the strings of life, blended with the saying 'To hang by a hair (or thread)' (*ODEP* 343b).

58 **module** lifeless image or counterfeit; i.e. fleshly remains fit for a grave. Compare *R2* 3.2.153–4 'that small model of the barren earth / Which serves as paste and cover to our bones'. 'Module' and 'model' were interchangeable spellings.

58 **confounded** shattered.

60 ***God He knows** God only knows.

62 **upon advantage** to gain an advantage.

63 **Were** See 5.6.39–40 for the plural verb with 'power' as subject.

64 **flood** high tide.

SALISBURY You breathe these dead news in as dead an ear.   65
    My liege, my lord! – But now a king, now thus.
PRINCE HENRY Even so must I run on, and even so stop.
    What surety of the world, what hope, what stay,
    When this was now a king and now is clay?
BASTARD Art thou gone so? I do but stay behind   70
    To do the office for thee of revenge,
    And then my soul shall wait on thee to heaven,
    As it on earth hath been thy servant still. –
    Now, now, you stars that move in your right spheres,
    Where be your powers? Show now your mended faiths,   75
    And instantly return with me again
    To push destruction and perpetual shame
    Out of the weak door of our fainting land.
    Straight let us seek, or straight we shall be sought;
    The Dauphin rages at our very heels.   80
SALISBURY It seems you know not then so much as we.
    The Cardinal Pandulph is within at rest,
    Who half an hour since came from the Dauphin,
    And brings from him such offers of our peace
    As we with honour and respect may take,   85
    With purpose presently to leave this war.
BASTARD He will the rather do it when he sees
    Ourselves well-sinewèd to our defence.
SALISBURY Nay, 'tis in a manner done already,
    For many carriages he hath dispatched   90
    To the sea-side and put his cause and quarrel
    To the disposing of the cardinal,
    With whom yourself, myself, and other lords
    If you think meet, this afternoon will post
    To consummate this business happily.   95

---

65 ear.] F4 *(subst.);* eare F   88 well-sinewèd] *Rowe (subst.);* well sinew'd F   91 sea-side] F2; *no hphen in* F

65 **dead news** news of death. See p. 42 above.
66 **But now** Just now.
68 **stay** support.
72 A promise the Bastard soon forgets.
72 **wait on** attend.

74 **stars . . . spheres** nobles who have returned to your old loyalties.
75 **powers** troops.
90 **carriages** wagons, gun-carriages.
94 **post** hasten.

BASTARD Let it be so. – And you, my noble prince,
        With other princes that may best be spared,
        Shall wait upon your father's funeral.
PRINCE HENRY At Worcester must his body be interred,
        For so he willed it.
BASTARD   Thither shall it then,   100
        And happily may your sweet self put on
        The lineal state and glory of the land!
        To whom with all submission on my knee
        I do bequeath my faithful services
        And true subjection everlasting. [*Kneels*]   105
SALISBURY And the like tender of our love we make
        To rest without a spot for evermore.
                        [*Lords kneel*]
PRINCE HENRY I have a kind soul that would give thanks,
        And knows not how to do it but with tears.
BASTARD [*Rising*] O, let us pay the time but needful woe,   110
        Since it hath been beforehand with our griefs.
        This England never did, nor never shall,
        Lie at the proud foot of a conqueror,
        But when it first did help to wound itself.
        Now these her princes are come home again,   115
        Come the three corners of the world in arms,
        And we shall shock them. Nought shall make us rue,
        If England to itself do rest but true.

                                                Exeunt

---

108 give] F; give you *Rowe;* fain give *conj. Cam.*   110 time] *Rowe;* time: F

97 **princes** lords.

99 **Worcester** Where John's monument still stands.

102 **lineal** As the heir of a crowned king, Henry had a better title than John; just as Henry V's was better than his father's (Wilson).

103–5 This statement matches his first references to himself at 1.1.50 (Jones, *Origins*, p. 260).

106 **tender** offer.

107 **rest** remain; with the suggestion of 'lay to rest'.

108 **kind** (1) natural (and so inclined to respond appropriately), (2) loving, i.e. 'kind by kind'. Both are attributes of England's 'inward greatness' according to *H5* 2 Chorus 16–19.

110–11 'Let us not pay more than necessary sorrow to the present occasion, because time has made us pay in advance with an abundance of our tears'; i.e. after the formalities of the funeral, let us look to the future. 'To be beforehand' is to pay in advance (*OED* Beforehand *adv* 1b) or to have more than enough for present demands (1d).

116 **three corners** all the rest of the world (England being the fourth corner: 'that utmost corner of the west' (2.1.29)).

117 **shock** repel, throw into confusion.

117–18 **Nought . . . true** See supplementary note.

SUPPLEMENTARY NOTES

*Title The early quartos of *R2* and *R3* were titled *The Tragedy of Richard the second* and *The Tragedy of Richard the third*; moreover, Francis Meres (*Palladis Tamia*, 1598) listed those plays, along with *King John*, among Shakespeare's tragedies. But after Shakespeare's death, the editors of the Folio tried to distinguish a class of serious plays based on English history from those based on ancient and contemporary European sources. Whoever planned the Folio's 'Catalogue' and the running titles for the histories normalised the titles of two- and three-part plays according to the formula *The First part of King . . .* and *The Second part of King . . .*, and the rest of the histories were titled with equally bland names: *The life and death of . . .* or just *The life of . . .* (if the leading character did not die). In one instance in the Folio, the title that stood at the beginning of the text (the head-title) retained the earlier form: *The Tragedy of Richard the Third . . .* although *The Life and Death . . .* was used in running titles. Since the head-title of *King John* in the Folio was *The life and death of King John*, as was *The life & death of Richard the Second*, we have little reason to be confident that the Folio's title was Shakespeare's. His preference may well have been *The Tragedy of King John*.

1.1.11 According to Holinshed (11, 273–4), after the death of King Richard 1, Queen Eleanor persuaded the nobles of Poitiers (an error for what is now Poitou), Anjou, Touraine, and Maine to swear allegiance to her youngest son John. These lands had originally been part of her dowry as Eleanor of Aquitaine when she married Louis VII of France, and after the divorce she brought them to her next marriage with Henry II of England. Arthur claimed them by inheritance from his father Geoffrey, John's older brother, and Arthur did homage to King Philip for these lands, as well as for Brittany. Thus the King of France had a political interest in defending Arthur's rights, but Shakespeare expands Arthur's claims to include England and Ireland. He turns a dispute about family property into a challenge to John's very right to rule England and its territories.

1.1.170 **above** The Folio's 'something about a little from the right' is puzzling, with or without F4's addition of a comma after 'about'. Nearly all editors follow F4, and they usually gloss the phrase as 'by a rather roundabout road', or 'a bit off the course'. The *OED* has no example of 'something about'; however, if 'about' is a misreading of 'above', there is no need to add a comma after the phrase, and the Bastard's response is a mocking understatement, in this case meaning 'a little more than'. Compare *Ham.* 2.2.435: 'it was never acted, or if it was, not above once'. 'Something' followed by a comparative adverb was an established idiom – see *WT* 2.2.53: 'Please you, come something nearer'; or *MND* 3.2.304: 'she is something lower than myself'.

1.1.256–7 The passage as printed in the Folio is ambiguous: 'Heaven lay not my transgression to my charge, / That art the issue of my dear offence'. The tenor of Lady Falconbridge's speech is that she resisted but was overcome by long and vehement suit; but, depending upon the emendation, the specific meaning is (1) My son should not blame me ('Heaven! . . . my charge / That' – Knight, Honigmann subst., Riverside subst.); (2) God should not blame me ('Heaven . . . my charge! / Thou' – Wright, Kittredge, Alexander, Smallwood); (3) God should not blame you ('Heaven . . . thy charge / That' – Staunton, Wilson, Sisson).

Each meaning is possible. The third resembles the words of St Stephen as he was stoned by the Jews, Acts 7.60: 'Lord, lay not this sin to their charge'; so Lady Falconbridge seems to say 'May God not burden you, the issue of my dear offence, with my transgression.' The second implies that God should not blame her because her sin has cost her dearly and she has confessed it now on earth. Compare *A Larum for London* (1602), sig. G: 'The blood that I have spilt . . . / Heaven lay not to my charge.' The first seems preferable because it is simplest and it leads into the Bastard's response. If Lady Falconbridge imagines that her son accuses her of a transgression, that misunderstanding naturally provokes his reply – the reply of a bemused, proud, and forgiving son. In effect he says, 'I do not blame you, mother, for giving me such a father. I thank you.'

1.1.268–70 When the newly dubbed Sir Richard Plantagenet thanks his mother for the gift of such a father, he honours not only her and his illustrious begetter, but also the example of Hercules, the first bastard, son of Zeus and Alcmena. Andrea Alciati and subsequent Renaissance emblemists pictured him wearing the lion's skin and exhorted bastards: 'forever celebrate the honours of Hercules, / for he was the prince of your class' (*Andreas Alciatus*, ed. Peter M. Daly *et al.*, 2 vols., 1985, emblem no. 139). Iconographically King Richard too was identified with Hercules and Samson, both of whom subdued a lion bare-handed (see illustration 12, p. 40 above).

2.1.144 As great Alcides' shoes upon an ass The idea is that King Richard's lion skin lies as appropriately upon Austria as something of great Hercules lies upon an ass. Shakespeare conflates two proverbs (Tilley A351 and S366) after Gosson's *School of Abuse* (1579). sig. A3ᵛ: 'You will smile . . . to see how this moral philosopher toils to draw the Lion's skin upon Aesop's ass, Hercules' shoes on a child's feet.' Hamlet also puns on 'shoes' and 'shows' (*Ham.* 1.2.147–9): 'A little month, or ere those shoes were old / With which she followed my poor father's body / Like Niobe, all tears' (and Q2 spells 'shoes' as 'shows'), and see Thomas Kyd, *The First Part of Jeronimo*, in *Works*, ed. T. S. Boas, 1901, 2.1.83 (Maxwell, p. 75).

2.1.184–90 Eleanor is not only the sinner for whom Arthur, in the third generation, must suffer; she has begotten John, 'her sin', who, along with her, plagues Arthur. She has aroused God's wrath, making her and her son His scourge. Thus an innocent child is punished for her, by her, and by her son.

2.1.195 Peace . . . pause The Folio's 'pause' could be a misreading of 'peace' as in the common phrase, found for example in *Err.* 4.4.58: 'Peace, doting wizard, peace!'; and in *1H4* 2.4.397, 5.1.29; *2H4* 3.2.119; *R3* 2.2.17; and *Sir Thomas More*, Hand D, line 50: 'peace peace scilens peace'. 'Pause' in this context would normally mean 'take a breath', but John asks for silence or moderation. However, 'Pause' probably should stand, for if the manuscript read 'peace . . . peace' we would not expect the compositor or scribe to misread the second, having got the first corrrect.

2.1.249–50 arms, like to a muzzled bear . . . sealed up The proximity of 'arms', 'muzzled bear', and 'sealed' suggests a play on words for a heraldic device, coat-of-arms, or seal. A contemporary allusion, lost upon us, may be intended. In any case, the Dudley family, including the Earl of Leicester and his ne'er-do-well son, were prominent bearers of the badge – a muzzled bear rampant tied to a rough post – and Leicester was satirised in these terms for his policies toward religious and political factions in England and abroad. Compare *The copie of a letter . . . of the Erle of Leycester* (1584), sig. B1: 'You know the Bears love . . . which is all for his own paunch, and so this Bear-whelp turneth all to his own commodity and for greediness thereof will over turn all if he be not stopped or muzzled in time.' Leicester is a man (sig. B1ᵛ) 'nooseled in treason . . . fleshed in conspiracy against the royal blood of K. Henry's children . . .' If Philip of France resembles Leicester, the significance lies in Philip's sacrifice of Arthur's right for the sake of his own commodity later in this scene. *Leicester's Commonwealth*, as this book was later known, circulated widely for more than a century. See D. C. Peck's edition (1985).

2.1.335 roam on Many editors have emended to 'run on' (after F2) because of the resemblance to 5.4.54–7: 'Leaving our rankness and irregular course, / Stoop low within those bounds we have o'erlooked, / And calmly run on in obedience / Even to our ocean . . .' The latter passage implies that, after the nobles rebelliously roamed outside the banks, they will now run dutifully within the river banks. The situation is different in 2.1.335, for John threatens to 'roam on' again continuing like a destructive flood, overswelling the banks, if France continues to impede his way. Otherwise he will flow peacefully to the ocean. The proverb is 'The stream (current, tide) stopped swells the higher' (Tilley S929). 'Roam on' implies irregularity, 'run on' regularity (see Schmidt, *roam*).

2.1.366–7 bear . . . you John asserts the unity of his natural body ('our person') and the body politic (lord of 'Angiers, and of you'). Edmund Plowden, *Commentaries or Reports* (1571), 816 edn, p. 213 (cited by E. H. Kantorowicz, *The King's Two Bodies*, 1957, p. 9), explains the two-in-one nature of a king, who 'has a body natural, adorned and invested with the estate and dignity royal; and he has not a body natural distinct and divided by itself from the office and dignity royal, but a body natural and a body politic together and indivisible; and these two bodies are incorporated in one person, and make one body and not divers'.

2.1.371 Kinged of our fears The Folio reading is contradictory, for the Citizen says that they will wait until some certain king appears to resolve their fears; yet 'Kings of our feare' implies that they already have control over their fear. In the context, the Citizen has noted that God knows who is the true King of England, but they do not. The possibilities are: (1) Warburton's suggestion, 'Kings are our fears', which removes the contradiction, for two kings are troublesome to them. They will wait until there is only one acknowledged king. But the reading is inelegant, and it is hard to suppose that the word 'are' was misread as 'of'. (2) Tyrwhitt's happy suggestion (followed by Malone), 'King'd of our fears', that means 'Our fears rule us like a king, until they are purged and deposed by one of these kings.' This emendation creates one of Shakespeare's favourite figures of speech, chiasmus: kinged, fears, fears, resolved. (3) Honigmann thinks Tyrwhitt's reading is ingenious but unnecessary, for Abbott (168, p. 111) points out that 'of' may be used for internal motives, as 'by' is used for external agents: e.g. *2H6* 2.1.85–6, 'camest thou here by chance / Or of devotion'; *R3* 1.3.63 (Q1–6), 'The King of his own royal disposition'. However, these phrases and others cited by Abbott use 'of' in the sense 'as a consequence of' (see *OED* Of 15a), so Honigmann paraphrases, 'We must be our own kings on account of our fear, until our fears (and thus our kingship, which follows from our fears) be deposed.' It seems unlikely that they should be kings on account of their fear.

2.1.451–5 The sea enragèd . . . city A Senecan echo – *Medea* 406–14: 'never will my furor cease in its punishing, but will always increase. What savagery of beasts, what Scylla, what Charybdis swallowing the Ausonian and Sicilian sea, or what Etna crushing the breathing Titan will burn with such threats? Not the swift river, not the stormy sea or Pontus raging from the northwest wind or the power of fires fanned by the tempest can hold back my force and anger: I will destroy and overturn everything.' The same passage may be behind *Oth.* 3.3.453–62. See G. Braden, *Renaissance Tragedy and the Senecan Tradition*, 1985, pp. 175–7.

2.1.455 None of the plausible meanings of 'stay' is entirely satisfying. (1) It refers way back to the Citizen's call (416) for a parley – 'vouchsafe awhile to stay' = wait. (2) It anticipates the Bastard's metaphor in the following lines, if 'stay' suggests a sudden check or cessation of action, as when a horse stops short and shakes the rider out of his saddle. Compare Florio, *World of Words* (1611): 'Falchi, the pauses or stays when a horse doth rest upon his hinder parts.' (3) it may be the imperative sense of the verb 'Stay!' – 'Halt' – used as a noun (Schmidt, followed by Kittredge). The general meaning is that the Bastard's plan of attack is impeded. Therefore we need not emend, although Dr Johnson has proposed an appealing possibility: 'stay' could be a misreading of 'flaw' – 'a gust of bravery, a blast of menace. This suits well with the spirit of the piece.' Compare *Cor* 5.3.74: 'Like a great sea-mark, standing every flaw.'

2.1.477–9 zeal . . . was The passage is as ambiguous as the Folio punctuation: (1) lest zeal for this match, now warm and yielding, be cooled by renewed windy petitions, pity, and compassion for Constance. If the image is one of hardening wax ready to seal (punning on 'zeal') a contract of marriage or a treaty (Wilson), it implies 'Seal while the wax is soft, before Constance blows on it.' See *TGV* 2.4.201–3, *R2* 1.1.47–51. This interpretation accords with the feelings that zeal is warm and flowing, as at 3.4.149: 'This act so evilly borne shall cool the hearts / Of all his people and freeze up their zeal.' At 2.1.475–6 Eleanor presumes that King Phillip and the Dauphin's souls are susceptible to 'this ambition'. (2) lest zeal for Arthur's right now melted by peaceful petitions from Angiers should cool and harden. If the image is of melted steel rehardening (Steevens), or melted ice refreezing (Malone), it implies that King Philip's formerly hardened resolve to fight for Arthur will firm up again 'to what it was'. Although it is hard to imagine that the Citizen's proposal should appeal to 'pity and remorse', it is possible to think of zeal as cold and hard. Moreover, this interpretation makes something of the final phrase 'what it was', that the first cannot easily accommodate.

2.1.493 education Because 'education' replaces 'virtue' in the series beauty, virtue, and birth (428 above), it probably means 'upbringing'. Although many well-born women were instructed in book-learning, their basic education in the sixteenth century was moral and religious. Compare *Oth.* 1.3.183–4: 'My life and education both do learn me / How to respect you; you are the lord of duty.'

2.1.544 passionate If Constance has not yet learned of the marriage agreement and treaty, she has no obvious reason for sorrow (Smallwood), and if she were on stage at the beginning of this episode, she would not withdraw during the negotiations. It is evidence of Shakespeare's instinct for theatre to keep her out of sight until Salisbury breaks the news. See 2.1.299 n. In *TR* she is present and she often interrupts the deliberations. See *Shr.* 4.2.54 ff. where Tranio knows things that he has not been told.

2.1.574–8 bias of the world . . . sway of motion The astronomical metaphor, mixed with the one from bowls, implies a heliocentric universe; the world (earth) moves and the sun stands still. Honigmann suggests that Chapman imitated this passage, *Bussy D'Ambois* (1604), 5.1.161–5: 'Now is it true, earth moves and heaven stands still; / . . . The too huge bias of the world hath sway'd / Her back-part upwards, and with that she braves / This hemisphere.'

2.1.582 E. M. W. Tillyard, *Shakespeare's History Plays*, 1946, p. 219: 'When Shakespeare calls Commodity "this all-changing Word" [*sic*] he means what Pope meant at the end of the *Dunciad* when he spoke of Dullness quenching light by her "uncreating word". As God himself had created the world through the Word, the second person of the Trinity, so Commodity is the evil "Word" undoing the great act of creation. And this theological reference is clinched when the Bastard a few lines later brings in the familiar ambiguity of the word *angel* as both coin and heavenly ministrant.'

2.1.583 the outward eye C. St German, *Doctor and Student* (1554), dialogue 1, ch.14: 'When the first man Adam was create, he received of God a double eye, that is to say, and outward eye, whereby he might see visible things and know his bodily enemies and eschew them. And an inward eye, that is the eye of the reason, whereby he might see his spiritual enemies that fighteth against his soul, and beware of them'. See also *Digby Mysteries* (1485), *New Shakespeare Society*, ser. 7, no. 1, 4.1134–5: 'with thine inward eye / Seest the deepest place of man's conscience'. The 'eye' may also refer to the game of bowls, the hole in a bowl into which the lead for the bias was inserted.

3.1.70–4 To me . . . bow to it Constance's emblem of pride, established by Tamburlaine's demand for homage from kings, blends with the image of Christ the King of Grief (see illustration 10, p. 31 above). Shakespeare merged these two again in the proud woes of Richard II. See *R2* 4.1.169–71. Constance nursed her hopes partly in the dream of being queen mother so she could 'check the world' (2.1.122–3), and her grief naturally reflects that lost vision.

3.1.73 To emphasise the *weight* of her grief Constance may sit on the ground at 72–3. If an actress stresses her *proud* grief, she might sit as early as 69. But if she waits until after 74 (Theobald and most editors), she separates action from word.

3.1.107–12 Seneca's *Medea* (530–8) calls upon the gods to blight the wedding between her husband and King Creon's daughter. Earlier in the play the Chorus asks for peace to be sacrificed, and Medea's opening speech (17–19) curses Jason's new wife, his father-in-law, the whole royal stock, and her husband. In the rising tide of her furious rhetoric, she seems, like Constance, to pre-empt heavenly power.

3.1.113 War . . . Peace . . . war Compare Erasmus, *Enchiridion* (1503), trans. Himelick, 1963, pp. 39–40: 'As if this peace of ours were not actually the most shameful kind of war, for surely a man who has come to terms with his vices has violated the covenant he made with God at his baptism. You lunatic! You cry "Peace! Peace!" when you have God as your enemy, who alone is peace and the author of peace.' Constance probably has Jer. 6.13–15 in mind: 'For from the least of them, even unto the greatest of them, everyone is given unto covetousness, and from the prophet even unto the priest, they all deal falsely. They have healed also the hurt of the daughter of my people with sweet words, saying Peace, Peace, when there is no peace . . . they were not ashamed, no neither could they have any shame: therefore they shall fall among the slain: when I shall visit them, they shall be cast down, saith the Lord.' See p. 56 above.

3.1.128–9 lion's . . . calf's-skin Consistent with her idea of Austria as coward (115) and fool (121), Constance combines both in her final insult. She alludes to the fable by Avianus of the ass wearing a lion's skin, signifying a coward who hectors like a farcical actor and is noted for his mimic roar (i.e. braying). (See *Minor Latin Poets*, 1934, ed. Duff, pp. 589–91.) When the ass frightens the cattle, his master takes off the lion's skin and thrashes him, as the Bastard will do shortly. The association with a fool is suggested by the calf's-skin worn by children and natural fools.

3.1.138 cardinal Shakespeare and *TR* combine in the character of Pandulph a number of papal representatives from the chronicles. Historically Pandulph was neither cardinal nor archbishop of Milan, but a lawyer sent from Rome to adjudicate the quarrel about Stephen Langton. However, Pandulph's Elizabethan counterpart may have been the much less cunning Father William Allen, the pugnacious leader of English Catholics. Allen announced in *An Admonition to the Nobility and People of England* (1588), sig. D2–4, that the Pope made him a cardinal specifically 'intending to send me as his Legate, with full commission' to deal with Philip of Spain and his armies, to restore 'the Catholic religion' in England. He

called for a 'Holy War' against Elizabeth, at the landing of Spanish forces, to be joined by all 'noble and
valiant Champions of God's Church and honour of English knighthood'.

3.1.148 *task 'task' and 'taste' mean almost the same thing but their grammatical uses differ. (1) The
Folio's reading, 'tast' (taste), can mean 'to try' or 'to test' or 'put to the proof'. Compare *TN* 3.1.78:
'taste your legs, sir, put them in motion' (*OED v* 2). But the construction of John's speech is 'taste
to' + noun + direct object (taste to interrogatories the free breath of a sacred king). (2) Theobald's
emendation, 'task', fits that construction, and it carries the additional meaning: to compel, charge, or
submit, consistent with 151, 'charge me to an answer'. Compare *1H4* 4.1.9: 'task me to my word, approve
me, lord'; and *Temp.* 1.2.192: 'To thy strong bidding task / Ariel and all his quality.' See *OED* Task *v*
2b, 3.

3.1.176–7 meritorious . . . Canonised Acting under orders from Pope Innocent III, the bishops of
London, Ely, and Worcester declared that King John was accursed and excommunicated (Holinshed, II,
297); later Innocent declared him deprived of his throne, 'forsaken and condemned as a common enemy
to God and his church'; and 'whosoever employed goods or other aid to vanquish and overcome that
disobedient prince, should remain in assured peace of the church . . . also in suffrages for saving of their
souls' (Holinshed, II, 303). Shakespeare's Pandulph hews closer to the wording of the bull against Queen
Elizabeth, issued by Pope Pius V in 1570 and reaffirmed by later popes. By his apostolic power he declared
her 'an heretic' in 'sentence of anathema', deprived of her title to the kingdom, and he absolved her
subjects from 'allegiance and obedience' (quoted in J. H. Pollen, *The English Catholics in the Reign of
Queen Elizabeth*, 1920, pp. 150–1). There was no promise of canonisation in Holinshed's account, nor in
the bull of 1570, but a renegade priest confessed in 1589 to Walsingham's agents that he heard Pope
Gregory III say that killing the queen was a 'good work', and any Catholic who might suffer death simply
for that would be 'worthy of canonisation' (see also C. Read, *Mr Secretary Walsingham*, 1925, III, 24–5).
The murderer of Henry III of France in 1589 was proposed for canonisation, much to the indignation of
English Protestants. And after the murder of William the Silent, the Protestant Prince of Orange (1584),
there was widespread fear for the life of Elizabeth. Confessions extracted by Walsingham's agents alleged
that Dr William Gifford described the planned assassination of the queen as 'praiseworthy and
meritorious', and John Savage thought it 'very lawful and meritorious'; John Ballard held it to be 'lawful
and meritorious'. See J. H. Pollen, *Queen Mary and the Babington Plot*, 1922, pp. xlv, 57, 68, 73, 94.

3.1.259 chafèd I follow Theobald's emendation 'chafèd lion' because Pandulph focuses on the danger
of holding King John's hand like holding a snake's tongue, an angry lion's mortal paw, and a hungry tiger's
tooth. The lion's paw can kill with one blow, hence 'mortal paw'. The Folio's reading, 'cased lion', has
nothing to do with the danger of such a handclasp: naturally the lion is in his own 'case' (i.e. his own skin),
but that is not relevant to Pandulph's point. If the Bastard were speaking, we might expect a play on the
lion's skin once more, but Pandulph is deadly earnest and without a sense of humour. Therefore the
quotation from the Bastard's speech in *TR* (2.280) – 'the Lyons case, / Which here he holds' – is
irrelevant. The appropriate parallels are: *H8* 3.2.206: 'So looks the chafed lion / Upon the daring
huntsman that has galled him'; Beaumont and Fletcher, *Philaster* 5.3.64–7 (ed. Robert K. Turner, in
Beaumont and Fletcher, *Works*, I, 1966): 'And what there is of vengeance, in a lion / Chaft among dogs,
or rob'd of his dear young, / The same enforc'd more terrible, more mighty, / Expect from me.' (As Dyce
noticed in *Philaster*, Q1's 'Chaft' was corrupted to Q2's 'Chast' and in subsequent editions to 'Cast', which
shows how the corruption in 'John' could have occurred.)

3.1.277–8 fire cools fire . . . burned Paracelsian physicians recommended the new treatment of 'like with
like'; thus burns should first be placed 'by little and little, near the fire . . . one heat drawing forth another'
(H. J. Wecker, *A Compendious Chyrurgerie* (1585), sig. TI). Traditional Galenists recommended treatment
by opposites, such as cold applications to 'qualify the heat' of a hectic fever, a 'vehement heat . . . in the
blood' (Andrew Boorde, *The Breviary of Health* (1587), p. 55). Editors normally gloss this passage simply
as an example of the proverb 'One fire drives out another' (Tilley F277), but the image is precisely about
new medical treatment. *AWW* 2.3.11 suggests that Shakespeare knew the difference between Paracelsian
and Galenic methods.

3.2.0 SD Although the Folio text does not mention the lion skin here or later, in *TR* and *The Famous
History of George Lord Fauconbridge* (1616), the Bastard wears the skin after winning it from Austria. Many

actors have made that sensible choice, and something has to be done with the severed head, since it is likely to raise a laugh. Kemble devised a remedy (*John Philip Kemble Prompt Books*, vol. 5, ed. Shattuck, 1974) whereby the Bastard speaks his first two-and-a-half lines ending with 'pours down mischief'. Austria enters, they fight, and the Bastard drives him off-stage. He re-enters with the lion's skin in hand (not the head) saying 'Austria's head lie there, / While Philip breathes.' Macready did the same, except he had the Bastard throw the skin off-stage as he said those last words. Sometimes all reference to the head is omitted, and in a Stratford prompt-book of 1940 'head' was changed to 'hide' (A. C. Sprague and J. C. Trewin, *Shakespeare's Plays Today*, 1970, p. 27).

3.2.2 airy devil There may be an affinity between this image and Austria, if we consider how Thomas Nashe (*Terrors of the Night* (1594) in *Works*, ed. R. B. McKerrow, 1904, rev. edn 1958, I, 353) portrays aerial spirits as 'all show and no substance', mere glimmerings of our eyes. Airy demons 'converse with' men of similar traits, like carpet knights, whom they 'inspire with a humour of setting big looks on it, being the basest cowards under heaven, covering an ape's heart with a lion's case, and making false alarms when they mean nothing but a may game'.

3.2.6–7 My . . . her An example of Shakespeare's tendency to conflate historical sources and compress events. Holinshed reports that Arthur led an army against Eleanor who had withdrawn to the strong town of Mirabeau. She sent letters to John calling for help, but Arthur won the town and 'took his grandmother within the same'. Yet Holinshed believes that other historians 'write far more truly, that she was not taken but escaped into a tower' from which John rescued her and captured Arthur, in another of his speedy marches and surprise attacks (Holinshed, II, 284–5). In this scene the tower becomes a tent and the Bastard, not John, rescues her.

3.3.26 *time The Folio's 'tune' has been defended, meaning 'style' as in *Ado* 3.4.41, 'do you speak in the sick tune?' Thus John implies 'I will adorn my words when I can say it in better style' (i.e. not only speak, but give). John's distraught language later on (37–53) indicates a mood that is unfit for speech. But Pope's emendation, 'time', emphasises John's anxiety about the right time to say what is on his mind: the repetition of 'I had a thing to say' (25), 'I had a thing to say, but let it go' (33), and 'creep time ne'er so slow, / Yet it shall come for me to do thee good' (31–2). The bright day is not the time and the sun not the right audience for what he has to say.

3.3.39 *ear The Folio's 'race' is an easy misreading of 'care' in an Elizabethan hand. The king struggles to communicate his dark purpose to Hubert without actually saying what he means, and at 48–51 he wishes Hubert could read his mind: see him without eyes, hear without ears, reply without tongue. Therefore it is appropriate that he should speak of these organs in a conceit of the bell's iron tongue, its brazen mouth, sounding into the ear of night. The Folio's 'race of night' could mean the 'course of night', i.e. across the dark sky. Compare Spenser (*FQ* 1, 5, 44): 'The mother of dread darkness . . . took her wonted way / To run her timely race', but the metaphors of the eye, ear, tongue, mouth seem more consistent and expressive.

3.3.52 *broad-eyed It is a hard choice between the Folio's 'brooded' and Pope's 'broad-eyed', which I follow. F's 'brooded' presumably means vigilant, like a brooding fowl guarding her eggs. Cotgrave, sv Accouvé: 'Brooded; set close on . . . covered, hidden, overshadowed'; *Accouveter* 'to brood . . . as a hen over her eggs . . . and hence . . . to overshadow'. Editors usually illustrate this meaning with Milton's 'L'Allegro', 6–7: 'Where brooding darkness spreads his jealous wings / And the night-raven sings'. 'Brooded', however, if it implies darkness or overshadowing, conflicts with the distinction between night and day in the rest of John's speech. The day 'cannot be proud, wanton and full of gauds attended with the pleasure of the world . . . and at the same time brooded' (Ivor John). Support for 'broad-eyed' is found in Chapman's *Iliad*, ed. Nicoll, 8.173, where Juno plans to aid the Greeks and to 'hinder brode-eyd Joue's proud will', as John hopes to avoid the vigilance of the sun, the eye of eternal providence. If 'brooded' is an error, it could have arisen from a manuscript that spelled the word 'brod-eid' or 'brode-eyd' (Wilson).

3.4.2 *consorted Because the Folio's 'convicted', meaning defeated or conquered, does not contrast with 'scattered and disjoined from fellowship' editors have suggested 'collected', 'connected', 'convented', 'compacted', and the latest, 'conjuncted' (Maxwell). However, 'consorted' offers the contrast, it goes with 'fellowship', and it is associated with a group of ships in the passages quoted.

3.4.17–19 grave . . . breath The analogy implies that Constance's body (this walking grave) holds her soul; her vile prison of breath holds her eternal spirit. Vaughan and Honigmann suggest a further distinction between 'soul' and 'spirit': the Holy Spirit (the image of Christ in the soul) is imprisoned in her breath, the usual symbol of the soul, both of which are imprisoned in her body.

3.4.88 know Although Constance assumes that Arthur's resurrected body will bear signs of his sorrow at the time of death, the usual doctrine held that the soul in heaven will be clothed in a perfected body. However, there were long-standing dissenting opinions in popular thought. Compare Philip Stubbes, *A Christal Glass for Christian Women* (1592), sig. C2: 'that we shall know one another in the life to come . . . some of you . . . will hardly believe this doctrine to be so'.

3.4.110 *world's* For Lewis, life in this world has lost its sweetness and joy. The F reading 'word's taste' could mean the 'taste of life' (Malone) or delight in praise – sweet word – for my success (Riverside), but the obvious reference is to the joyless world mentioned in 107 (Smallwood).

3.4.135–6 sceptre snatched . . . gained Compare Seneca, *Hercules* 341–5: 'rapta sed trepida manu / sceptra obtinentur. omnis in ferro est salus; / quod civibus tenere te invitius scias / strictus tuetur ensis. alieno in loco / haut stabile regnum est'; restated by Marvell, 'Horatian Ode', 199–120: 'The same arts that did gain / A power must it maintain.' The Elizabethan translation (1561) is less faithful to the Latin than Shakespeare's paraphrase, especially *obtinentur* (be maintained) and *trepida manu* (unruly hand).

4.1.39 Must . . . burn out . . . eyes? Shakespeare clouds the warrant with a vagueness, whether John intends just to incapacitate Arthur by blindness or to have him killed. As Arthur reads the warrant, we are led to think that it authorises just blinding, but John expressly asks for death when he first speaks to Hubert (3.3.66). Hubert plans to report that the boy is dead (4.1.127), and while he does so, Pembroke (4.2.70, 81) says that Hubert showed the warrant 'to a friend of mine', and that the king charged Hubert to do the deed that will presumably 'issue' in the 'child's death'. Later Hubert justifies himself, for the king's hand and seal ordered what he did (4.2.215).

In Holinshed (II, 286) there is no mention of a warrant, but rumours of Arthur's death floated through France. In response to a belief at large that the kingdom would never be quiet as long as Arthur lived, it was reported that John 'appointed certain persons' to 'put out the young gentleman's eyes'. But Hubert his keeper prevented injury to Arthur and made it known in the countryside that the boy was dead according to the king's command. Thus, neither Holinshed nor Shakespeare's play says explicitly that blinding will cause death, but the impression is that one will lead to the other.

Coggeshall's *Chronicle*, which Shakespeare probably knew, says specifically that the king's counsellors recommended the noble youth be blinded and castrated (in folklore the two are often equivalent), so that he could never rule. *TR*, as usual, spells out the king's order literally, with a quotation from the warrant for blinding (7.50), which Arthur recognises as 'murder' (7.82), and Hubert reports to John that he blinded the boy, who died in one hour of extreme pain (8.209–12).

4.2.1 again crowned Historically this was John's fourth coronation, 3 April 1202, shortly after Arthur's death. Among the Angevin kings this oft-repeated ceremony allowed the king and nobles to reaffirm their oaths of trust and service, patching up differences after a crisis. In the play John asks for loyal support in anticipation of a crisis, and the nobles become suspicious, treating it as an occasion for complaint.

4.2.31 worser Because the line in the Folio lacks a syllable, most editors expand the elision to 'worse by the excuse', but it is unusual for a compositor to introduce an elision not in his copy unless the line is full. Thus 'the worser by th'excuse' is preferable (Maxwell, pp. 473–4).

4.2.42 *when lesser is my fear* I follow Tyrwhitt's emendation of the Folio's 'then', because 'when' goes with 'Meantime' in the next line. John's promise to give more and stronger reasons which he does not want to reveal at the moment is typical of his artful vagueness. Dover Wilson noted that John seems to be thinking of Arthur ('my fear') and Arthur's impending death, after which he will explain more freely. Sisson accepts this interpretation but favours a simpler emendation: 'the lesser is my fear' (after Pope), supposing that the compositor mistook 'the' in the copy for the abbreviation 'the'. Wright and Kittredge retain 'then' and treat 'then lesser is my fear' as a parenthetical remark. Collier, Honigmann, and Evans have chosen 'than lesser is my fear', since 'then' and 'than' were spelling doublets. This most conservative emendation results in an awkward construction.

4.2.46 grant . . . requests Modern audiences expect something here or at 168 about the Magna Carta. Although Holinshed tells of the struggle for that short-lived agreement between barons and king, Shakespeare's play is silent about it. John Bale's *King Johan* and *TR* mention the Charter but are otherwise indifferent. See May Mattsson, *Five Plays about King John*, Uppsala, 1977, pp. 109–10. John's contemporaries, also, probably thought of the Charter as an extension of the baron's coronation oath, and their rebellion another broken vow.

4.2.55 in rest Since Pembroke and Salisbury load their speeches with double meanings, 'rest' may suggest 'wrest'. But compare Holinshed (II, 279–80): 'King John being now in rest from wars with foreign enemies, began to make war with his subjects' purses at home . . . which alienated the minds of a great number of them from his love and obedience.'

4.2.79–81 His . . . death Compare Holinshed (II, 148), life of Henry II: 'the rancour which King Henry the son had conceived . . . was so ripened, that it could not but burst out . . . the sooner to pour out his poison which he had sucked before' (Honigmann).

4.2.99–100 That . . . all this isle . . . hold A traditional reflection on the death of a great or ambitious person, here scaled down for the irony of Arthur's death. Compare *1H4* 5.4.90–2: 'A kingdom for it was too small a bound [for Hotspur's spirit] / But now two paces of the vilest earth / Is room enough.'

4.2.117 care The Folio's 'care' should stand because it reminds us of John's mother's habitual vigilance as his adviser. When the initial letter *c* was thought to be a broken *e*, several editors emended to 'ear'. But Charlton Hinman (*Printing and Proof-Reading*, I, 430) found that the letter was originally a *c*, intact in some copies but broken in others at sig. T6 b55, 'because'. Hereafter compositors used the broken letter as a *c* thirty-five times, twice as an *e*.

4.2.125 Occasion This emblem of John's predicament is a personification of opportunity and penitence, often depicted with winged feet, a shock of hair in front, and bald behind. She stands on a wheel of fortune or a globe surrounded by stormy seas (G. Whitney, *A Choice of Emblems* (1586), sig. z3). If one does not grasp Opportunity in front, she slips by, and the advantage passes to others (see 61–2 above and 3.1.324). Penitence and Furor, son of Occasion, naturally follow (*FQ* II, 4, 4–5). For John she is ugly, 'dreadful Occasion' – having passed by; but at 5.2.58 and 5.4.51, Fortune in prospect is a 'fair occasion'.

4.2.144–8 strangely . . . Pomfret Foxe, pp. 252–3, describes this atmosphere: 'rumour was the larger . . . new tales were invented, fables were added to fables, and lies grew upon lies'. Peter of Pomfret is described as 'an idle gadder about . . . a counterfeit sooth-sayer . . . a very idle vagabond . . . fantastical prophet'.

4.2.151 Ascension Day John was first crowned on this day, but Ascension Day is also part of Rogation Week, which emphasises man's need to depend on God, and the need to protect boundaries. Emrys Jones (*Origins*, p. 256) thinks that from this point on to the end of the play 'a more general theme of human dependence on God is more certainly established. Everyone in the fifth act, the Bastard included, seems dwarfed by events, at the mercy of unforeseeable consequences . . . men are shocked into acknowledging their weakness and lack of self-sufficiency'. Perhaps so, but God seems rather distant – leaving events to chance and conscience. (See pp. 50–7 above.)

4.2.210 house of life Traditionally 'house of life' allows two meanings: (1) the temple of life which is the sacred body of a Christian. Even the servants of the king cannot violate it without warrant. Compare *Mac.* 2.3.67: 'Most sacrilegious murder hath broke ope / The Lord's anointed temple, and stole thence, / The life of the building!' (2) The Platonic conception of the body as the dwelling-house of the soul: *Ant.* 5.2.51, 'This mortal house I'll ruin.' Compare Cicero, *Tusculan Disputations*, I.xxii.51: 'the nature of the soul, the conception of it in the body, as it were a home that is not its own'. See 5.7.2–3 where the 'pure brain' is the 'soul's frail dwelling-house'.

4.2.237–8 signs . . . sin The pun on 'sin' and 'sign' was widely known in the Renaissance. See Barclay, *The Ship of Fools* (1874 edn), p. 294, and *Paradise Lost*, II, 760. Erasmus, *The Praise of Folly*, trans. Thomas Chaloner (1549), ed. C. H. Miller, 1965, pp. 89–90, makes fun of the preachers who discourse upon the name of Jesus dividing the word 'as it were by geometry into two equal parts, leaving S . . . in the middle: which letter in the Hebrew's ABC . . . they call it sin. "Now sin", quoth he, "in English is as much to say as a deadly offence against God: so hereby it appeared, that Jesus was the . . . mediator, that took on him the sins of this world."'

4.3.16 *privity The Folio's 'Whose private with me of the Dauphin's will' is the only example recorded in the *OED* of 'private' in the sense of private counsel or secret thoughts. Wilson suggested that 'private with me' should be 'private warrant'. But 'privity' (sometimes spelled 'privite', 'private' or 'privitie') was frequently used (*OED* sv 1a and 1c) from the fourteenth to the seventeenth century. Compare *H8*

1.1.74: 'without the privity of the king' (meaning private knowledge); Spenser, *FQ* II, 4, 20: 'My friend . . . I did partake / Of all my love and all my privitie'; Jonson, *Every Man in his Humour* 4.7.63–4: 'I will tell you, sir, by the way of private, and under seal.'

4.3.159 heaven . . . frown . . . land Compare Holinshed (II, 300). A preacher incensed the king greatly to cruelty to his subjects, 'affirming that the general scourge wherewith the people were afflicted, chanced not through the prince's fault, but for the wickedness of his people, for the king was but the rod of the Lord's wrath', on account of their disobedience 'to their natural prince King John'.

5.1.1–2 William Charles Macready's staging of the first few moments of this scene illustrates his care for detail. As the curtain rises, John and Pandulph are discovered in the Templars' Church; organ music is heard while Pandulph sits in the chair of state on a low dais at stage left, and bags of money are on the steps. 'John is in the act of giving his crown to Pandulph, who places it on a cushion, held by a Bishop' on the right. 'K John, kneeling, then places his hands between those of Pandulph, as doing homage. Organ ceases.' John rises at the end of his first speech, and Pandulph returns the crown, which John gives to Hubert on his right, who receives it on a cushion and gives it to an abbot. At the rear stand twenty-four supers, in rows; four priests with banners, four monks, two knights, seven bishops, two abbots, an archbishop, and an apostolic notary. On stage right are six Templars, the Grand Master of the Templars, and two Knights Hospitallers. Centre stage are three noblemen (Hereford, Oxford, Essex), standing behind Hubert, who is behind John. Two heralds stand on either side of the dais, and at stage left front are two more knights templar and a priest with a crosier (*Macready's 'King John'*, ed. Shattuck, pp. 270–1).

By comparison, J. P. Kemble's prompt-book (after 1804) for the same scene specified the set as just 'The Palace' – a stock set used several times in the play – with a table, a chair of state where Pandulph sat, and a footstool probably for John to kneel on. In addition to John and Pandulph, there were two attendants to the cardinal, four English gentlemen, and a herald. The crown was passed back and forth on a cushion, which was then placed on the table (*John Philip Kemble Prompt Books*, vol. 5, *King John* (1804), ed. Charles Shattuck, 1974). See pp. 15–21 above.

5.1.8 discontented counties John may be thinking of his discontented peers (4.2.127), his 'distempered lords' (4.3.21). However, Shakespeare uses 'county' or 'counties' in this sense only in an Italian setting. But if weight is given to events later in this scene (30–2), when Kent yields and London receives the Dauphin, the shires may be intended.

5.1.25–9 The decay of John's self-respect runs apace. He has given up even before he is sure Arthur is dead or Lewis has been elected. But in *TR* his capitulation to the Pope is much less 'voluntary', and in Bale's play John mitigates the terrible decision by doing it to save the suffering of his kingdom. Shakespeare's John at this time thinks most of his security.

5.1.41 some damned hand A theatre audience should have little difficulty with this apparent change of mind, because we know John's guilty intent and his responsibility for giving the order. The accusatory tone, therefore, seems appropriate, although the Bastard formerly was unsure that Arthur's death was the work of any hand, and he seems convinced that Hubert was not directly responsible (43).

5.1.78–9 Yet . . . may well meet a prouder foe This speech should be an aside. Except for Dr Johnson, whom I follow, editors have taken the speech as self-evident or have construed it as 'I know that we are still able to encounter even a prouder enemy than the French' (Wright). Such an interpretation is possible if the Bastard's confident tone must be maintained. 'May well' could mean 'can satisfactorily or honourably' do something (*OED* Well *adv* 1b), and 'yet' was often used for 'still' or 'even'. It is difficult, nevertheless, to imagine an actor getting the idea across to an audience, much less to John. Steevens objected to Johnson's reading because a realistic assessment of the situation would 'dispirit the king whom he means to animate', and certainly the immediately preceding exhortation, 'Away then with good courage!', is meant to lift the king's spirits after the bad news. But the objection can be overcome if the Bastard finishes the couplet with an aside, 'Yet I know / Our party may well meet a prouder foe.' He ended the previous scene with a confession of his private doubts and fears about John's 'wrested pomp' and the imminent decay of the kingdom. He guessed that someone might have ordered and someone might have consented to the killing of Arthur – if it were the work of any hand. In any case, Providence frowns upon the land, and there are only a few uncertain friends among the king's party. (For another of his gloomy, closing speeches see 5.6.37–44.) It is, therefore, fitting that he end this scene with a private, rueful confession to the audience, as the Bastard did in the BBC production.

5.2.36 *grapple The Folio's 'cripple' is probably a misreading of 'crapple', and an unrecorded spelling variant of 'grapple'. Compare Hall's *Chronicle* (1548), 1809 edn, p. 534: 'the *Regent* crappeled with her a long boord . . . so these two noble ships, which were so crappled together that they could not part, were consumed by fire'. Therefore, Pope's emendation is the best modern equivalent. Elsewhere in the Folio the word is spelled 'grapple', as it is in *John* 5.1.61.

5.2.58 Fortune . . . feasts The Dauphin's superior tone, when he chides Salisbury for an immature view of Fortune, marks a change in his character. He has grown from the green and fresh youth that we see in 3.4 into one who lectures his elders in the way of the world. Salisbury should put aside the naïve conception of Fortune suitable only to 'baby eyes' – Fortune as simply a happy and bountiful goddess with her cornucopia. A man of the world should understand that capricious and ironic goddess in her fullness. This is precisely what he has learned from Pandulph: that 'when Fortune means to men most good / She looks upon them with a threat'ning eye' (3.4.119–20). Now the Dauphin instructs Salisbury not to be distressed by the hard choice between a nobleman's duty to the state and his need to revolt against an illegitimate king. Rather, he should bury his scruples, seize Fortune (presumably by the forelock, since she offers occasion momentarily; see 4.2.125 n.). If he does that, he and the nobles can 'thrust [their hands] deep / Into the purse of rich prosperity', knitting their sinews to Lewis's cause. (See Edgar Wind, *Pagan Mysteries*, rev. edn, 1968, pp. 101–4, and E. Panofsky, *Studies in Iconology*, 1962 edn, p. 72 n., on the union of Occasion and Fortune.)

5.2.104 banked their towns None of the proposed interpretations is entirely convincing. (1) The Dauphin's troops threw up banks or entrenchments around the towns. Assuredly, the historical Dauphin besieged and won Rochester Castle, but the line in the play suggests that he was acclaimed *as* he banked their towns, not after. (2) 'Banked' may mean 'sailed along' on a river, by analogy with 'coasted' or 'skirted', although no other use of 'banked' in this sense is recorded. However, this meaning would not have occurred to modern editors without the comparable passage in *TR* and supported by the general belief that it was Shakespeare's source. Several commentators since Steevens have assumed that the passage implies that Lewis sailed up a river while he received shouted greetings from the towns along the banks.

> Your city Rochester with great applause
> By some divine instinct laid arms aside;
> And from the hollow holes of Thamesis
> Echo apace replied *Vive le roy*.
> From thence, along the wanton rolling glade
> To Troynovant your fair metropolis . . .
>   *TR* 11.172–7

Although Dover Wilson claimed that 'banked their towns' could 'only be understood by reference to *TR*' upon which it is based, the Dauphin in *TR* says that the echo reverberated from the 'hollow holes' of the Thames, its banks. It is not clear that he sailed along the banks at all, because 'along the wanton rolling glade' seems to refer to a march toward London by land. (3) 'Banked their towns' means 'won their towns, put them in the bank', as in a gambling game of cards (Staunton's suggestion). 'Bank' was a term of card-playing in other languages during the sixteenth and seventeenth centuries, but in English, apparently, the closest meaning was a 'pile of money' (*OED* sv *sb*³ 3; the earliest quotation is of 1515, but its use in association with gambling is unrecorded until about 1720, and as a verb in this sense not until the early nineteenth century). Florio, *World of Words* (1598), p. 38, cites *Banco fallito* as a game at cards, and Charles Cotton, *Complete Gamester* (1674), p. 153, mentions 'Bankofalet', as a game on the cards (Honigmann, p. 170). On internal evidence – the consistency of the card-playing metaphors and the Dauphin's overblown style – I am inclined toward this interpretation. And *Vive le Roy* in the same line refers to the name of a card in French decks. (See H. R. D'Allemagne, *Les Cartes à Jouer*, 1906, ii, 445; i, 91; R. Merlin, *Origine des Cartes à Jouer* 1869, plate 36; W. Gurney Benham, *Playing Cards*, 1931, p. 135, with illustrations of early cards inscribed 'Vive le Roy' and 'Vive La Raine' (Honigmann).)

5.2.119–20 speak, . . . king: The Folio's punctuation cuts the sequence of clauses into awkward units. Wilson justified this division by suggesting that 'I am sent to speak' means 'not to fight, in spite of my loud trumpet'. But Theobald's simpler punctuation, transposing the colon to the end of the following line, may very well reveal the intended sense. The Bastard must speak guardedly and precisely until he knows the situation.

5.2.132–6 masque . . . circle The underlying conceit likens the invasion to a grotesque antimasque performed by dwarfs and children for the entertainment of a king. At the end the pygmies are driven from the playing 'circle' to make way for the main part of the show. See Sidney's 'Proteus and the Adamantine Rock', *Gesta Grayorum* (1595), ed. W. W. Greg, 1914.

5.2.139 like buckets in concealèd wells The Bastard means hiding in wells that offer concealment. The proverb 'like two buckets in a well' (Tilley B695) is relevant, since it suggests rapid change of fortune or mood, as in *R2* 4.1.184–9.

5.2.144 nation's crow If the Bastard refers to the crow of a cock, it is another barnyard metaphor. However, the 'crying of your nation's crow' may imply that the crows jeer at the French, as in *Edward III* 4.6.4–12, when a prophetic flight of ravens struck terror in the French soldiers just before the battle of Poitiers. 'The amazed French / Are quite distract with gazing on the crows.' And Prince Edward says, 'What need we fight, and sweat, and keep a coil, / When railing crows out-scold our adversaries?'

5.2.152–3 Neroes . . . mother England A commonplace in Armada pamphlets. Compare G. D.'s *Brief discovery* (1588), sig. H2: 'he that will not stick to rip up the womb, and to tear and rake out the bowels of his own mother, he that will endeavour to bring in an invasion, to the utter spoil, ruin, and depopulation of his dear country . . . what impiety will he leave unattempted?' (Honigmann). Chaucer's *Monk's Tale* (*Works*, ed. F. N. Robinson, 2483–6) popularised the notion that Nero slit open his dead mother's womb to 'behold / Where he conceived was'.

5.2.173 deep-mouthed thunder Instead of the musical discord of the hunt (*MND* 4.1.105–17), the Bastard selects only the deep-throated and loud-barking hounds. He is thinking of a 'double hunt', two armies like two packs of hounds: 'the babbling echo mocks the hounds . . ./ As if a double hunt were heard at once' (*Tit.* 2.3.17–19).

5.4.11–12 Unthread . . . faith The literal meaning is clear enough, and Salisbury repeats it moments later (52): 'We will untread the steps of damnèd flight.' (Theobald's emendation of 'Unthread' to 'Untread' just changes the expression without altering the literal meaning. On stage the two words may sound the same.) Moreover, with 'Unthread the rude eye' Shakespeare varies the biblical saying (Luke 18.25) 'Surely it is easier for a camel |or 'rope': the Geneva gloss| to go through a needle's eye, then for a rich man to enter into the kingdom of God.' Since it is easy to unthread a needle, the reversal of the saying implies that the passage back to the barons' traditional loyalty will be easier than the way to their treasonous revolt. Hence the importance of Salisbury's painful soul-searching (5.2.8–39) when he signs the agreement with Lewis. Now that the traitors are betrayed, they must fly from 'paying the fine of rated treachery, / Even with a treacherous fine', and the return will be a happy 'new flight' of obedience to 'old right' (37–8, 60–1).

5.4.24–5 as a form of wax . . . the fire Melun telescopes two ideas in this image: (1) the dissolution of his body when the principle of life, his form or soul, departs; (2) the danger of his dying without a clear conscience, because he must soon answer to God, and 'as wax melteth the fire, so shall the wicked perish at the presence of God' (Ps. 68.2). Commentators following Steevens usually gloss the metaphor as a reference to a witch's killing an enemy by melting his waxen image at the fire, but in Melun's situation the Christian connotations are more appropriate (see also Ps. 97.5: 'The mountains melted like wax at the presence of the Lord'). Shakespeare uses the image of a form of wax elsewhere to suggest a god's imprint upon a person, and in *MND* 1.1.47–51 there is also the threat that the god could destroy the form he has created: 'To you your father should be as a god; / One that composed your beauties; yea, and one / To whom you are but as a form in wax, / By him imprinted, and within his power, / To leave the figure, or disfigure it.' It is this disfiguring of his body (by death) and of his soul (by guilt) that Melun considers as his life bleeds away. Also see *Ham.* 3.4.60–2 and *Rom.* 3.3.126–7.

5.4.57 our ocean The controlling image here is the obedient return to the sea of tidal waters that overflowed river banks. Compare *2H4* 5.2.129–33, King Henry V's forgiveness of the Lord Chief Justice for arresting him in his wild youth, because the arrest was a just and impartial act by one who represented the authority of the king. Hereafter, Hal, like Salisbury and the nobles, will 'stoop and humble' his intentions according to that authority, for 'The tide of blood in me / Hath proudly flowed in vanity till now; / Now doth it turn and ebb back to the sea, / Where it shall mingle with the state of floods, / And flow henceforth in formal majesty.'

5.6.12 *eyeless night Theobald's emendation of the Folio's 'endless night' sharpens the complaint against darkness and bad memory. Hubert is not concerned with the endlessness of night and not yet with death, but with the 'black brow of night' (17). He cannot see the person he is talking to. Compare *The Rape of Lucrece* 675: 'blind concealing night', and *Edward III* 4.4.8–9: 'sullen dark / And eyeless terror of all ending night'. The Dauphin has just called it 'stumbling night' (5.5.18); and in a comparable passage (*TR* 13.42–3) the Bastard describes the occasion: 'By this time night had shadowed all the earth, / With sable curtains of the blackest hue.' However, Schmidt, Moore Smith, Honigmann, and Smallwood think the emendation is unnecessary because 'endless night' means infinite or impenetrable, hence dark, as dark as can be. To say with Honigmann that 'endless night' was a cliché only makes the misreading easier. Moreover, the cliché is a euphemism for death, not darkness, and how could death do Hubert shame? Therefore, the emendation seems necessary.

5.6.23 The king, I fear, is poisoned Shakespeare allows the audience to share the uncertainty about John's death, whether caused by fever (5.3.3) or poison (5.6.23), just as Holinshed (II, 335–6) reports that 'some have written' that he took such grief for the loss of much of his army that he died of an ague exacerbated by a surfeit of peaches and new cider, and 'There be which have written' that he was poisoned by a monk 'moved with zeal for the oppression of his country', or that one of his own servants induced a convert of the abbey to poison him with a dish of pears. This hovering between alternative reports is typical of the way Elizabethan historians and poets handled conflicting sources.

5.6.38 tempt us not In reaction to the news about the king's impending death – a sign of God's indignation – the Bastard petitions God not to afflict the English with more than they can bear. 'Tempt us not' implies 'do not try us', and a passage in 1 Cor. 10.13 (Bishops' Bible) reassures the faithful: 'God . . . shall not suffer you to be tempted above your strength: but shall with the temptation make a way, that ye may be able to bear it.' Honigmann also cites L. Wright, *Display of Duty* (1589), sig. E2^v (1614 edn): 'God . . . never faileth his children in necessity: nor suffereth them to be tempted above their power.' It is difficult to imagine with Calderwood (p. 356), Matchett (pp. xxxiv–xxxviii) and Smallwood (p. 340) that the Bastard is tempted to take over the reins of government, especially since he says 'tempt us' and 'our power'. Moreover the heir, Prince Henry, has already been mentioned.

5.7.16 insensible Although the Folio's 'inuisible' is probably an error, no single substitute has won general approval, and several editors retain the Folio reading, not without some doubt.

I adopt Hanmer's emendation because it is intelligible, it is the harder word, and it presents the fewest difficulties in the context. Its meaning concurs with Prince Henry's meditation on the 'vanity of sickness' as evidence of his father's oncoming death. Henry comments on the one strange moment when his father sings, explaining this odd behaviour by reference to the principle that prolonged anguish destroys a person's capacity to feel his own misery. He is numbed or confused. Death began his attack on the body, the outworks of the fortress, where he has preyed so thoroughly that he has left the body insensible to pain, and now he attacks the mind where legions of 'strange fantasies' so rush upon the inner fortress that they destroy themselves. In more lucid moments John feels his pain, like Constance, who raves but declares that she is sane so long as she is 'sensible of grief' (3.4.53). But when John's body is insensible and his mind nearly so, Death takes charge, and he makes the king sing his own funeral hymn.

An emendation closer to the appearance of the word in the Folio is Steevens's suggestion, 'invincible' (see *2H4* 3.2.313 for 'invisible' misread as 'invincible'). Smallwood, who follows Steevens, explains that Death has done his worst against the body and found it finally incapable of further suffering. According to this interpretation the body is numbed, and thus 'invincible' to further attack, and Death turns his ferocity onto the mind. (But since Death may attack the body with impunity if he wishes, the body is hardly invincible.)

The Folio's 'invisible' has the least in its favour, since it is obscure in sense and grammar. Malone thought the word is used adverbially and that Death, having glutted himself, leaves the body 'in such secret manner that the eye cannot *precisely* mark his progress'. W. A. Wright thought that 'invisible' is an adjective modifying 'Death'. In either case, the grammar is ambiguous.

5.7.26–7 indigest . . . shapeless . . . rude The phrase comes from the opening lines of the *Metamorphoses*: *chaos, rudis indigestaque moles.* Shakespeare adapted it again in *2H6* 5.1.157 describing Gloucester, a 'heap of wrath, foul indigested lump, / As crooked in thy manners as thy shape'. John's decomposition into chaos in the rest of this scene echoes Golding's translation (1567), lines 1–18 (equivalent words italicised): 'Of shapes transformed to bodies *strange* (18) . . . / Which chaos hight, a huge *rude* (27) heap, and nothing else but even / A heavy lump and clottred *clod* (57) of seeds together driven / Of things at strife among themselves for want of order due. / No sun as yet . . . the *shapeless* (27) world did view . . . / No kind of thing had proper shape, but each *confounded* (20, 58) other. / For in one self same body strove the *hot* (45) and *cold* (41) together.'

5.7.117–18 Nought . . . true A biblical commonplace. Compare Matt. 12.25: 'Every kingdom divided against itself shall be brought to naught; and every city or house divided against itself shall not stand' (also Mark 3.24, Luke 11.17). Dent (L54.1) cites a resonant example by W. Seres, *An Answer to the Proclamation of the Rebels in the North* (1569), sig. A8ᵛ: 'A proverb old, no land there is / that can this land subdue, / If we agree within ourselves / And to our realm be true.' The phrasing in *TR* 16–45, 'Let England live but true within itself', is almost identical with that of *The True Tragedy of Richard Duke of York* (1595), sig. D3ᵛ: 'Let England be true within itself'.

TEXTUAL ANALYSIS

The First Folio, the sole authority for the text of *King John*, was reprinted serially, F2 from F, F3 from F2 and F4 from F3, with various accretions and minor corrections. Similarly, Rowe based his edition on F4, Pope based his on Rowe, and so forth. Not until Edward Capell did editors return to the First Folio as a basis for the text because it is closest to the author's manuscript.[1] Otherwise, the textual history is mainly a history of conjectural emendation; inspection of the supplementary notes to this edition shows that there are several credible and ingenious emendations that have stood the test of time, and there is still room for new ones. But first we must determine, as best we can, the nature of the manuscript copy that went to the printer of the First Folio.

The names of characters in the Folio text vary so greatly that they would present difficulties in a prompt-book. In stage directions Eleanor is called *Queene Elinor, Eleanor, Queene*; in speech headings, *Elea., Elin., Eli., Qu.Mo., Qu.*, and *Old Qu*. At his first entrance the King of France is called *Philip King of France*, but his headings are *Lewis* (twice) and *King* (three times); when John enters, France's speech headings are *Fran.* or *Fra.*, then *Lewis* again, and he is addressed by Austria once as 'King Lewis'. By Act 3 the French king's name is established as *France* or *Fra.*, and in dialogue 'Philip of France' or 'France'. Lewis's headings are also stabilised as *Dau.* and *Dolph.*, and in dialogue he is called 'Lewis' and 'Daulphin'. In the stage directions of the first act the Bastard is called *Philip*, and his speech headings are *Phil.* and *Philip*, but his headings become *Bastard* as soon as he is recognised as the son of Cœur-de-lion, although he is knighted 'Sir Richard Plantagenet'. At the end of Act 1, he jokingly refers to himself as 'Sir Richard' (185) and denigrates his old name 'Philip' (231). In Act 2 he is known in the dialogue, headings, and entries simply as a 'Bastard of the King's deceast', *Bastard*, and one among many bastards. Yet in the third act his entry is indicated as *Philip*; he speaks to himself in 3.2 'While Philip breathes', and John addresses him in 3.2 as 'Philip'. Henceforth, throughout Acts 4–5 his entries and headings continue as *Bastard* or *Bast.*, but he is addressed with more dignity now as 'Falconbridge', 'Faulconbridge' or 'Sir Richard', and the king calls him 'Cosen'.

Apparently Shakespeare was undecided about what to name certain major characters, and he improvised as he composed. In the haste of writing, he realised that he could not have two characters on stage both identified as 'Philip', but elsewhere he altered the names experimentally to fit immediate roles and events. Someone else could tidy up the details later. Much the same indecision about names is found in

---

[1] Alice Walker, 'Edward Capell and his edition of *Shakespeare*', Annual Shakespeare Lecture, 1960, *PBA* (1961), 135–6.

early texts of *Romeo and Juliet, Much Ado*, and *Love's Labour's Lost*. I agree with Honigmann that this is part of the openness and fluidity of Shakespeare's mind while he wrote.[1] The point to be recognised here is that the instability of these names runs through much of the script, occurring in dialogue, not just in speech headings. With such evidence we may assume that the author's foul papers were somewhere behind the printed text.

The evidence of stage directions is not nearly so clear, for there are no distinctly authorial or theatrical directions. Occasionally a direction comes later than the action itself. Mute characters' names are omitted from entrances, and once Constance's name is among those entering even though she has not left the stage (3.1.74). Exits are sometimes left out. A few directions have a slight untheatrical flavour, as if the writer is not imagining the play on a stage: *Enter before Angiers, Citizen upon the walles, Enter . . . to the gates*, and *Arthur on the walles*. There are some vaguely theatrical directions too: *powers, at severall doores, Enter (in Armes) Dolphin, Bastard with Austria's head, Iohn brought in*, and some '*Allarums, Excursions*' (as Greg noted).[2]

In any case, other evidence about transmission of the text implies that the foul papers were copied by at least two scribes. The signs of their work are found in the change of spelling habits from the predominance of 'O' to 'Oh'. Fortunately this exclamation is so common a word that we can see one distinct pattern before 4.2.171 and another after 4.2.260 of the printed text, where the frequency of 'O' suddenly decreases, and 'Oh' increases. Somewhere in this 89-line stretch of the script the scribes appear to have changed.[3] The shift in spelling is hard to attribute to the two Folio compositors B and C. Their spelling habits were distinctly different from each other, but they were indifferent about 'O' and 'Oh'. Thus they seem to have preserved some of the copy spellings, enough to leave a shadow of the scribes' assignments. The table below lists the comparative frequencies before and after this

Scribe I: 1.1.1–4.2.c.219[4]			Scribe II: 4.2.c.220–5.7.118	
Word	Frequency	Ratio 1 per	Frequency	Ratio 1 per
O	41 *2	45 lines	3	243 lines
Oh	7 *1	263 lines	17	43 lines

division. A few lesser signs add to the probability of this division of labour on the manuscript. Throughout the play Jaggard's two compositors, B and C, regularly spell 'sweet' without a final 'e' (C five times before and once after the division, B once before, twice after, not counting this spelling in justified lines), but on one page after

[1] 'Shakespeare as a reviser', in *Textual Criticism and Literary Interpretation*, ed. J. J. McGann, 1985, pp. 12–13.
[2] W. W. Greg, *The Shakespeare First Folio*, 1955, pp. 251–2.
[3] Stanley Wells, Gary Taylor *et al.*, *William Shakespeare: A Textual Companion*, 1987, p. 317.
[4] Since the exact place is uncertain where Scribe I stopped and Scribe II began, the division is assumed to be mid-way between the *O* at 171 and the *Oh* at 267. Starred numbers in the table indicate the spellings that occur in justified lines, not included in the ratios.

the division, Compositor B spells it 'sweete' three times (sig. b3). Again, Compositor B early in the play expands the titles in 'Saint *George*' and 'Saint Maries', but after the division he twice abbreviates 'S. *Edmondsbury*' where there is plenty of room (sigs. b2 and b4ᵛ), and neither compositor normally uses abbreviations except to justify a long line. Therefore the discrepancies suggest the influence of scribal copy.[1]

There has been speculation that Ralph Crane, who transcribed several of the comedies for the printers of the First Folio, prepared the text of *King John* too.[2] However, I see nothing of Crane's distinctive stage directions and few of his spelling habits as described by Howard-Hill.[3] Certainly, the preposterous act divisions should disqualify Crane as a candidate. The early quartos of other plays testify that Shakespeare had little interest in act divisions. Except for the choruses in *Henry V* and possibly in *Romeo and Juliet* and *Pericles*, he did not follow neoclassic divisions. None of the quartos, except for the 1622 *Othello*, has any act or scene division.[4] This stands to reason, for the imposition of acts was primarily an editor's or printer's responsibility in the Folio. Even so, only the Folio comedies are regularly divided into five acts, and act divisions in the histories and tragedies are irregular.

In *King John* the first two scenes are headed *Actus Primus, Scæna Prima* and *Scæna Secunda*, extending 'Act 1' to 874 lines (Acts 1 and 2 of the present edition). Even more unlikely, *Actus Secundus* constitutes only the first 74 lines of what is Act 3, Scene 1 in this edition.[5] At the end of *Actus Secundus* the stage is not clear, for Constance sits on the ground and waits until the members of the wedding party enter to her from the city. Nevertheless, someone designated this entrance as the beginning of *Actus Tertius, Scæna prima*– line 3.1.75 in the present edition. Taylor and Jowett suggest in *A Textual Companion* (p. 317) that someone else may have been responsible, perhaps after about 1608, when the King's Men began to be concerned with act divisions. If these absurd divisions were marked for theatrical use, they would have been provisional at best.

Another kind of scribal error, this time probably the work of Scribe II, is the misplaced speech heading in 5.6.1–6, where Hubert and the Bastard meet in

---

[1] Another feature of the text is the peculiar way the oaths were purged. References to God were carefully edited out by the scribes, someone in the printing house, or a book-keeper, presumably to satisfy the censor, except in 2.1 where eight instances of 'God' or 'God's' remain. We can hardly blame one of the compositors for nodding over his work, because three of these instances are in C's stints and five in B's. Therefore the erratic purging probably occurred on the manuscript copy. In the present edition, I have attempted to restore the name of God in several passages similar to those left standing in Act 2: where the meaning is religious ('we under God are supreme head', 3.1.155), in familiar expressions like 'I would to God I were your son' (4.1.23–4) or 'God He knows how we shall answer him' (5.7.60), and where the deity is addressed ('O God, that there were but a mote in yours', 4.1.91). Not all references to 'heaven' implying 'God' should be emended, for even in 2.1, apparently untouched by censorship, there are many uses of 'heaven' and one of 'heaven-moving' sprinkled through the dialogue. (I assume that 'God', 'heaven' and 'heav'n' are metrically interchangeable.)

[2] J. M. Nosworthy, *Shakespeare's Occasional Plays, Their Origin and Transmission*, 1965, p. 230.

[3] T. H. Howard-Hill, *Ralph Crane and Some Shakespeare First Folio Comedies*, 1972, pp. 64–8, 75–81.

[4] Emrys Jones summarises these matters in *Scenic Form in Shakespeare*, 1971, pp. 66–8.

[5] It is also strange that *Actus Secundus* is not followed by the usual *Scæna prima*.

darkness. In what follows, I have laid out the assignments of speeches as they are found in the Folio, but aligned as they would appear in a manuscript.

> *Hub.* Whose there? Speake hoa, speake quickely, or I shoote.
> *Bast.* A Friend. What art thou?
> *Hub.* Of the part of England.
> *Bast.* Whether doest thou go?
> *Hub.* What's that to thee?
>   Why may not I demand of thine affaires,
>   As well as thou of mine?
> *Bast.* *Hubert*, I thinke.
> *Hub.* Thou hast a perfect thought:

Several editors and commentators have found a difficulty in the fifth speech, where Hubert seems to answer his own question. Among the emendations proposed I follow substantially Dyce's elegant solution (1866). Since scribes normally wrote the speeches for a whole page first before they inserted the headings in the margin, it was easy for a heading to be misplaced above or below where it should be. In this case, the sixth heading, *Bast.*, should be moved up a line and a half:

> *Bast.* Why may not I demand of thine affaires,
>   As well as thou of mine?
>   *Hubert*, I thinke.
> *Hub.*   Thou hast a perfect thought:

(In the present edition, a dash has been added after 'mine?') A short line in mid speech remains, but that is not unusual; compare *Rom.* 2.2.11.[1] Although I wish I were as certain as Dyce that the emendation is 'absolutely necessary', it makes better sense than leaving the assignments of the Folio. Moreover, Dyce's solution does not imply many secondary hypotheses like the bolder reassignments that have been proposed. W. W. Lloyd, who first pointed out the difficulty, suggested that three headings be moved. And Karl Elze, *Notes on Elizabethan Dramatists*, 1st series (1880), pp. 63–5, made six reassignments, because he assumed that the Bastard should open the dialogue, for he is hot-headed, aggressive and overbearing whereas Hubert is sedate and defensive. Dover Wilson and Smallwood follow Elze's scheme generally, but they do not break up the second speech or join the third and fourth.

> *Bastard.* Who's there? speak, ho! speak, quickly, or I shoot.
> *Hubert.* A friend . . . What art thou?
> *Bastard.*   Of the part of England.
> *Hubert.* Whither dost thou go?
> *Bastard.* What's that to thee?
> *Hubert.*   Why may not I demand
>   Of thine affairs, as well as thou of mine?
> *Bastard.* Hubert, I think.
> *Hubert.*   Thou hast a perfect thought:

[1] Dyce matches the half-lines somewhat differently from my scheme, leaving the short line as Hubert's 'Whither dost thou go?'

Such a wholesale rearrangement implies deep corruption, and the editors offend against Occam's razor: avoid unnecessary multiplication of secondary hypotheses. In any case, if the Bastard is to have the first question, and if Hubert says he is 'A friend', this drastic overhauling of the dialogue is consistent within itself, but in conflict with the following speech, where Hubert declares 'I will upon all hazards well believe / Thou art my friend that know'st my tongue so well.' This is apparently a response to the Bastard's claim to be 'A friend'. Thus falls the house of cards.

So far, the evidence implies that the printer's copy was prepared by two scribes who followed Shakespeare's foul papers rather closely. Their work leaves the impression that they were not attempting to make a prompt copy, just a readable script, perhaps, for the company to look over and assign parts, to consider the cuts or other changes. Once an official prompt-book was made, the intermediate transcript would be expendable. The players would naturally prefer to hold on to their prompt-book, but they were presumably willing to supply an intermediate transcript to the printer.[1]

If these assumptions are valid, we can move with some confidence to the process of setting the play in type. Charlton Hinman's careful investigations have established that *King John* was set by two compositors, B and C, and that they worked from a manuscript that was 'cast off' – that is, before composition began, the master printer or an assistant in the printing-house counted off the lines to determine exactly what segments of the text should go on each page. Because casting off enabled the compositors to set by formes rather than to set from the beginning of the play and go straight through to the end, they started with the pages that were destined to be printed first. Since the Folio was to be gathered in quires of three sheets, six leaves, and twelve pages, if a compositor began setting at page one and proceeded in order, he could not supply the press with a completed forme until pages six and seven were finished. Therefore, it was common to begin setting type with that portion of the text slated for the inner forme of the inner sheet of a gathering: pages six and seven of each quire. In the case of *King John*, Compositor B began setting type for the first quire, pages six (sig. a3^v, 1.1.302–426) and seven (sig. a4, 2.1.427–552), then pages five (sig. a3, 2.1.179–301) and eight (sig. a4^v, 2.1.553–3.1.74), while Compositor C set pages one to four (sigs. a1–a2^v, 1.1.1–2.1.178) and ten to twelve (sigs. a5–a6^v, 3.1.75–3.4.122). For the second quire, Compositor C set just the inner forme of the inner sheet (sigs. b3^v–b4, 4.1.142–5.2.143), and Compositor B set all the rest (sigs. b1–b3 and b4^v–b5^v, 3.4.123–4.3.141 and 5.2.144–5.7.118). Apparently, this order of setting was economical because less type was tied up waiting to be printed, and the balance between composition and press work was easier to achieve.[2] Above all,

---

[1] Fredson Bowers proposed the 'reasonable assumption' that acting companies preferred a fair copy rather than foul papers. And it 'could well have been expedient, in lieu of the author's fair copy, for a theatrical scribe to make an intermediate transcript . . . for consideration, revision, submission to the censor, copying for parts or sometimes for marking and cutting in preparation for the final prompt book' (*On Editing Shakespeare and Elizabethan Drama*, 1955, pp. 18–21).

[2] Charlton Hinman, *The Printing and Proof-Reading of the First Folio of Shakespeare*, 1963, I, 47–51, 72–3.

casting off had to be accurate, because the compositors needed to know exactly where each page started and ended. (The task is not so difficult, however, if the text is in verse rather than prose.) By tracing distinctive bits of damaged type through the Folio, Hinman showed that normal composition proceeded in the way I have sketched.

This procedure allows us to reconsider an important and controversial emendation in Act 2 of *King John*, where the speech headings are muddled. At the entrance of the Citizen of Angiers (sig. a3) his headings at lines 201, 267, 270, and 282 identify him first as *Citizen*, then *Cit.* But on the next two pages (sig. a3ᵛ–a4) his headings become *Hubert* (325) and later *Hub.* (363, 416, 423, and 480).[1] With the exception of Knight, editors since Rowe have, until recently, assigned all these speeches to *Citizen, First Citizen* or the like. J. P. Collier was the first to suggest that 'Possibly the actor of the part of Hubert also personated the citizen, in order that the speeches might be well delivered, and this may have led to the insertion of his name in the MS.' In other words, one actor could have doubled as Citizen and Hubert, for the Citizen does not appear on stage after 2.1, and Hubert comes on first in 3.3. As several editors mention, the Folio's faulty speech headings may have been caused by a playhouse annotation in the margin.

Later commentators – John Hunter (1871), C. Porter (1910), and John Dover Wilson (1936) – thought that the name did not come into the text by way of someone's marginal note but that Shakespeare meant the Citizen to be one and the same person as Hubert. Wilson used this interpretation to buttress another conjecture, concerning King John's 'baffling' profession in the next act (3.3.20–4) that his mother and he owe Hubert much, and that Hubert has given a 'voluntary oath' to John. If Hubert and the Citizen are the same person, 'the speech obviously refers back to the great service performed by the spokesman of Angiers in 2.1 in bringing about the match between John's niece and the French Dauphin'.[2]

Wilson granted that doubling was a normal feature of Elizabethan acting, and 'may in this case go back to *The Troublesome Reign* [which he presumed was Shakespeare's source]. If so, and if Shakespeare had himself played in that drama, as I am inclined to think possible, he may have come to the writing of *King John* with the identification of the two characters firmly in mind. In any event, there can be little doubt that the confusion in the text originated with him, and not with the prompter of the company' (p. xlvi). Enough doubt remained, apparently, for Wilson did not put the theory to work in his text. Quite the reverse; he uniformly emended the *Hubert* and *Hub.* speech headings in Act 2 to *Citizen*, but in a note he restated his case, more fancifully: 'At this point [in revising], I think, Sh. made up his mind that Hubert de Burgh, under whose charge [John] left Arthur in France, was the chief citizen of Angiers (as his name "de Burgh" suggests)' (p. 121).

Subsequent editors have generally accepted that the Citizen and Hubert are the same character; thus Honigmann (1954) assigned all the Citizen's speeches to

---

[1] At 368 a speech by the Citizen is given to France, but that is an obvious mistake.
[2] Wilson, p. xlvii.

Hubert, as did Matchett (1966), Smallwood (1974), and Riverside (1974). Honigmann justified the choice by asserting that the manuscript that went to the printer was Shakespeare's own foul papers, in which he had not yet decided on the names of his characters. Moreover, he thought that the mixture of speech headings is not really like any other cases of textual confusion on account of doubling, because 'In those plays where doubling is thought to have caused confusion of names only isolated instances of confusion are known'; there is 'no comparable parallel in the canon'. He denies the parallel with the difficulties in the Folio text of *MND* 5.1, where Egeus's name replaces all of Philostrate's speech headings, because 'Philostrate disappears altogether' (Honigmann p. xxxvii).

On the contrary, Philostrate remains in Act 1 as a mute master of the revels, Theseus orders him by name to prepare for the revels, and although someone has systematically changed his speech headings in Act 5, it was probably not what Shakespeare preferred, because more confusion exists when Theseus calls for Egeus – 'our usual manager of mirth'.[1] If we did not have the quarto text of *MND*, a few editors might have smelled something fishy and wished to emend the Folio's speech headings. The Folio texts of both *John* and *MND* contain extensive alteration of headings, in effect reducing the number of actors for speaking parts, and yet maintaining something of what must have been an original distinction between the dramatic roles. Therefore, doubling in *King John* remains the simplest and the most adequate explanation.

Moreover, a bibliographical detail lends weight to this conjecture. Why do all the *Hubert* headings and none of the *Citizen* headings occur on two facing pages in the same forme (sigs. a3ᵛ–a4, 2.1.302–552)? Compositor B set these pages, the very first forme of the play put into type. Then B set the second forme (a3–a4ᵛ, 2.1.179–301; 2.1.553–3.1.74) which contains all the headings for *Citizen* and *Cit.* (The compositor's spelling habits alone are inconclusive, but, with the typographical evidence. Hinman (II, 474) says there is no room for doubt that B set the first two formes.)[2]

With greater confidence we may now imagine how the speech headings became muddled: Compositor B came cold to his first stint of setting *King John*, without having read the preceding pages of his copy, and after the long speeches by the Heralds (who address the citizens as just 'men of Angiers') B saw a heading for *Cit.* and in the margin a notation 'Hubert'. Thinking that Hubert was the character's name, the natural reaction for Compositor B – who often made arbitrary changes in the text – was to adopt the proper name, which he spelled out in full in the first heading. Thereafter he set the heading *Hub.* four times, replacing *Cit.* each time. But when B composed the second forme (a3–a4ᵛ) and came upon the unambiguous stage direction *Enter a Citizen upon the walles*, he decided that *Cit.* was a proper heading. Since he was the undismayed Compositor B, he did not go back to correct the error in the first forme, which may have been in the press. (Only one trivial press-

[1] See Harold F. Brooks (ed.), *MND*, 1979, p. xxxii and n. 1.
[2] The compositor could not have been B's partner C, because these two pages lack C's most obvious habit: the frequent insertion of a space before a comma at the end of a short line. See T. H. Howard-Hill, 'The compositors of Shakespeare's Folio comedies', *SB* 26 (1973), 68–9.

correction has been found in *John*, and literal errors abound.) This conjecture at least explains why only half the names were changed, whereas in *A Midsummer Night's Dream* all were changed. It implies, moreover, that the agent of the muddled change in identity of the Citizen was not Shakespeare but the compositor, who misunderstood his copy when he came upon a marginal note while he was setting by formes.

If we think of the play as a drama to be seen and heard on stage, the identification of the Citizen with Hubert seems equally unlikely. The Citizen in Act 2 is one of several on the walls, and he speaks for the group, using 'us' and 'we' repeatedly; the characters below address them as 'you men of Angiers', 'Citizens', 'kind citizens', and 'townsmen'. Their spokesman refers to himself once as 'I' (417), and after his long speech the Bastard refers to him as 'he' (462–3), but the kings return to the general address immediately – 'Now, citizens of Angiers' – when the marriage has been agreed upon. As Emrys Jones has noticed, the audience has no way from the dialogue alone to recognise that the Citizen and Hubert are the same character.[1] The Citizen is impersonally conceived by the playwright, and he speaks as a type. After he has performed his part he disappears, and is forgotten. He is absent from the stage directions even in 3.1, when the wedding party emerges from the gates of Angiers. But Hubert enters 'exactly where he does in Holinshed: when John invites him to dispose of Arthur' (Jones, *Origins*, pp. 283–5). His name is repeated many times in his first appearance (3.3) as if identifying a new character for the audience. After all, Hubert was a historically important person – chief justiciar to John and his son, Henry III, and he served King Richard, John, and Henry as a distinguished soldier and public official. His name is prominent in both Holinshed and Foxe. In short, the dialogue does not give the slightest hint to the audience that Hubert comes from Angiers, and a reader of chronicles as savvy as Shakespeare had good reason to keep the two separate.

It remains to explain how the notation 'Hubert' could have come into the manuscript. Occasionally the names of obscure actors were written in a prompt copy, indicating bit parts they were to play, and were carried over by accident into the speech headings and stage directions of early printed texts. But in this instance Hubert and the Citizen are names of characters, not actors. A similar example of interloping characters' names (aside from Egeus/Philostrate in *MND*, mentioned above) appears in *Romeo and Juliet*, Q2–3, F, 5.3.21, where 'Peter' – a clownish servant to the Nurse, played by Will Kemp – appears in a stage direction instead of 'Balthasar', Romeo's servant. W. W. Greg thought that doubling may also explain why in *Hamlet* Q, 5.2.373, 'Voltemar' – an ambassador from Norway in 1.2 – appears in the embassy from England, accompanying Fortinbras.[2] The examples of Egeus/Philostrate and Peter/Balthasar as well as Citizen/Hubert suggest that a playhouse book-keeper was compiling a cast list, determining what supporting roles could be

---

[1] Of course, in performance it is possible that Hubert, with a ghastly disfigurement on his face, could be identified visually with the Citizen. John refers to Hubert's 'abhorred aspect' which 'the hand of Nature marked, / Quoted, and signed to do a deed of shame' (4.2.221–2). However, the Citizen remains anonymous, and there is no point in his having a huge birthmark or tumour.

[2] W. W. Greg, *The Editorial Problem in Shakespeare*, 1951 edn, pp. 61 and 66. See G. B. Evans (ed.), *Rom.*, 1984, p. 28 and 5.3.21 SD. 2 n.

doubled for a company of about twelve men and four boys, who had to play twenty-nine speaking parts and several mutes. Aside from the major roles of John and the Bastard, which could not be doubled, the others had to be parcelled out in twos and threes to each of the remaining members of the troupe. In any case, the importance of doubling in sixteenth-century English plays is now widely recognised, and the example in *King John* should be added to the instances in the Shakespeare canon.[1]

Dover Wilson and editors who have followed his emendation, making the Citizen and Hubert into one character, were misled by the assumption that there were just two choices of copy-text: foul papers and prompt copy. But once we have evidence for an intermediate transcript, as in *King John*, a transcript that preserves many of the author's irregularities but is unsuitable for the official prompt copy, annotation by other hands could occur.

The general inaccuracy of the two compositors casts a light on some less complicated but still troubling errors. Since B throughout the Folio does not follow copy carefully, his pages contain many mistakes, particularly substitution and sophistication of words or phrases. Sometimes B makes wild guesses at difficult words such as 'Symet' for 'sygnet', the presumed spelling in the printer's copy (5.7.21); he substitutes similar words like 'once against crown'd' for 'once again crown'd' (4.2.1), and 'rights of marriage' for 'rites of marriage' (2.1.539). He transposes phrases such as 'you haue beheld' for 'haue you beheld' (4.3.41) or 'Kings of our feare' for what was probably 'Kinged of our fears' (2.1.371). His punctuation is sometimes ridiculous, such as 'mercy, lacking' for 'mercy-lacking' (4.1.120). Several of B's pages contain as many as four substantial errors – for example, sigs. a3 (2.1.99–301), a3^v (2.1.302–426), a4 (2.1.427–552), and b5 (5.4.59–5.7.28). He apparently tried to hold so much in his head that he omitted, interpolated, repeated, and anticipated.

Superficially, it seems that Compositor C followed copy somewhat better than B, but he was prone to literal errors, the omission of letters and words, and an occasional sophistication; and in a play that survives in only one authoritative text, his errors seem easier to rectify. For example, he set 'words' for 'worlds' (3.4.110), 'center' for 'centure' (4.3.155), 'hast fought' for 'hast thou fought' (5.2.43), 'In any beast' for 'In any breast' (2.1.113), 'It would' for 'I would' (1.1.147). His sophistications are 'This vn-heard sawcinesse' for 'This vn-haired sawcinesse' (5.2.133) and 'This expeditious charge' for 'This expedition's charge' (1.1.49). However, when the same compositor set from a quarto, as he did for the Folio's *Ado, LLL, MND*, and *MV*, and we can compare his version with his copy, the picture darkens. His large number of memorial errors and almost all his substitutions make sense, so they are 'nearly

[1] See W. A. Ringler, 'The number of actors in Shakespeare's early plays', *The Seventeenth-Century Stage: A Collection of Critical Essays*, ed. G. E. Bentley, 1968, pp. 110–34. W. J. Lawrence, 'The practice of doubling and its influence on early dramaturgy', *Pre-Restoration Stage Studies*, 1927, pp. 43–78. David Bevington, *From Mankind to Marlowe*, 1962. Incidentally, Bevington points out (p. 268) that in the old play of *King Johan* by John Bale there are stage directions from which a partial pattern of doubling can be determined: for example, Private Wealth is directed at line 1060 *Here go owt and dresse for Nobylyte* and at line 1533 *Here Nobelyte go owt to dresse for the Cardinall.*

impossible to detect without referring to copy'.[1] He omits many pronouns and prepositions, smooths out the metre, changes words to solve problems of spacing. In his 42 pages set from quarto copy among the comedies, 18 pages contain five or more errors each. That is a high figure indeed, and although C appears not to have been as independent and inventive as B, we have little chance in a one-text situation to know exactly where many of C's errors are to be found. There is little for an editor to do with this kind of information, except to be alert to the evident signs of corruption in these classes, and to emend with good reason.

The text of *King John* probably contains more than an average amount of corruption for an Elizabethan play, but that corruption is not especially deep. If these examples of readings that need emendation are typical, the errors of transmission seldom call for drastic action. In spite of the lapses of attention by compositors or scribes, Shakespeare's foul papers were transcribed and set in type with enough fidelity, it seems, for the faults to be sometimes within range of correction. Consequently, an editor need not adhere too strictly to the received text, for he has a certain liberty of emendation.

As W. W. Greg pointed out, an editor has generally a greater liberty to emend what appear to be mistakes or corruptions when there is just one authoritative text. In a two-text situation (as with *Troilus* and *Othello*), where a good quarto and a somewhat independent Folio text survive, emendations are mostly limited to a choice between variants in one or the other authoritative witness. But with only one substantive text, those constraints do not hold. Nevertheless, conjecture does not operate in a vacuum, for much depends upon the context, a knowledge of the idioms of Elizabethan English, and a knowledge of Shakespeare's habits with words. Greg defined a good emendation as one that strikes a trained intelligence as supplying 'exactly the sense required by the context, and which at the same time reveals to the critic the manner in which the corruption arose'.[2] This is a rigorous standard that few emendations meet, but in any case the explanations for our conjectures should be consistent with the evidence and the assumptions we have about the transmission of the text.[3]

Since the evidence is accretive, the assumptions about compositors, scribes, playhouse annotator, and Shakespeare's habits of writing have emerged gradually. This analysis is not meant to prove, but only to suggest what may have happened to the text of *King John*.

[1] See John O'Connor, 'A qualitative analysis of Compositor C and D in the Shakespeare First Folio', *SB* 30 (1977), 59–60.
[2] W. W. Greg, 'Principles of emendation in Shakespeare', Annual Shakespeare Lecture, 1928, *PBA* 14 (1929), 4.
[3] *Ibid.*, pp. 7–11.

APPENDIX: DATE, SOURCES, AND *THE TROUBLESOME REIGN*

The only certainties about the date of *King John* are that it was first printed in the 1623 Folio and written sometime after the second edition of Holinshed's *Chronicles* (1587) but before 1598, when Francis Meres listed it in *Palladis Tamia* among Shakespeare's tragedies. Historical allusions, like the mention of the destruction of a 'whole armado' by a 'roaring tempest' (3.4.1–2), or the probable reference to Secretary Davison's use of Queen Elizabeth's 'hand and seal' in ordering the execution of Mary Queen of Scots (4.2.215–17) move the early limit to 1588. Internal evidence suggests that the play's declamatory style resembles the dialogue of Shakespeare's first tetralogy, which could be no later than 1589–90 if *The Troublesome Reign* (1591) borrows lines and phrases from *Richard III*.[1] But signs of an increasingly mature style may be found in some of John's and the Bastard's speeches, which create the illusion of a person thinking and comprehending, like certain speeches by Richard II[2]. However, much depends on the relationship between Shakespeare's play and the anonymous *Troublesome Reign of John, King of England*, reprinted in 1611 as the work of 'W.Sh.' and in 1622 as by 'W. Shakespeare'.[3] The troublesome question is whether *Troublesome Reign* is Shakespeare's source or whether *King John* is the source of *TR*.

Although opinion is divided, most who have written about the subject favour *TR* as Shakespeare's main source, especially Dover Wilson, Kenneth Muir, Alice Walker, and R. L. Smallwood.[4] However, Peter Alexander, E. A. J. Honigmann, William H. Matchett, and a few others have suggested that Shakespeare's play is the original and *TR* is somehow indebted to it.[5] (Years ago it was thought that *TR* was Shakespeare's first draft.) Amidst the often conflicting evidence, unshakeable proof one way or the other is not possible. But if we put greater weight on the evidence of dramatic construction, as I think we should, it is more likely that Shakespeare's play came first and that *TR* is an adaptation of *John*. Before explaining this hypothesis, I will sketch the various difficulties that the mixed evidence presents.

[1] See E. A. J. Honigmann, *Shakespeare's Impact on his Contemporaries*, pp. 78–88.
[2] See pp. 26–37 above.
[3] The title page indicates its appeal to popular taste: *The Troublesome Raigne of John King of England, with the discoverie of King Richard Cordelions Base sonne (vulgarly named, The Bastard Fawconbridge): also the death of King John at Swinstead Abbey. As it was (sundry times) publikely acted by the Queenes Maiesties Players, in the honourable Citie of London.* There is no record of its entry in the Stationers' Register, nor was Shakespeare's *John* entered prior to its printing in the First Folio, presumably because *TR*'s publication was thought to be an edition of the same play.
[4] Wilson, pp. xix–xxxiv; K. Muir, *Sources of Shakespeare's Plays*, 1977, pp. 79–90; A. Walker, review of Honigmann, *RES* n.s. 7 (1956), 421–3; Smallwood, pp. 365–74.
[5] Peter Alexander, *Shakespeare's Life and Art*, 1939, p. 85, and *Shakespeare*, 1964, pp. 167–71. Honigmann, pp. xi–xxxii, and *Shakespeare's Impact*, chs. 3–4. W. Matchett (ed.), *John*, 1966, pp. 153 ff., and Suzanne Tumblin Gary, 'The Relationship between *The Troublesome Reign of John King of England* and Shakespeare's *King John*', unpublished dissertation, University of Arizona, 1971.

Contradictions and inconsistencies

Troublesome Reign and *John* each contains incidental details traceable to Holinshed's
Chronicles (1587) and to John Foxe's *Acts and Monuments* (1583) that are not present
in the other play (see Honigmann, pp. xii–xviii; and J. W. Sider's edition of *TR*, pp.
xxxii–iii); and at least once the two plays use divergent sources for a small detail: when
Peter of Pomfret forecasts that the king will give up his crown, *John* follows Foxe in
having him do it publicly, whereas *TR* follows Holinshed in making him say so
privately to John (Honigmann, p. xv). Both plays contain their share of inconsistencies
and puzzling contradictions that are clearer in the other (see Wilson, pp. xxi–xxiv;
Honigmann pp. 167–73). Yet the plays match so closely in the selection of characters,
the sequence of events, and the management of scenes that they cannot have been
written independently. Sometimes they parallel not just scene for scene but
(substantially) speech for speech.

Parallel passages

If *TR* is derived from *John*, it is strange that the anonymous author did not reproduce
more of the language. He has not even remembered the Bastard's repeated taunt of
Austria, 'And hang a calf's-skin on those recreant limbs'(3.1.131).[1] And if the author
witnessed a performance of Shakespeare's play (obviously, he has not relied upon an
actor's memory, which is one explanation of the transmission of the texts of the 'bad'
quartos), we still should expect more of Shakespeare's language to come through. As
it is, *TR* possibly echoes no more than about twenty to twenty-five lines or half-
lines,[2] and they are not the stunning passages. Most are as pedestrian as this:

> Hubert, what news with you?   *John* 4.2.68
> How now, what news with thee   *TR* 8.207[3]

Several of the parallels are just lists of place-names in the same order, numbers, and
routine forms of address. In both plays only two lines come through essentially the
same: *John* 2.1.528, *TR* 2.410; *John* 5.4.42, *TR* 12.117.

Evidence of *TR*'s habit of repeating undistinguished lines and phrases is found
elsewhere in the play, for the author seems to appropriate at least six passages from
3 Henry VI, five recognisable phrases from *Richard III*, four from *Titus Andronicus*,
and a handful of others from plays by Peele, Kyd, and Marlowe.[4] As Honigmann
says, 'Are we to suppose that Peele, Marlowe, Shakespeare, and others all pilfered
phrases and ideas from *TR*, a play strangely uncelebrated by its contemporaries?'
(*Shakespeare's Impact*, p. 81). They are phrases like

> *Set down, set down* your honourable *load*   *R3* 1.2.1
>
> *Set down, set down* the *load* not worth your pain   *TR* 13.1

---

[1] Smallwood, p. 368.
[2] See Wilson's list, pp. xxvi–xxvii; Suzanne Gary has added seven more, pp. 155–7.
[3] I follow the scene and line numbering of *TR* in Sider's edition.
[4] Honigmann, *Shakespeare's Impact*, pp. 79–83.

But several are strong examples, not easily reversible; for example, Shakespeare adopts a phrase from his immediate source in Holinshed:

> before such great things, *men's* hearts of a secret *instinct* of nature misgive them; as the sea without wind *swelleth* of himself sometime before a tempest . . .
>
> Holinshed, III, 379

> *By divine instinct men's* minds mistrust
> Ensuing danger; as by proof we see
> That water *swell* before a boist'rous storm. *R3* 2.3.42

Shakespeare apparently coined the phrase 'By divine instinct', and *TR* uses it in a different context:

> Your city Rochester with great applause
> *By* some *divine instinct* laid arms inside *TR* 11.172

From a dozen or more of such borrowings the impression is that the author of *TR* has his head full of scraps of plays which he regurgitates, and it is unlikely that *TR* is the lender.

Transpositions

Aside from the more obvious parallels between the two plays, there are about twenty passages that appear to be unconscious transpositions of images, words, and phrases from one context into another.[1] Two examples will suffice.

(a) The Bastard addresses the barons who have joined the Dauphin in *John* 5.2.151–3:

> And you degenerate, you *ingrate* revolts,
> You bloody Neroes, ripping up the *womb*
> Of *your* dear *mother* England . . .

In a later scene of *TR* the dying Melun speaks to the barons in much the same terms (12.127–30):

> Back warmen, back, *embowel* not the clime,
> Your seat, your nurse, your birthday's breathing place,
> That bred you, bears you, brought you up in arms.
> Ah! be not so *ingrate* to dig *your mother's* grave . . .

Elsewhere *TR* uses the image of ripping the womb of one's mother (1.133) and 'As cursed Nero with his mother did' (1.373). But the idea of an *ingrate* who embowels his nurse, his birthday's breathing place, then digs *your mother* England's grave seems to come from Shakespeare.

(b) In another passage it may be that the author of *TR* has the gist of the Bastard's Commodity soliloquy in mind, but he omits the whole soliloquy and gives a summary of it to Constance addressing the two kings:

---

[1] Wilson collected a few, pp. xxviii–xxxii, and Gary cites several more, pp. 83–114.

BASTARD Mad world, mad *kings*, mad composition! . . .
   And France . . . rounded in the *ear* . . .
         . . . that wins of all,
   Of *kings*, of beggars, old men, young men, maids –
   Who having no external thing to *lose* . . .
   That smooth-faced gentleman, *tickling* Commodity . . .
   Since *kings* break faith upon commodity,
   Gain, be my *lord*, for I will worship thee!   *John* 2.1.561–98

CONSTANCE What *kings*, why stand you gazing in a trance?
   Why how now *Lords*? accursed Citizens
   To fill and *tickle* their ambitious *ears*,
   With hope of *gain* that springs from Arthur's *loss*.   *TR* 2.360–3

This sort of borrowing is usually associated with tricks of memory, while a person writes, after reading or hearing the phrases in a different context, but it does not establish priority.

Shakespeare's handling of dramatic sources

Let us suppose that Shakespeare took the design of his play straight from *TR*, simply omitting a few scenes, moving a few entrances and exits, but revamping the dialogue and building up the roles of Constance and the Bastard (since *TR* has neither of his soliloquies nor much of her magnificent lamentation). In this case Shakespeare would have departed from his way of handling dramatic sources, for in no other of his plays does he fail to make large structural changes when he works from a dramatic source. In *The Comedy of Errors* and *Measure for Measure*, for example, he doubles the plots or creates a frame plot, he adds major scenes from other plays, he compresses and synthesises events and unrelated characters in the source play. And in his history plays, working from the *Chronicles*, he boldly telescopes and invents. Must we presume that he found in *TR* a ready-made, carefully articulated plan that fitted his own habits of plotting? This is odd, indeed, since no other playwright of the time – not Marlowe, Peele, Greene, Kyd, or Lyly – has the combinative and structural powers of the early Shakespeare; yet the preternaturally gifted author of *Troublesome Reign* has supposedly done his basic work for him.

This survey of the evidence for the relationship of the two plays so far suggests that a simple solution is no solution at all.

Construction

I think it is improbable that *John* is indebted to *Troublesome Reign* for its design because the author of *TR* seems insensitive to the very principles on which his play is constructed. A greater dramatic artist conceived the design by which the scattered historical events were synthesised from the *Chronicles*. Nor does it seem likely that the symmetries of the play and the mirroring actions should have been the anonymous author's work: the three mothers and their three sons, and the three power-brokers, if not the three innocents; the English invasion of France that reaches a stalemate and the French invasion of England that ends in a stand-off.[1] Moreover, the ironies and the dilemmas that are built into the scenes of the two plays are too sophisticated to have been invented by the author of the dialogue and of the monastic episodes in *TR*. This interpretation of the evidence is a development of Peter Alexander's idea that started the reinvestigation of these two plays:

Powers of construction and integration . . . cannot be acquired, though they may be developed. Yet it is precisely here that the author of *The Troublesome Raigne* is supposed to have shown the way to Shakespeare. In all that can be put under the heading of vocabulary or versification or atmosphere the plays are worlds apart; in their construction and unity of impression they are as close together as two very differing pieces can be.[2]

If we follow Alexander's lead and look carefully at the way that the two plays are put together from the major source in the *Chronicles*, assuming that one of the two writers made the basic decisions about what to include and what to leave out, a reasonable case can be made for the priority of Shakespeare's play – that is, a case not easily reversible.

First we must cast aside the abbreviated versions of Holinshed's *Chronicles*, whether they be in the old Boswell–Stone or the new Bullough selections, because they are confined to passages that most resemble characters and events in the plays, as if source study amounts to little more than a search for stolen property. The abbreviated versions create a false impression of contiguity and relevance, giving us a collection of tasty bits, not the vast feast of action, anecdote, sermons, letters, formal declarations, and odd details about storms and apparitions. If we read the full text of Holinshed's account of King John's reign, now available in a reprint of Ellis's edition, we can see that the chronicler's usual method was to conflate the received accounts of each king's rule, year by year, making a vast sprawling collection of miscellaneous information and unreconciled contradictions. One of Holinshed's virtues as a historian is that, for important matters, he will often print variant or conflicting reports, the consequent uncertainty of which interested Shakespeare. So a playwright could with such material depict on the stage something of the indeterminacy of life: for example, the mixed impressions of King John's death – did he die of a fever, by poison, for grief, or all of these? And the mystery of Arthur's death, the real circumstances of which are known only to the audience, distinguishes each character at a dramatic moment according to his guess at the fearful truth.

Fortunately even the abbreviated versions pass on many of those local indeterminacies, but if we are to reconstruct the playwright's larger artistic choices we must also know what he chose to leave out, what he synthesised, and how he shifted emphasis. That is the important reason for knowing the whole historical

---

[1] See pp. 37–46 above.
[2] Alexander, *Introductions to Shakespeare*, 1964, p. 99. He said much the same in *Shakespeare's Life and Art*, p. 85, and there he mentioned the half-assimilated phrases in *TR* taken from *3H6*, *R3*, and *John*.

account. For the reign of John there are sustained stretches of historical narrative, like the developing chaotic state of affairs when the Dauphin invaded and almost conquered England, and there are dispersed accounts of John's rapid, frenetic movements back and forth within the kingdom, across the Channel, into Scotland, Wales, and Ireland to cope with each sudden crisis. It is surprising to see how well the author of *TR* or *John* has created the impression of these events and a sense of sporadic warfare, letting three battles (2.1, 3.2–3, and 5.3–6) stand for numerous campaigns. Broken treaties, alliances, vows, and shifting loyaltes that recur in the two plays are but a sample of the political and moral turmoil recorded in Holinshed.

Both plays leave out most of John's worst qualities: his cruelty to his subjects (except for his treatment of Peter of Pomfret), his rapaciousness (aside from squeezing money from the abbeys), and his ruthless use of foreign mercenaries in the kingdom, but they preserve his military prowess, his dissimulation, his explosive temper, his pride, his fears, his subsequent regrets for rash acts, and his growing dependence upon a few loyal servants, when his support from the nobility dwindles. He shows, indeed, that he is a true son of Henry II and Queen Eleanor. There is enough in the two plays to warrant Holinshed's assessment that he had a 'princely heart', and like Coriolanus he tasted 'of fortune both ways', 'bountiful and liberal unto strangers, but of his own people . . . a great oppressor' (Holinshed, II, 339). However, except for his once complaining about his mistaken submission to the Pope, there is very little in the *Chronicles* to support the helpless, desperate, guilt-ridden King John that emerges in the second half of the two dramas. Holinshed's John fights his enemies vigorously and with some success up to the last few days; he does not delegate to anyone the responsibility for 'the ordering of this present time' (*John* 5.1.77).

If we consider the whole of John's reign, as Holinshed lays it out, we have a chance to imagine the playwright's structural intentions, how he transforms this hodgepodge of events into dramatic scenes that fit into a large plan. About all the chronicle offers by way of order is a natural division into three periods. First, the years 1199–1202, when among a thousand troubles there is intermittent strife over Arthur's rights to territories that John also claims, ending with Arthur's death. Second, John's protracted quarrel with the Pope, 1205–13, over the appointment of the archbishop of Canterbury, which led to interdiction, excommunication, and an order to depose the king.[1] This period ends with the king's capitulation to Rome. Third, the years 1213–17 of growing disaffection among the nobility and the Dauphin's invasion, which continued beyond John's death. The playwright's problem was how to link these discrete periods, for, although the cast of characters for the most part remains the same, the events in the *Chronicles* are disconnected.

One of the two playwrights solved the problem by creating a sequence of scenes that intercalates the events of the three periods, making one action depend upon another that is quite remote in the source. Not all the connections are well-fitted,

---

[1] Some of this is in John Foxe's *Acts and Monuments of Martyrs*, 1583 edn, but Holinshed incorporated most of the same material from the same sources – Coggeshall, Matthew Paris, Polydore Vergil, Grafton, and Stow.

such as Pandulph's unprepared entry at 3.1.135 and *TR* 3.63, and Prince Henry's sudden appearance, a *deus ex machina*, in the last scene (second-to-last in *TR*). But the major links are so skilfully made that contingent actions and characters form a network that continues from scene to scene. In what follows, I will attempt to describe the strategies of invention that affect the construction of scenes.

Act I of *John* or the opening scene in *TR* is strikingly original, for, although the historical John and his mother were busy in the first year of his reign garnering support for his new kingship, and King Philip backed Arthur in the cities and provinces of north-western France, King Philip did not send an embassy to John at this time challenging his legitimacy and championing Arthur's lineal right to the throne of England. The closest parallel in the *Chronicles* occurs in 1204, two years after Arthur died, when John sends an embassy to King Philip to try to settle their differences, but Philip swears that he will never cease fighting to revenge Arthur's death, until he deprives John of his whole kingdom (II, 289). Nor does Holinshed say anything of two brothers Falconbridge bringing a similar quarrel for him to resolve, since they are fictional characters, almost wholly original inventions.[1] What we have in the scene is a fine example of Shakespearean opening moves in which he ever so briefly introduces a central theme, then dramatises it in a minor key. With only a fifth of the dialogue given to the embassy and John's defiant reply, the rest is a serio-comic dispute over a modest inheritance that parallels the royal family's problem. The low-mimetic dispute involves a widowed mother, a younger son who claims to be the legitimate heir, and an elder bastard son – the relationships just similar enough to cast an oblique light on the dispute between the other two pairs of mother and son – Eleanor and John, Constance and Arthur. Chatillon announces flatly that by primogeniture Arthur, son of John's elder brother, has the stronger right, and, in *John* but not *TR*, Eleanor as much as admits the charge, in a whispered aside. In Shakespeare's play the two disputes over lineal right are linked by another parallel in the second scene – the dying father's will disinheriting the elder son or his grandson, and passing the property rights to the younger son (*John* 1.1.109–15, 2.1.191–4; in *TR* 2.98–107 only King Richard's will is mentioned).

Are we to suppose that the author of *TR* invented this elaborate high/low juxtaposition that Shakespeare was to exploit again in the opening scenes of *1* and *2 Henry IV*, and *Julius Caesar*? A lesser dramatist might have stuck closer to his source and used a less theatrical juxtaposition from the *Chronicles*: the threatened invasion by the King of Scotland. The historical John was troubled by this potential enemy in his first year, and Scotland sent a threatening embassy. But the playwright responsible for the design of *John* and *TR* economises by transferring the formal challenge to a French embassy, which compounds the danger to John because

---

[1] The Bastard was suggested by the single mention that Philip bastard son of King Richard killed the Viscount Limoges 'in revenge of his father's death' in the year 1199. Shakespeare also modelled him on Dunois, the Bastard of Orleans, as depicted in Hall's *Chronicle*, fol. civ, who renounced his inheritance from his mother's family and affirmed his bastardy. See Jacqueline Trace, 'Shakespeare's Bastard Fawlconbridge: an early Tudor hero', *S.St.* 13 (1980), 59–69, who has found another bastard of that name among the *Letters and Papers of Henry VIII*.

Arthur's right is involved. The wording of Chatillon's speech is taken in part from a later face-to-face parley between John and King Philip (Holinshed, II, 277). The only other important detail in Act 1 that comes from Holinshed essentially unchanged is Eleanor's belief that Constance hungers for power while she promotes her son's claim (Holinshed, II, 274; *John* 1.1.31–34; 2.1.122–3; *TR* 1.54–6).

TR's handling of Lady Falconbridge's part in the first scene raises another problem. Since the anonymous author of *TR* has brought her on stage earlier than in *John* to protest against her younger son's slurs upon her honour, she witnesses the Bastard's open confession that he is the son of King Richard. In a trance he hears voices that tell him of his paternity, and he publicly announces that fact. But her presence early in the scene renders otiose the private interview that follows between her and the Bastard, for she speaks to him as if he does not know the identity of his true father, and as if she has not witnessed his miraculous confession moments earlier. Such duplication of actions suggests that the less competent playwright had Shakespeare's scene roughly in mind, but in the first half of the scene he forgot or omitted Eleanor's offered choice to the Bastard because he preferred the more spectacular trance, and he included Lady Falconbridge's protests to eke out the dialogue. Yet he seems otherwise to have followed his model mechanically, retaining the now unnecessary private confrontation between the mother and her bastard.[1]

Acts 2 and 3 and *TR* Scenes 2–5 compress scattered events from Holinshed between the years 1199 and 1213 into action that occurs on one day and in one place. Almost all characters in the play are massed on stage before the walls of Angiers, and they are carefully arranged in antagonistic pairs.[2] But why Angiers? Passing over England's internal disputes about loyalty to Arthur or John, one of the two writers has combined a half-dozen battles between the French and English over the continental cities and provinces, some loyal to King Philip, to Arthur, or to John. Angiers was one of the many cities that changed hands in these disputes, but nothing particular happened there, except that once, when Constance and Arthur were temporarily reconciled to John, they became suspicious and fled to Angiers. And in 1206 John was so furious at the losses that he suffered at the hands of King Philip that he levelled the city, among others, but he soon felt remorse, 'because he was descended from thence', and he rebuilt the city at great cost. Then Holinshed reflects upon John's uncontrollable wrath.

But what will not an ordinary man do in the full tide of his fury; much more princes and great men, whose anger is resembled to the roaring lion, even upon light occasions oftentimes, to satisfy their unbridled and brain sick affections, which carry them with a swift full stream into such follies and dotages as are undecent for their degrees.   (II, 295)

Although these details are sheared off by the dramatist, he may have felt that Angiers had conflicting emotional resonances for Arthur and King John. In any case the city

---

[1] See Emrys Jones, *Scenic Form in Shakespeare*, 1971, pp. 99–104, for Shakespeare's re-use of this interview pattern in the closet scene of *Hamlet*, where the son questions his mother about his father. It is hard to imagine that Shakespeare learned the pattern from *TR*.

[2] Gary makes much the same point about these scenes, pp. 138 ff.

was one of those bell-wether towns whose allegiance was crucial to both King Philip and John. Is should be noticed, however, that historically their battles were mainly for French or English hegemony on the mainland, not over Arthur's rights. And when Arthur is mentioned, France usually fights for his rights to specific continental territories, not, as in the two plays, for the crown of England, Ireland, and Wales. In this way the playwrights exaggerate Arthur's threat at this moment.

Moreover, the marriage alliance in 1200 between Blanche and Lewis is not formally proposed by anyone, much less a citizen of Angiers, and according to the *Chronicles* it is not the perfidious betrayal of Arthur that we see in the plays. It seems to have nothing to do with Arthur, for King Philip continues to support his claims to various provinces. Even John accepts homage from Arthur for Brittany and other lands (Holinshed, II, 279). In 1205, Constance's last husband, who became Duke of Brittany after Arthur's death, fought loyally for John. In the two plays (*John* 3.2 and 3.3, *TR* 3.159 ff.) the important battle of Mirabeau (1202) is transferred to Angiers, when Eleanor is captured and is speedily rescued by John, as in *TR* (not by the Bastard), and when John captures Arthur. *TR* includes John's generous offer if Arthur will forsake his alliance with the French king, but the boy gives a cheeky reply, as in the *Chronicles*; in *John* Arthur is not defiant, just sorry that his capture will break his mother's heart. From this point on John is more fearful and sinister and Arthur more of a victim.

The dramatic purpose of the changes common to both plays is to focus on relationships in the first three acts, and much of the fourth, that magnify the danger of Arthur's claims to England, the opportunistic motives for French support of those claims, and John's fear of them. Both plays omit or subordinate as side issues the particular problems and cross-loyalties. This is the selective principle for the actions of both plays: nearly everything done by John, King Philip, and their entourage seems contingent upon Arthur.[1]

The danger is compounded by the sudden appearance of Pandulph, another key figure, who has been moved up from the third period of John's reign.[2] He stands for several messengers, legates, and cardinals who pop up in the *Chronicles* between 1205 and 1216, carrying orders from Pope Innocent III to both kings, but mostly to John, threatening interdiction, excommunication, and finally deposition if he is not obeyed. Historically the Pope and his agents had nothing to do with the messy situation concerning Arthur because the boy was dead by 1203. John's troubles with Rome began at the death of the old archbishop of Canterbury (1205) and gradually worsened until his capitulation in 1213. It was in 1213 that King Philip prepared to invade England at the suggestion of Pandulph – a move that John thwarted by a *blitzkrieg* on his ships and men before they ever left their French port. But when Philip later backed his son's invasion (1216), he did it against the wishes of the Pope.

---

[1] Sider, p. xlii, notes that Charles Knight first suggested that this is the principle of selection in *King John*; everything turns on Arthur's fate. See Knight's supplementary notice to *John* in *The Pictorial Edition of the Works of Shakspere*, 1839, 1, 72.

[2] Honigmann suggested to me privately that Pandulph, like Arthur, also pulls dispersed events together.

For by that time John had humbled himself to Rome, and the papacy was his champion against all enemies. Consequently, Shakespeare or the author of *TR* telescoped several legates' roles, and ten years of John's vicissitudes with the church. Above all he implicated poor Arthur in Pandulph's schemes for bringing John to his knees (*John* 3.1–4; *TR* 3.63–5.46).

The execution of these scenes in *TR* is the critical evidence that the author did not realise exactly what the momentous artistic choices entail, for, if every major action in the dovetailed events depends upon the fate of Arthur and the influence of Pandulph, the anonymous author failed to make much of John's order to kill Arthur.

> Hubert de Burgh take Arthur here to thee,
> Be he thy prisoner: Hubert keep him safe,
> For on his life doth hang thy Sovereign's crown,
> But in his death consists thy Sovereign's bliss:
> Then Hubert, as thou shortly hearst from me,
> So use the prisoner I have given in charge.   4.30–5

That is the long and short of the order—no qualms, no hesitation, no puzzled reaction from Hubert. Pandulph's advice to Lewis that he exploit inevitable popular anger at the boy's death is even less emphatic:

> Now Lewis, thy fortune buds with happy spring,
> Our holy father's prayers effecteth this.
> Arthur is safe, let John alone with him,
> Thy title next is fairest to England's crown . . .   5.36–9

Unless something more is said, the audience could easily overlook the main purpose of the two scenes leading up to the prison scene.[1] Are we to presume that the playwright who designed these scenes would not know the importance of those speeches? It looks rather as if the author of *TR* was all too eager to get on with the high-jinks of the nun in the abbot's money-chest and other fascinating matters.

Once more, the barons' revolt, hanging upon Arthur's fate, becomes crucial to the structure of Act 4 and the comparable scenes in *TR* (scenes 7, 8 and 9), although the source says nothing about his connection.[2] Historically, King Philip justified his son's later invasion (in 1216) partly on the pretext than John was not the lawful ruler of England 'having first usurped and taken it away from his nephew Arthur the lawful inheritor' (Holinshed, II, 330). But in 1213–14 the English barons were concerned only with their legal and property rights. However, one ominous though small event earlier, in 1208, may have influenced the dramas. When John was asking for hostages from the nobility lest they should rebel, an imprudent mother said she would not give up her two sons to a king who had already slain his nephew. Her husband harshly rebuked her and the family fled to Ireland 'for the safeguard of their lives'

---

[1] Matchett, pp. 154–5, comments on *TR*'s missing the thematic point of the dialogue between Lewis and Pandulph.
[2] The Magna Carta is not mentioned in either play, although in Holinshed it is an important part of the barons' protracted struggles with the king.

(Holinshed, II, 293). After the mother and her sons were captured, they were confined in Windsor Castle until, it was rumoured, they starved to death (Holinshed, II, 301). This defiance and cruelty suggests that there was smouldering resentment about Arthur, but in later episodes that concern the open rebellion of the nobility, nothing is said of him. Thus one of the playwrights adopted this issue for the barons and dramatised it in two scenes depicting their anger with the king about Arthur's imprisonment, his apparent murder (*John* 4.2; *TR* 8.108–30, 8.217–27), and their rage when they discover the body (*John* 4.3; *TR* 9.33–109). In *John* they also grumble about the second coronation and the king's neglect of their counsel, and in *TR* they complain about the banishment of Chester. But these are perfunctory nods at historical fact, for the obvious interest of the playwright who put the scenes together was the effect of Arthur's death. Hubert's white lie (that much is in the historical record, along with the king's subsequent troubles, Holinshed, II, 286), the barons' hasty conclusions from the discovery of the body (pure fiction), and the Bastard's wise suspension of judgement (fiction) – all of these are woven masterfully into a network of contingent events and characters in *King John*.[1] Much the same is in *TR* without the Bastard in the confrontation scene between the barons and Hubert over the boy's body.

Other telescoped events in the plays link the barons' revolt directly to the impending invasion by Lewis, whereas historically a civil war went on for about two years after the gathering of the nobles at St Edmundsbury (1214), and it was John who used 'strangers' from the continent to fight his own lords. After John raised the siege of Rochester, the nobles were holed up in London, and the Pope excommunicated them at the behest of an obedient John. The barons in desperation, therefore, invited Lewis to claim the English crown (1216). Historically it was described as a painful but necessary decision under the circumstances (Holinshed, II, 328).

Of the two playwrights Shakespeare has a better sense of the implied moral and political ambiguities in the *Chronicles*. Salisbury's long regretful speech (5.2.8–39) becomes in *TR* a cheerful welcome of their prince who will heal all the wounds of the kingdom (*TR* 11.190–8, 216–20). To Melun's dying confession, with details from Foxe, only Shakespeare adds the gratuitous remark that Melun is a friend of Hubert. In the comparable scene with Melun and the English nobles, as elsewhere, *Troublesome Reign* flattens the characters and irons out the moral dilemmas that the choice of scenes implies. Similarly the scenes in Swinstead Abbey, found only in *TR*, are coarse-grained dramaturgy appropriate for an amateur playwright. The scenes are enlivened by one bit of humour: the abbot overhears the monk's soliloquy and imagines that the monk plans to kill him, not John (*TR* 23.99 ff.). The poisoning scene is gross, and even when the author of *TR* has some of the design in other scenes common to *John*, he muddles or neglects the opportunities implicit in the construction of both plays. This writer is apparently not the same person who invented the Bastard Falconbridge or who conceived of Constance's grief. He is more interested in dramatising the spectacle of the five moons, the Bastard's trance, and

---

[1] See pp. 50–6 above.

other thrills that are consistent with the scenes that he alone depicts. His play appeals to the instincts of tabloid journalism not to the intelligent interest in moral and political dilemmas that beset the characters in Shakespeare's play. Therefore it seems likely that the constructive imagination which selected and compressed the material from historical sources, as we have noticed, is the same mind that executed the dialogue and the fine interplay of conscience and political necessity that makes *The Tragedy of King John*.

The propaganda play

If *The Troublesome Reign* is a derivative play, the anonymous author's purpose was not to reproduce the dialogue of Shakespeare's drama but to hang his own play on Shakespeare's framework. Higgledy-piggledy he turned it into an odd sort of *de casibus* tragedy about the punishment of a tyrant who becomes a Protestant martyr.[1] As a consequence, the poised dilemmas in Shakespeare's play were tipped toward doctrinaire solutions in *TR*. The Bastard reproves the barons with arguments from the 'Homily against Disobedience and Wilful Rebellion' (1571). Even if John had killed Arthur, 'Yet subjects may not take in hand revenge' and usurp God's proper power. The Pope cannot authorise such rebellion, and if a man dies in the belief that any rebellion is lawful he 'sells his soul perpetually to pain' (*TR* 11.118–27).[2]

In the prison scene Arthur and Hubert debate the related question whether a subject should passively disobey a king's order that violates God's law. Arthur insists that Hubert must answer to God if he commits murder. So he asks Hubert to consider that it is hard 'to lose salvation for a king's reward' (*TR* 7.78). The same exception to the rule of obedience is expounded in the homily 'Concerning Good Order and Obedience to Rulers and Magistrates'. Although a subject must leave to God the judgement of kings and magistrates, 'Yet let us believe undoubtedly . . . that we may not obey king's magistrates, or any other (though they be our own fathers) if they would command us to do anything contrary to God's commandments.' We must obey God not man. 'But nevertheless in that case we may not in any wise withstand violently, or rebel against rulers.'[3]

Much like the pamphlets that flooded England in the late 1580s and early 1590s, *TR* appeals to popular fear of seditious 'popelings' who would kill the English monarch. This fear was reinforced by Pope Sixtus V's renewal of the death sentence

---

[1] See Sider, pp. liv–lix, for this point about the play's form. V. M. Carr, *The Drama as Propaganda; A Study of 'The Troublesome Raigne of King John'*, Salzburg Studies in English Literature, 1974, identifies the popular themes from Elizabethan politics and religious controversy.

[2] The homily contains an example from the reign of King John, in which the Bishop of Rome is cast as a usurper who incensed the French king against John. The nobles would not have rebelled if they knew, according to scripture, their duty to their natural prince, and they would not have driven John to such straits that he was forced to submit his crown to Rome (1582 edn, sigs. 3B2–3). *The Second Tome of Homilies* was originally printed in 1563, and the homily 'Against Disobedience and Wilful Rebellion' was added to the volume in 1571.

[3] *Certain Sermons* (first printed 1547), 1582, edn, sig. F8.

against Queen Elizabeth, to coincide with the sailing of the Great Armada.[1] It was also thought that the execution of Mary Queen of Scots emboldened Catholic traitors who endangered Elizabeth's life. The most influential idea about King John in the age was, however, the one found in the homily 'Against Disobedience', that *TR* exploits more than Shakespeare does. John not only defies the Pope and all his minions vociferously; he deceives Pandulph, and on his deathbed he predicts a Tudor victory over the whore of Babylon.

> From out these loins shall spring a kingly branch
> Whose arms shall reach unto the gates of Rome,
> And with his feet tread down the strumpet's pride,
> That sits upon the chair of Babylon.   *TR* 15.104–7

Like the example of King John in the homily, he emerges as a misunderstood victim of papal tyranny and the precursor of Henry VIII.

This is vintage material for the anonymous playwright, suggesting that *Troublesome Reign* is not an imitation of Shakespeare's play but an adaptation. It is a quasi-independent work, not exactly a bad quarto but a propaganda piece awkwardly draped over Shakespeare's structure.

Transmission

Yet a difficulty still remains; how could the adapter learn of the design of Shakespeare's play without unconsciously picking up more of the texture of his language. Granted that, as an adapter rather than a plagiarist, he may not have cared about such things, how could he have passed over something as obvious as 'hang a calf's-skin on those recreant limbs'? Peter Alexander suggested that the method of pirating *The Taming of the Shrew* that resulted in *The Taming of a Shrew* might have been like the pirating of Sheridan's *Duenna* in eighteenth-century Dublin. After seeing a performance, someone sketched the scenes and wrote down all the jokes he could remember; he cribbed the rest from other sources.[2] As an explanation for *TR*'s derivation from *John*, this has been questioned because, as Alice Walker noticed, certain stage directions in *TR* are unusually close to those in *John*, so close as to imply a documentary link.

1 *Enter . . . Pembroke, Essex, and Salisbury*   *John* 1.1.1
   Enter . . . William Marshal Earle of Pembroke, The Earles of Essex, and of Salisbury
                                                                   TR 1.1

2 *Enter Pembroke, Salisbury, & Bigot*   *John* 4.3.10
   Enter Pembroke, Salisburie, Essex   *TR* 9.26

3 *Enter a Sheriffe*   *John* 1.1.43
   Enter the Shrive   *TR* 1.65

---

[1] Sider reprints 'A Declaration of the Sentence of Deposition of Elizabeth, the Usurper and Pretended Queen of England', pp. 212–19.
[2] Peter Alexander, *Shakespeare's Henry VI and Richard III*, 1927, p. 69.

4   *Enter a Citizen upon the walles*   *John* 2.1.200
    the Citizens appeare upon the walls   *TR* 2.249

5   *Enter Arthur on the walles*   *John* 4.3.1
    Enter yong Arthur on the walls   *TR* 9.1[1]

Since Essex and the Sheriff are never identified by name in the dialogue, a spectator who wanted to pirate Shakespeare's play could not recognise them, but their names are spoken in *TR*. The identical phrasing of Citizen(s) 'upon the walls' and Arthur 'on the walls' are distinct enough not to arise spontaneously. Miss Walker thought that items 1, 2, 4, and 5 confirmed her conclusion formed 'many years ago' that Shakespeare wrote his play with *TR* at hand. Mr Thomas thinks item 3 comes as close as possible to 'absolute proof' that *TR* preceded *John*. But if there are other responsible explanations of how the wording of these directions may have been passed on, we should keep an open mind. Strictly speaking, the evidence implies simply that the wording was not transmitted orally on the stage, and probably not by memory. They probably depend upon some sort of manuscript or printed sources. Among the various possibilities, items 1 and 2 could have been found in Holinshed where the two characters twice appear in that order in the opening pages of the reign (William Marshall and Geoffrey Fitzpeter, elsewhere called Pembroke and Salisbury). *TR* may have copied any of these from a prompt-book of *John*; or the Folio compositors may have consulted *TR* to supply omitted stage directions in their copy, especially items 4 and 5; or the author of *TR* may have worked from a 'plot' of *King John*. The analogy with duplicated phrases in stage directions in *The Shrew* and *A Shrew* and the evidence that compositors occasionally consulted bad quartos for alternative readings in their copy, as Honigmann points out, make his explanation a distinct possibility.[2] The other possibility that should be considered is transmission by way of a scenario or an 'author's plot', which appeals to me because it may not only account for the five parallel stage directions but also explain how the author of *TR* missed so much of the dialogue, while he remained comparatively faithful to scenic construction. This hypothesis was first put forth but withdrawn by Matchett and later expanded by Suzanne Gary.[3] In surviving theatrical records, there exist at least two kinds of plots, one a 'dramatic plot', as W. W. Greg calls it, and the other an 'author's plot'. A dramatic plot, of which four Elizabethan examples survive in manuscript, was used in the theatre and probably hung by the stage doors as a means of keeping the actors on their toes, ready to enter at the correct moment with suitable props and the like. It was usually on a large sheet of paper, divided into scenes, each scene beginning with the word *enter* and ending with *exeunt*. Between them were the names of characters and actors, with linking phrases like 'Dick to them' or 'to the Cardinal'. Internal exits were usually omitted, and we suppose that the actor once on

[1] A review of Honigmann, *RES*, n.s. 7 (1956), 421–3. Miss Walker cited items 1, 2, 4, and 5, Sidney Thomas, item 3: '"Enter the Sheriffe"', *SQ* 37 (1986), 98–100; and see Honigmann, '*King John. The Troublesome Reign*, and "documentary links": a rejoinder', *SQ* 38 (1987), 124–30.
[2] Honigmann, *Shakespeare's Impact*, pp. 60–2.
[3] Matchett, p. 156; Gary, pp. 13–28. I am much indebted to Gary in what follows.

stage could get himself off well enough. Occasionally there are descriptions of events like a dumb-show and stage noises. Obviously, a play as complicated as *TR* could not be written from one of these dramatic plots, but a stage direction in the prison scene uses the formula often found in this kind of plot, seldom in published scripts of the age: *Enter Arthur to Hubert de Burgh* (*TR* 7.14).[1]

An author's plot, however, was more detailed, going beyond the bare entrances, exits, and props. *Henslowe's Diary* contains several references to loans that were made to playwrights on the basis of a plot. On 3 December 1597 Henslowe advanced twenty shillings to Ben Jonson 'upon a book which he showed the plot unto the company which he promised to [deliver] unto the company at Christmas next'.[2] John Day writes to Henslowe 'about the plot of the Indies [i.e. *The Conquest of the West Indies*] I have occasion to be absent therefore pray deliver it to Will Hauton fiddler'. Sometimes a plot was used in collaborations, as, for example:

Lent unto Robert Shaw and Juby the 23 of October 1598 to lend unto Mr Chapman on his play book and two acts of a tragedy of Benjamin's plot . . . iii[li]

A fragment of what appears to be an author's plot was detached from a document and inserted in the manuscript of *The Faithful Friends, c.* 1614, sometimes attributed to Massinger.

[*The Plot of a Scene of mirth. to conclude this fourth Act.*]

Enter Sir Pergamus the foolish knight like a Bridegroom leading Flavia his Bride, Bellerio the singing soldier, Black Snout the Smith, Snipp Snapp the Taylor and Caulskin the Shoemaker.
An altar to be set forth with the image of Mars. Dindimus the Dwarf bearing Sir Per[gamus's] lance and shield which are hung up for trophies, and Sir Perg. vows for the love of Flavia never to bear arms again, the like does Bla. Snout who hangs up his sword and takes his hammer vowing to God Vulcan never to use other weapon, The Taylor and the Shoemaker to vow the like to God Mercury Then Bellario sings a song how they will fall to their old trades, a clap of thunder and run off/   finis 4 Act[3]

Unlike the dramatic plots, this resembles a scenario, indicating the entrances, props, stage business, and a summary of what the characters say in the scene, but it does not contain much of the language in the corresponding scene in *The Faithful Friends*, that runs to 56 lines of dialogue. If this is the kind of documentary link between *John* and *TR*, it is natural that some stage directions and a rough idea of the plan of each scene could be passed on to the adapter's manuscript. In *The Faithful Friends* only a few words that appear in the plot, aside from proper names, were incorporated in the ensuing dialogue, such as *hang, soldier, hammer, sword, trade*, and a few synonyms like

---

[1] See W. W. Greg, *Dramatic Documents from the Elizabethan Playhouses*, 1931, 1, 70–93.

[2] *Henslowe's Diary*, ed. R. A. Foakes and R. T. Rickert, 1961, p. 85. Subsequent references are to pp. 295 and 100.

[3] *The Faithful Friends*, ed. G. M. Pinciss and G. R. Proudfoot, 1975, pp. 93–4. The editors note that the handwriting of the fragment may be that of the author or part-author and that it 'provides sufficient basis for the composition of the dialogue' of the accompanying scene by another hand. They discount (p. xii) Greg's speculation that it was for a scene to be improvised or that it was composed from recollection of a performance.

pike, marry, and *wife*. That is just about what the author of *TR* seems to pick up from Shakespeare in many passages.

If we may suppose that *TR* is based on a plot or a scenario like this that had fallen into the hands of a writer with little talent and a lot of conventional opinions, his independent use of the *Chronicles* makes sense. With only a scenario in front of him (and perhaps a memory of a performance), he would need something to eke out his invention and pad the speeches. So he turned to Holinshed and Foxe for miscellaneous details. Smallwood thinks it is difficult to imagine *TR*'s using more historical material if the point is clear enough in Shakespeare's play, as when he supplies more motives for the rebellious barons, especially their complaint about John's banishment of Chester.[1] But if the adapter worked from a scenario, he would have had to fill in the blanks with something vaguely relevant from the *Chronicles*. Typically, his invention is most impoverished at those places where Shakespeare fictionalises, that is, in the non-historical speeches by the Lady Constance and in almost all the Bastard's major speeches, because the adapter cannot depend on the historical sources. This constraint offers a possible explanation for the fact that when Shakespeare's invention is at its highest, the anonymous author's is in the pits.

Chronology

One other matter should be mentioned that worries some judicious critics. It is often said that if the case could be proved that *King John* was the source of *TR* and hence written before 1591, the chronology of Shakespeare's early plays would have to be greatly overhauled. The implication is that such an eventuality would be unpleasant, onerous, or otherwise undesirable. However, the conventional dating, based presumably on 'hard' evidence uncovered by Edmond Malone, modified slightly by Dyce, and established by E. K. Chambers in *William Shakespeare: A Study of Facts and Problems*, 1930, depends upon very little for the start of Shakespeare's dramatic career. Robert Greene's reference to the 'upstart crow' (1592) is the earliest substantial evidence that Shakespeare was a practising playwright. So ultra-conservative literary historians have attempted to squeeze the composition of twelve or thirteen plays, two long poems, and the *Sonnets* between 1592 and 1598, when Meres's list was published. Only *2* and *3 Henry VI* and possibly *1 Henry VI* are usually dated before 1592.

There are many weak links in the chain of evidence and inference about the chronology of the early plays, and the resistance to a hypothesis that *TR* is derived from Shakespeare's play should not rest on the fancied assumption that Chambers's dates are set in concrete. F. P. Wilson argued persuasively that Shakespeare may have taught Marlowe how to write a history play, and he warned that 'the chronology of Shakespeare's early plays is so uncertain that it has no right to harden into an orthodoxy'.[2] Since Honigmann has handsomely re-examined the arguments for an early start v. the late start and for the possible place that *King John* may occupy in

---

[1] Smallwood, p. 368.
[2] *Marlowe and the Early Shakespeare*, 1953, p. 113.

the complicated network of the historical evidence, his demonstration need not be repeated here.[1]

For the date and sources of *John*, an important point must be emphasised. The case for the priority of *John* should not be prejudiced by the illusory authority of Chambers's early chronology. And since proof is not often possible in the establishment of memorial reconstructions, adaptations, or other pirated versions of plays, the best we can do is to arrive at a conclusion that is more or less probable. The case for the priority of *John* is no more provable than the case for *The Taming of the Shrew* as prior to *A Shrew*, but the weight of evidence and opinion about *A Shrew* has now shifted, after several generations of scholars have worked on the problems: Peter Alexander, Dover Wilson, G. I. Duthie and Richard Hosley.[2] They have not proved anything hard and fast except that it now seems more likely that *A Shrew* is an adaptation of Shakespeare's play, and *The Shrew* should probably be dated earlier than usual, though it is not mentioned by Meres.

The priority of *King John* seems likely, once we recognise evidence that *TR* has few of the signs of a memorial reconstruction like the bad quarto of *Hamlet*, but it resembles an adaptation, like *A Shrew*. We will probably never know exactly how the specific links in stage directions occurred between *TR* and *John*, but taking full measure of the structural evidence of *John* and *TR*, I am inclined to favour Shakespeare's play as the source of *Troublesome Reign*.[3] If this argument is persuasive, the composition of *King John* may be dated no later than about 1590.

[1] *Shakespeare's Impact*, chs. 3–4.
[2] See Ann Thompson (ed.), *Shr.*,1984, pp. 164–73, for a cogent summary of the case.
[3] It is also possible that *TR* has adapted Shakespeare's play from a lost early version or a scenario of it, but since we know nothing of that hypothetical script, speculation is fruitless. Certain passages in *John* that have a relatively mature style suggest at least the possibility of later revision. See pp. 26–8 above.

READING LIST

This list includes details of books and articles referred to in the Introduction, Commentary and Appendix, and may serve as a guide to those who wish to undertake further study of the play.

Alexander, Peter. *Introductions to Shakespeare*, 1964; originally published in *William Shakespeare, The Complete Works*, 1951

Berry, Edward I. *Patterns of Decay: Shakespeare's Early Histories*, 1975

Boklund, Gunnar. 'The troublesome ending of *King John*', *SN* 40 (1968), 175–84

Bonjour, Adrien. 'The road to Swinstead Abbey: a study of the sense and structure of *King John*', *ELH* 18 (1951), 253–74

Boris, Elna Z. *Shakespeare's English Kings, The People and the Law*, 1978

Burckhardt, Sigurd. '*King John*: the ordering of this present time', *ELH* 33 (1966), 133–53; reprinted in his *Shakespearean Meanings*, 1968

Calderwood, J. L. 'Commodity and honour in *King John*', *UTQ* 29 (1960), 341–56

Downer, Alan. *The Eminent Tragedian: William Charles Macready*, 1966

Erasmus, Desiderius. *The Education of a Christian Prince* (1516), trans. L. K. Born, 1936

   Enchiridion militis Christiani (1503), trans. Raymond Himelick, 1963

Frye, Northrop. *Fools of Time: Studies in Shakespearean Tragedy*, 1962

Hibbard, G. R. *The Making of Shakespeare's Dramatic Poetry*, 1981

Honigmann, E. A. J. Introduction to his edition of *King John*, 1954

   Shakespeare's Impact on his Contemporaries, 1982

Jones, Emrys. *The Origins of Shakespeare*, 1977

   Scenic Form in Shakespeare, 1971

Jones, Robert C. 'Truth in *King John*', *SEL* 25 (1985), 397–417

Kelly, Henry Ansgar. *Divine Providence in the England of Shakespeare's Histories*, 1970

Leggatt, Alexander. 'Dramatic perspective in *King John*', *ESC* 3 (1977), 1–17

Lindenberger, Herbert. *Historical Drama: The Relation of Literature and Reality*, 1975

Matchett, William H. 'Richard's divided heritage in *King John*', *EIC* 12 (1962), 231–53 (substantially the same as his introduction to the Signet edn of *King John*, 1966)

Prior, Moody E. *The Drama of Power: Studies in Shakespeare's History Plays*, 1973

Sanders, Wilbur. *The Dramatist and the Received Idea: Studies in the Plays of Marlowe and Shakespeare*, 1968

Shattuck, Charles H. (ed.). *William Charles Macready's 'King John'*, 1962

Sider, J. W. (ed.). *The Troublesome Raigne of John, King of England*, 1979

Smallwood, R. L. Introduction to his edn of *King John*, 1974

    'Shakespeare unbalanced: the Royal Shakespeare Company's *King John*', *SJH* 112 (1976), 79–99

Talbert, E. W. *The Problem of Order*, 1962

Waith, Eugene. '*King John* and the drama of history', *SQ* 29 (1978), 192–211

Wilders, John. *The Lost Garden: A View of Shakespeare's English and Roman History Plays*, 1978

Made in the USA
Lexington, KY
26 September 2017